izombie

Six Feet Under and Rising

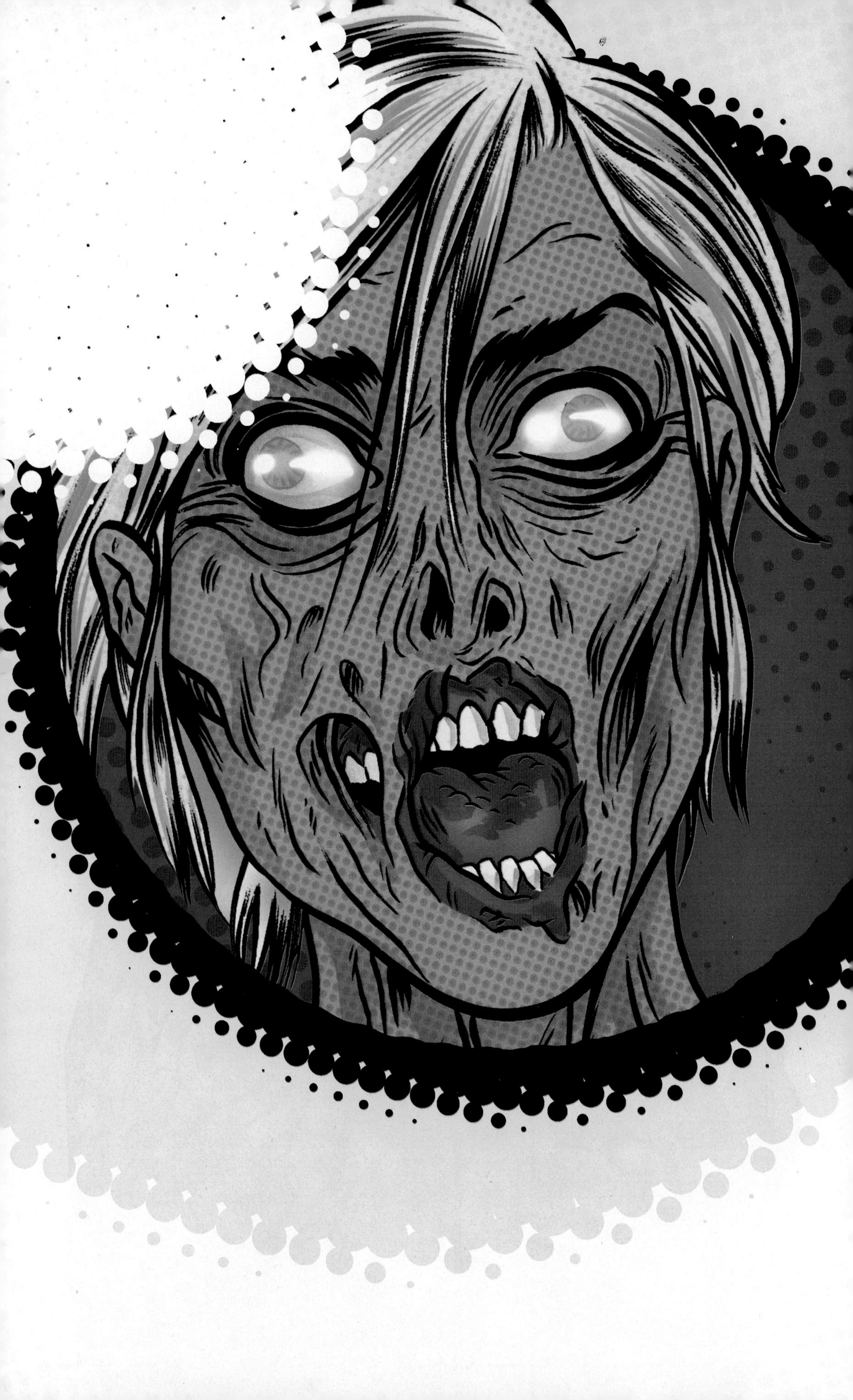

izombie
Six Feet Under and Rising

Chris Roberson
Writer

Michael Allred
Art and Covers

Jay Stephens
Guest Artist — "Vampire Queen of the Amazon"

Laura Allred
Colorist

Todd Klein
Letterer

iZombie created by **Roberson** and **Allred**

Shelly Bond Editor – Original Series

Gregory Lockard Assistant Editor – Original Series

Ian Sattler Director – Editorial, Special Projects and Archival Editions

Robbin Brosterman Design Director – Books

Curtis King Jr. Publication Design

Karen Berger Senior VP – Executive Editor, Vertigo

Bob Harras VP – Editor-in-Chief

Diane Nelson President

Dan DiDio and **Jim Lee** Co-Publishers

Geoff Johns Chief Creative Officer

John Rood Executive VP – Sales, Marketing and Business Development

Amy Genkins Senior VP – Business and Legal Affairs

Nairi Gardiner Senior VP – Finance

Jeff Boison VP – Publishing Operations

Mark Chiarello VP – Art Direction and Design

John Cunningham VP – Marketing

Terri Cunningham VP – Talent Relations and Services

Alison Gill Senior VP – Manufacturing and Operations

David Hyde VP – Publicity

Hank Kanalz Senior VP – Digital

Jay Kogan VP – Business and Legal Affairs, Publishing

Jack Mahan VP – Business Affairs, Talent

Nick Napolitano VP – Manufacturing Administration

Sue Pohja VP – Book Sales

Courtney Simmons Senior VP – Publicity

Bob Wayne Senior VP – Sales

iZOMBIE: SIX FEET UNDER AND RISING

Published by DC Comics. Cover and compilation
Copyright © 2012 Monkey Brain, Inc. and Michael Allred.
All Rights Reserved.

Originally published in single magazine form in iZOMBIE 13-18
Copyright © 2011 Monkey Brain, Inc. and Michael Allred.
All Rights Reserved. VERTIGO is a trademark of DC Comics.
All characters, their distinctive likenesses and related elements
featured in this publication are trademarks of DC Comics. The stories,
characters and incidents featured in this publication are entirely fictional.
DC Comics does not read or accept unsolicited ideas, stories or artwork.

DC Comics, 4000 Warner Blvd., Burbank, CA 91522
A Warner Bros. Entertainment Company.
Printed in the USA. 4/10/15. Second Printing.
ISBN: 978-1-4012-3370-9

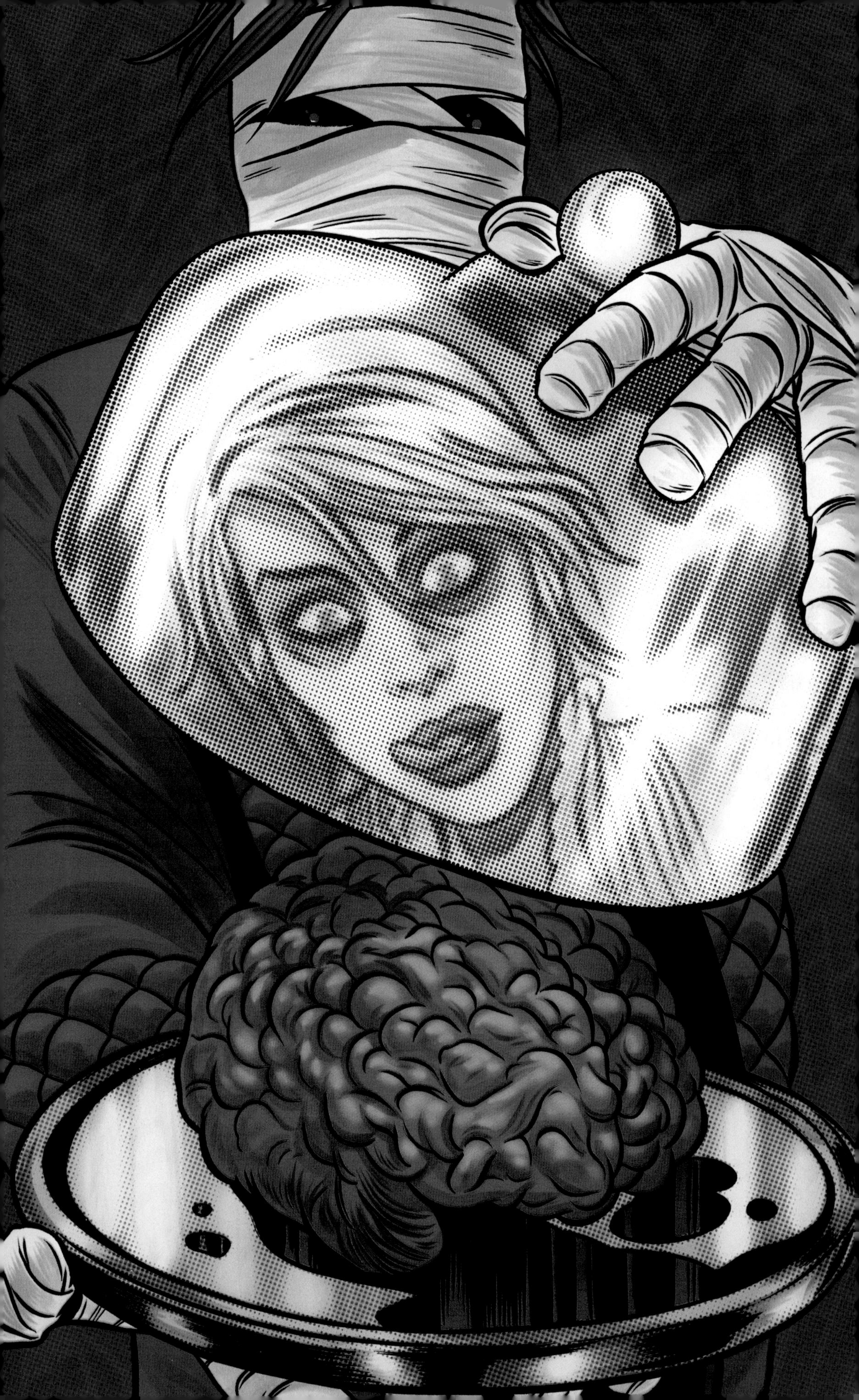

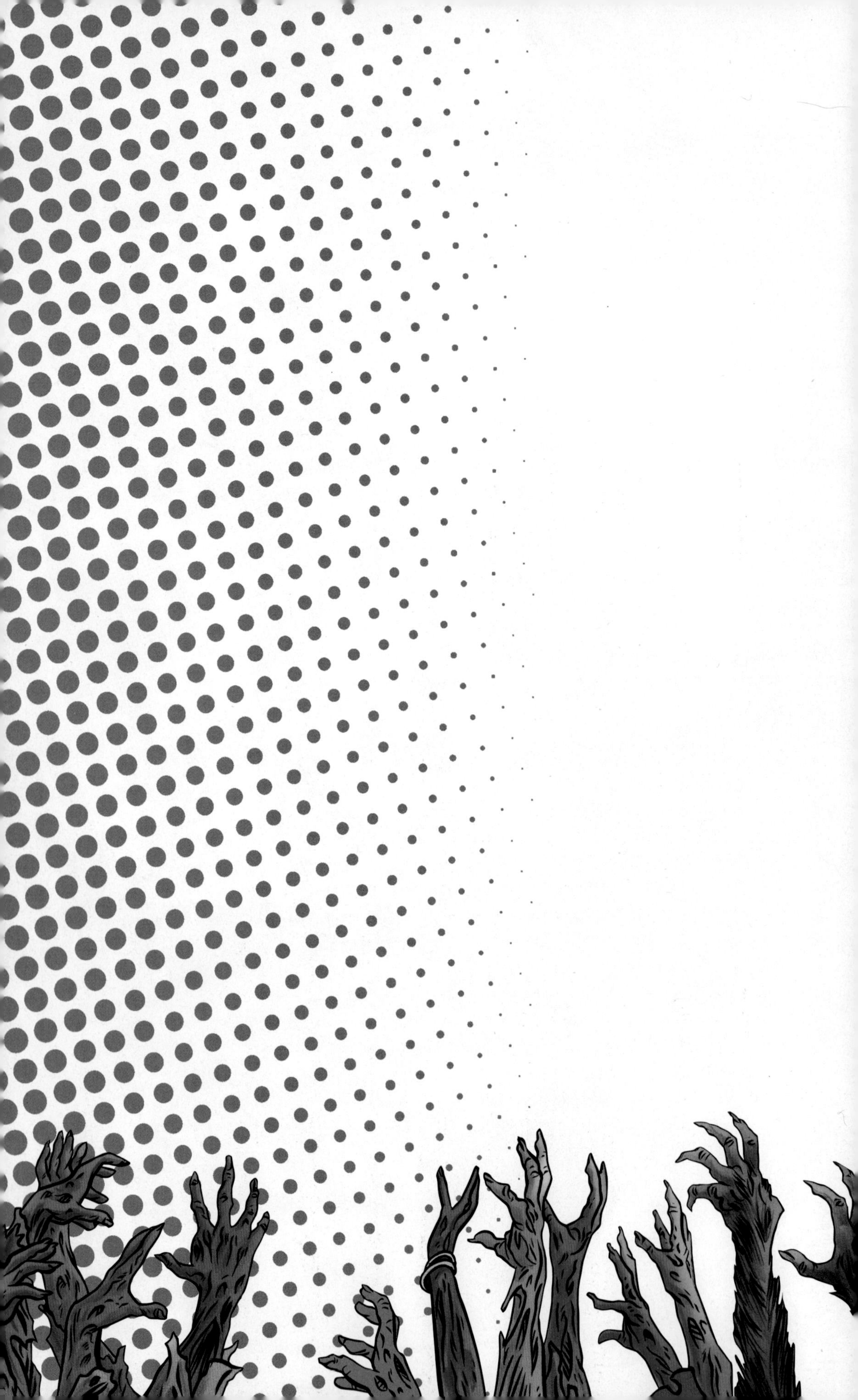

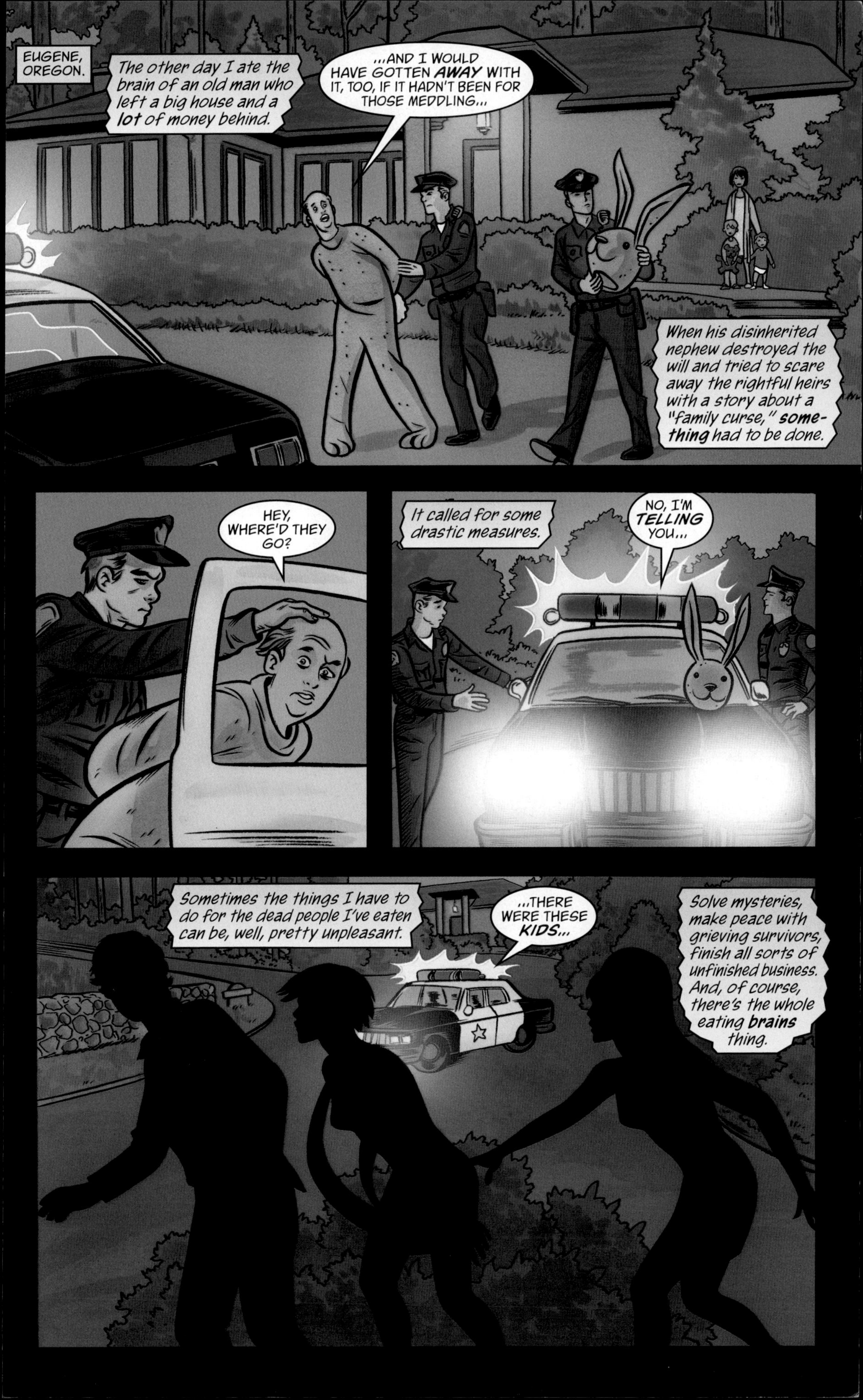
EUGENE, OREGON.
The other day I ate the brain of an old man who left a big house and a **lot** of money behind.
...AND I WOULD HAVE GOTTEN **AWAY** WITH IT, TOO, IF IT HADN'T BEEN FOR THOSE MEDDLING...
When his disinherited nephew destroyed the will and tried to scare away the rightful heirs with a story about a "family curse," **something** had to be done.
HEY, WHERE'D THEY GO?
It called for some drastic measures.
NO, I'M **TELLING** YOU...
Sometimes the things I have to do for the dead people I've eaten can be, well, pretty unpleasant.
...THERE WERE THESE **KIDS**...
Solve mysteries, make peace with grieving survivors, finish all sorts of unfinished business. And, of course, there's the whole eating **brains** thing.

But this was *fun.*

ARRIVALS AND EXITS

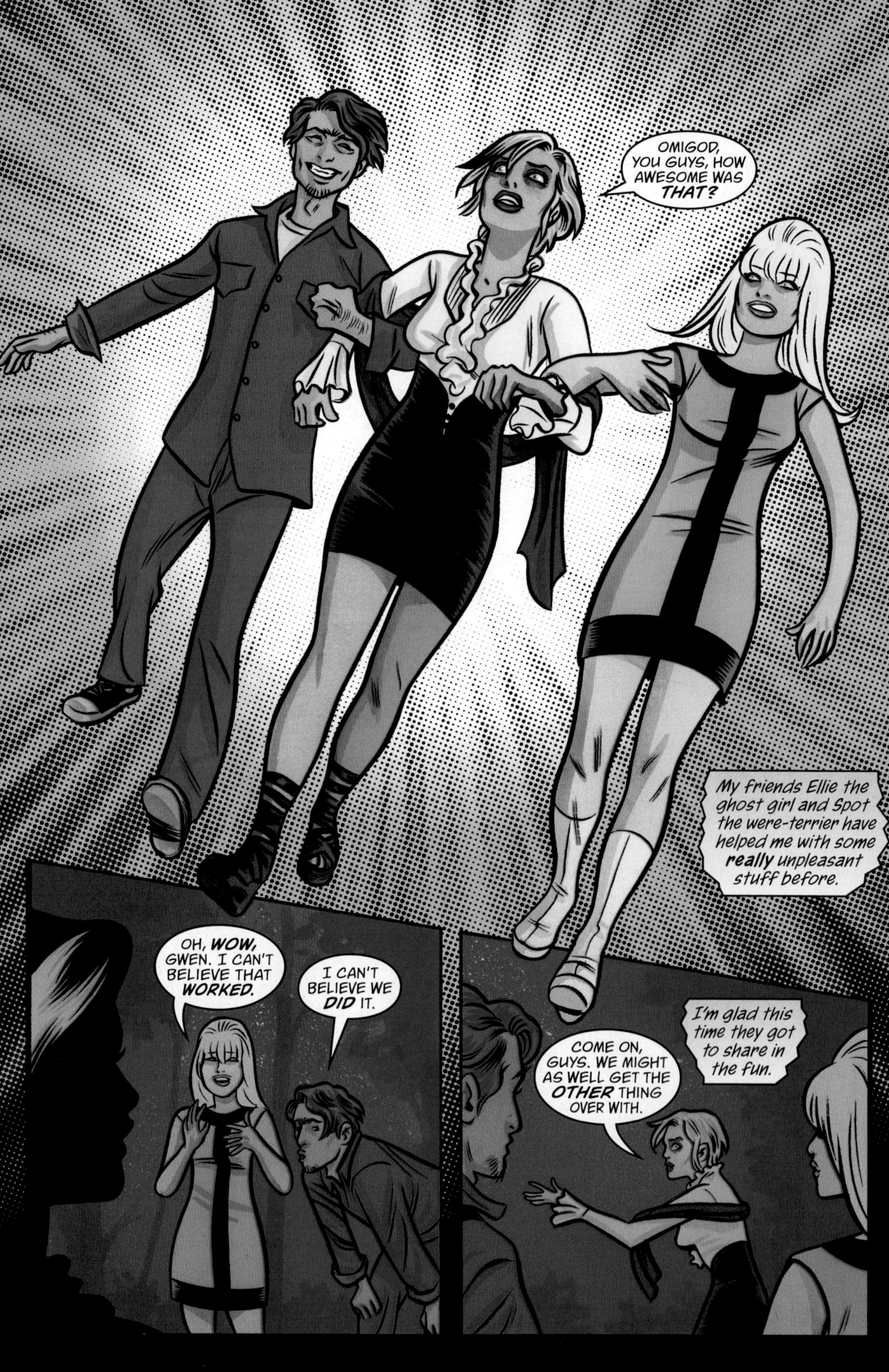

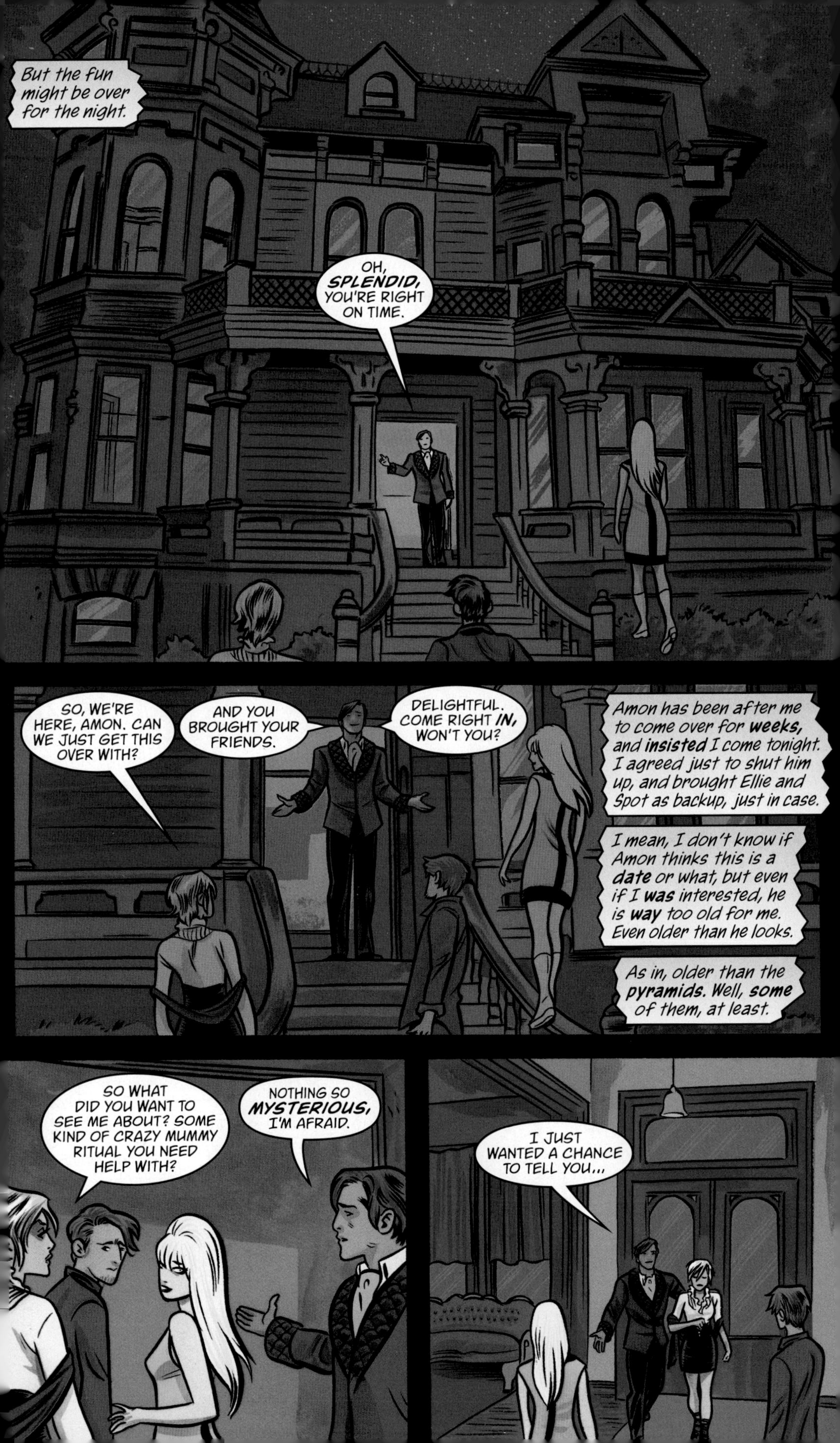
But the fun might be over for the night.
OH, SPLENDID, YOU'RE RIGHT ON TIME.
SO, WE'RE HERE, AMON. CAN WE JUST GET THIS OVER WITH?
AND YOU BROUGHT YOUR FRIENDS.
DELIGHTFUL. COME RIGHT IN, WON'T YOU?
Amon has been after me to come over for weeks, and insisted I come tonight. I agreed just to shut him up, and brought Ellie and Spot as backup, just in case.
I mean, I don't know if Amon thinks this is a date or what, but even if I was interested, he is way too old for me. Even older than he looks.
As in, older than the pyramids. Well, some of them, at least.
SO WHAT DID YOU WANT TO SEE ME ABOUT? SOME KIND OF CRAZY MUMMY RITUAL YOU NEED HELP WITH?
NOTHING SO MYSTERIOUS, I'M AFRAID.
I JUST WANTED A CHANCE TO TELL YOU...

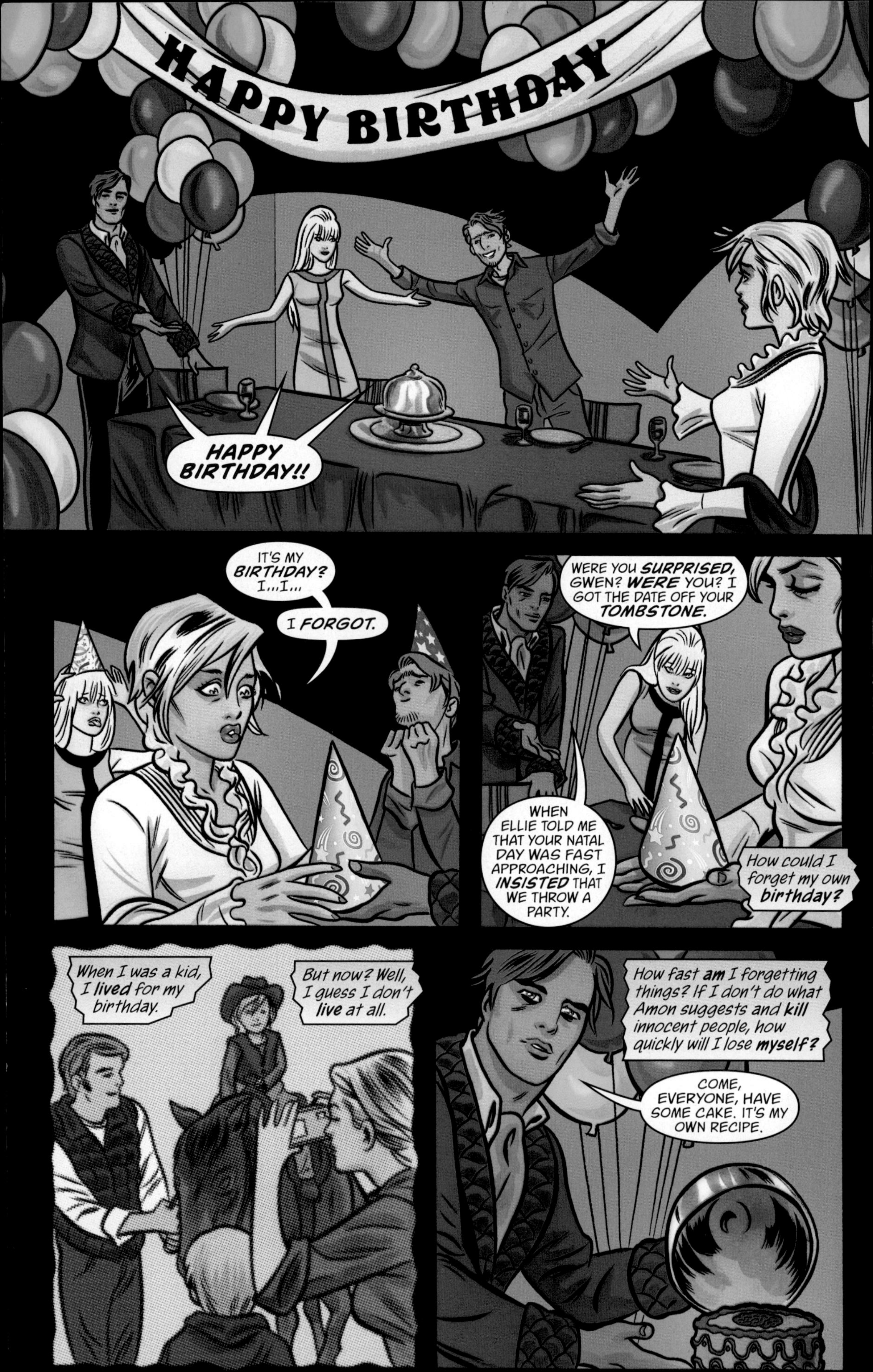
HAPPY BIRTHDAY
HAPPY BIRTHDAY!!
IT'S MY BIRTHDAY? I...I...
I FORGOT.
WERE YOU SURPRISED, GWEN? WERE YOU? I GOT THE DATE OFF YOUR TOMBSTONE.
WHEN ELLIE TOLD ME THAT YOUR NATAL DAY WAS FAST APPROACHING, I INSISTED THAT WE THROW A PARTY.
How could I forget my own birthday?
When I was a kid, I lived for my birthday.
But now? Well, I guess I don't live at all.
How fast am I forgetting things? If I don't do what Amon suggests and kill innocent people, how quickly will I lose myself?
COME, EVERYONE, HAVE SOME CAKE. IT'S MY OWN RECIPE.

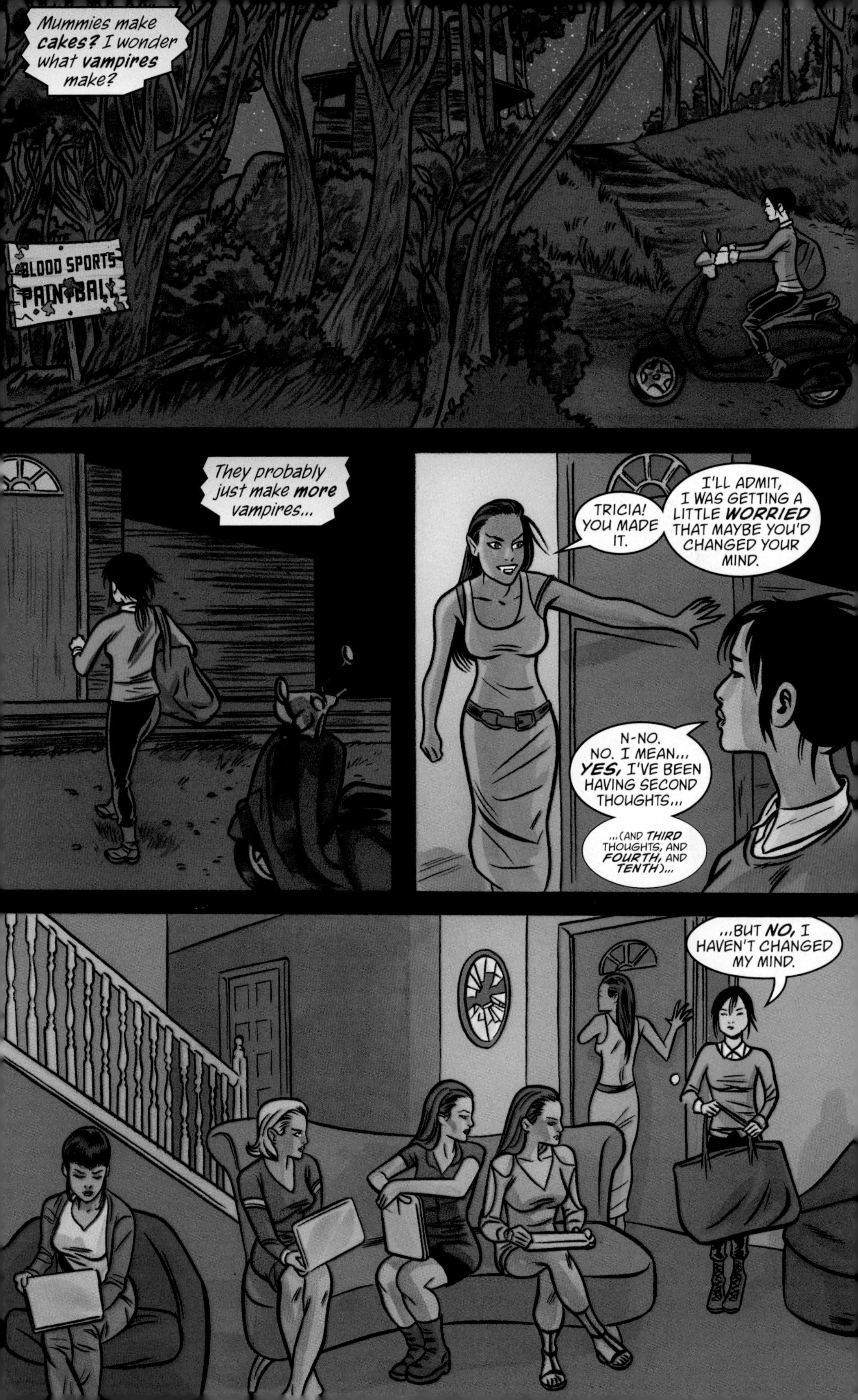
Mummies make cakes? I wonder what vampires make?
BLOOD SPORTS PAINTBALL
They probably just make more vampires...
TRICIA! YOU MADE IT.
I'LL ADMIT, I WAS GETTING A LITTLE WORRIED THAT MAYBE YOU'D CHANGED YOUR MIND.
N-NO. NO. I MEAN... YES, I'VE BEEN HAVING SECOND THOUGHTS...
...(AND THIRD THOUGHTS, AND FOURTH, AND TENTH)...
...BUT NO, I HAVEN'T CHANGED MY MIND.

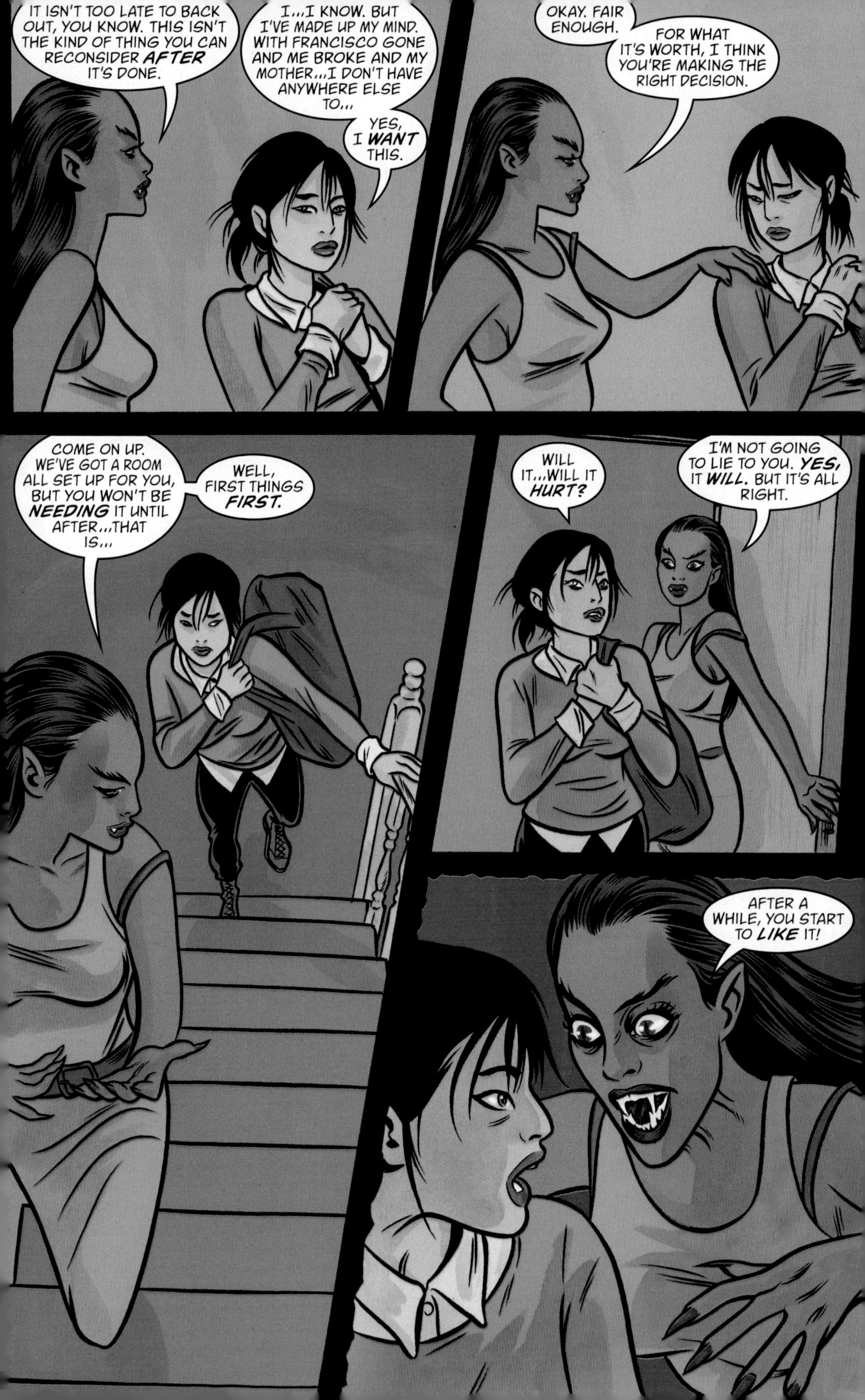
IT ISN'T TOO LATE TO BACK OUT, YOU KNOW. THIS ISN'T THE KIND OF THING YOU CAN RECONSIDER *AFTER* IT'S DONE.
I...I KNOW. BUT I'VE MADE UP MY MIND. WITH FRANCISCO GONE AND ME BROKE AND MY MOTHER...I DON'T HAVE ANYWHERE ELSE TO...
YES, I *WANT* THIS.
OKAY. FAIR ENOUGH.
FOR WHAT IT'S WORTH, I THINK YOU'RE MAKING THE RIGHT DECISION.
COME ON UP. WE'VE GOT A ROOM ALL SET UP FOR YOU, BUT YOU WON'T BE *NEEDING* IT UNTIL AFTER...THAT IS...
WELL, FIRST THINGS *FIRST*.
WILL IT...WILL IT *HURT?*
I'M NOT GOING TO LIE TO YOU. *YES,* IT *WILL.* BUT IT'S ALL RIGHT.
AFTER A WHILE, YOU START TO *LIKE* IT!

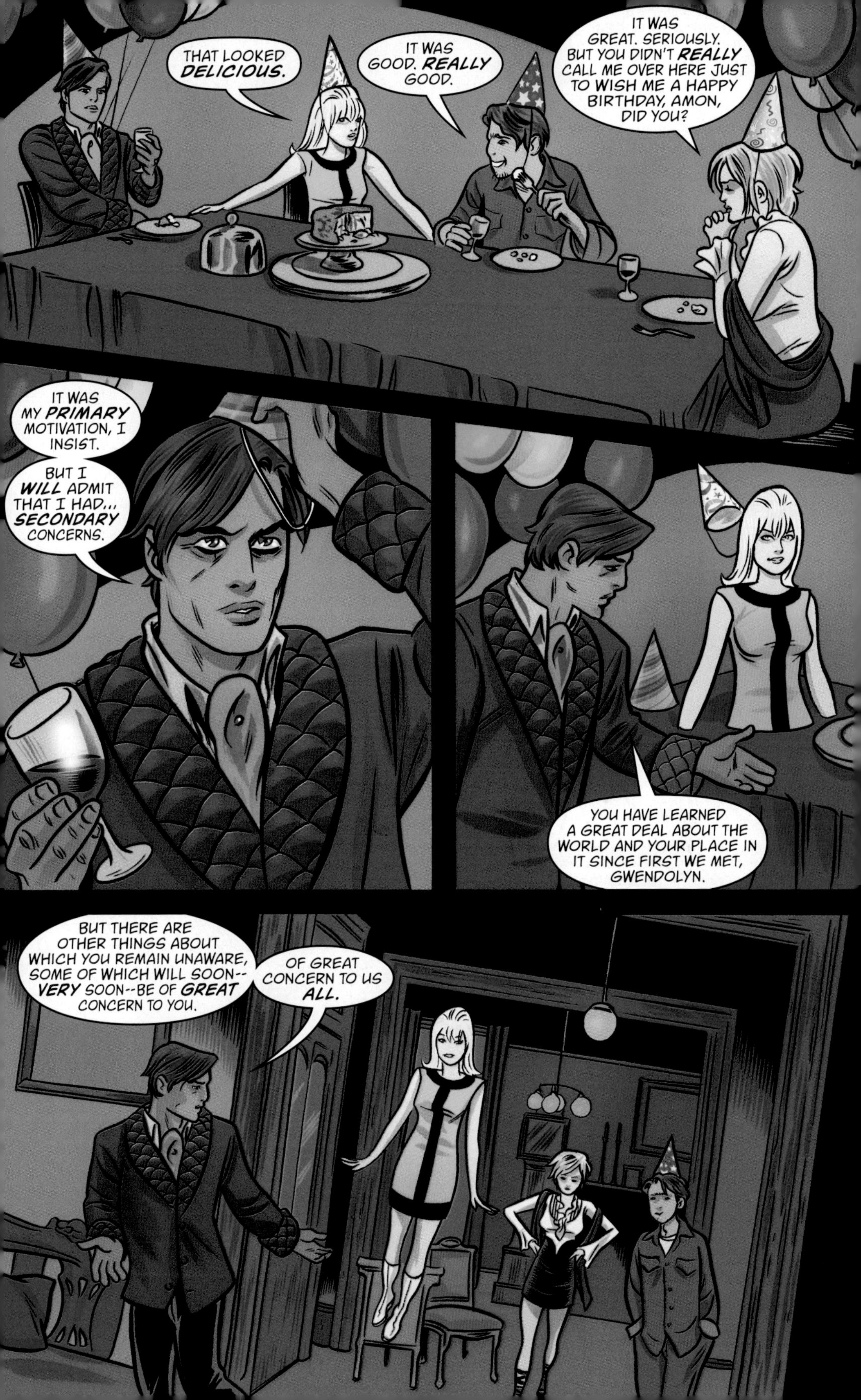
THAT LOOKED DELICIOUS.
IT WAS GOOD. REALLY GOOD.
IT WAS GREAT. SERIOUSLY. BUT YOU DIDN'T REALLY CALL ME OVER HERE JUST TO WISH ME A HAPPY BIRTHDAY, AMON, DID YOU?
IT WAS MY PRIMARY MOTIVATION, I INSIST.
BUT I WILL ADMIT THAT I HAD... SECONDARY CONCERNS.
YOU HAVE LEARNED A GREAT DEAL ABOUT THE WORLD AND YOUR PLACE IN IT SINCE FIRST WE MET, GWENDOLYN.
BUT THERE ARE OTHER THINGS ABOUT WHICH YOU REMAIN UNAWARE, SOME OF WHICH WILL SOON--VERY SOON--BE OF GREAT CONCERN TO YOU.
OF GREAT CONCERN TO US ALL.

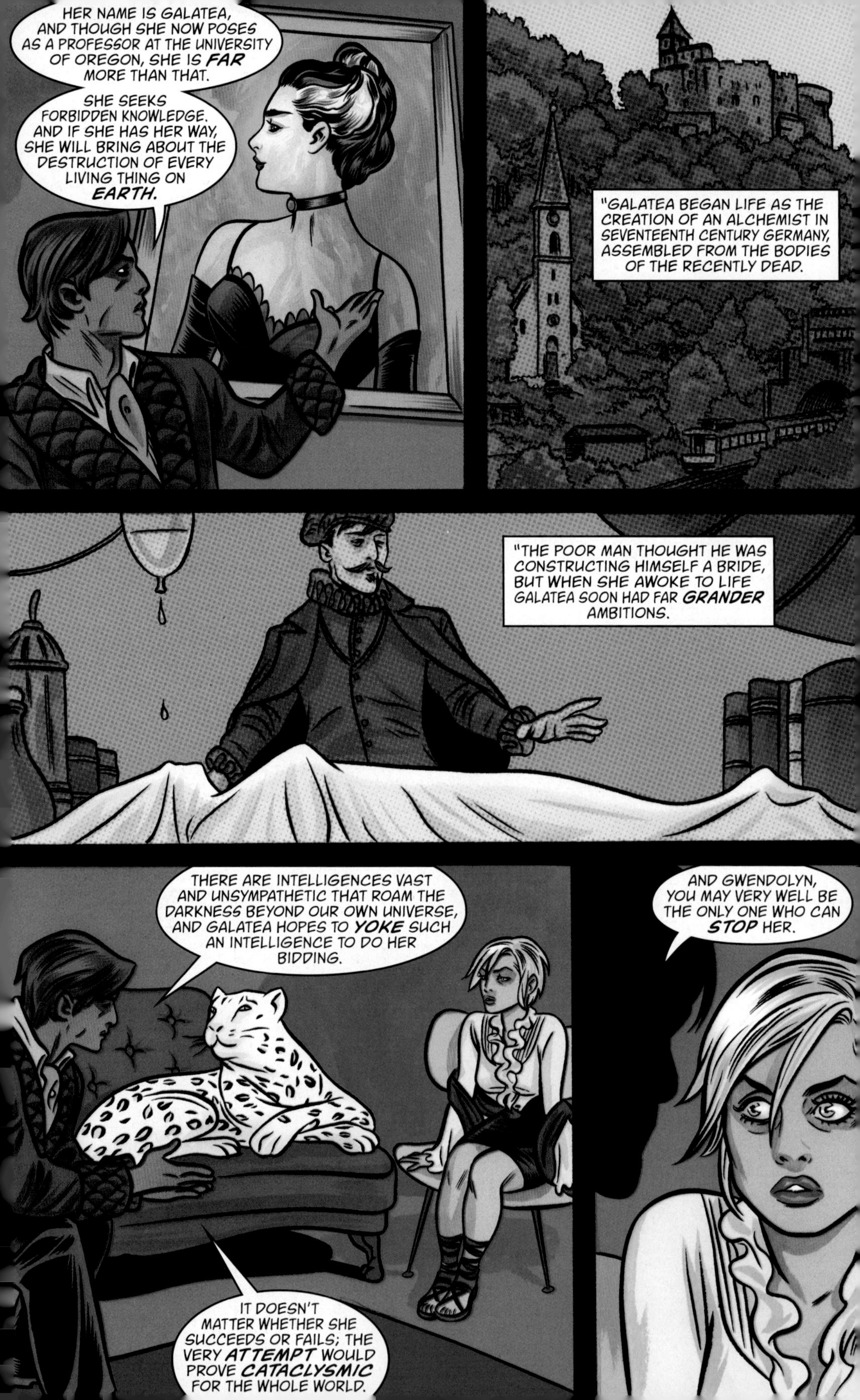
HER NAME IS GALATEA, AND THOUGH SHE NOW POSES AS A PROFESSOR AT THE UNIVERSITY OF OREGON, SHE IS FAR MORE THAN THAT.
SHE SEEKS FORBIDDEN KNOWLEDGE. AND IF SHE HAS HER WAY, SHE WILL BRING ABOUT THE DESTRUCTION OF EVERY LIVING THING ON EARTH.
"GALATEA BEGAN LIFE AS THE CREATION OF AN ALCHEMIST IN SEVENTEENTH CENTURY GERMANY, ASSEMBLED FROM THE BODIES OF THE RECENTLY DEAD.
"THE POOR MAN THOUGHT HE WAS CONSTRUCTING HIMSELF A BRIDE, BUT WHEN SHE AWOKE TO LIFE GALATEA SOON HAD FAR GRANDER AMBITIONS.
THERE ARE INTELLIGENCES VAST AND UNSYMPATHETIC THAT ROAM THE DARKNESS BEYOND OUR OWN UNIVERSE, AND GALATEA HOPES TO YOKE SUCH AN INTELLIGENCE TO DO HER BIDDING.
IT DOESN'T MATTER WHETHER SHE SUCCEEDS OR FAILS; THE VERY ATTEMPT WOULD PROVE CATACLYSMIC FOR THE WHOLE WORLD.
AND GWENDOLYN, YOU MAY VERY WELL BE THE ONLY ONE WHO CAN STOP HER.

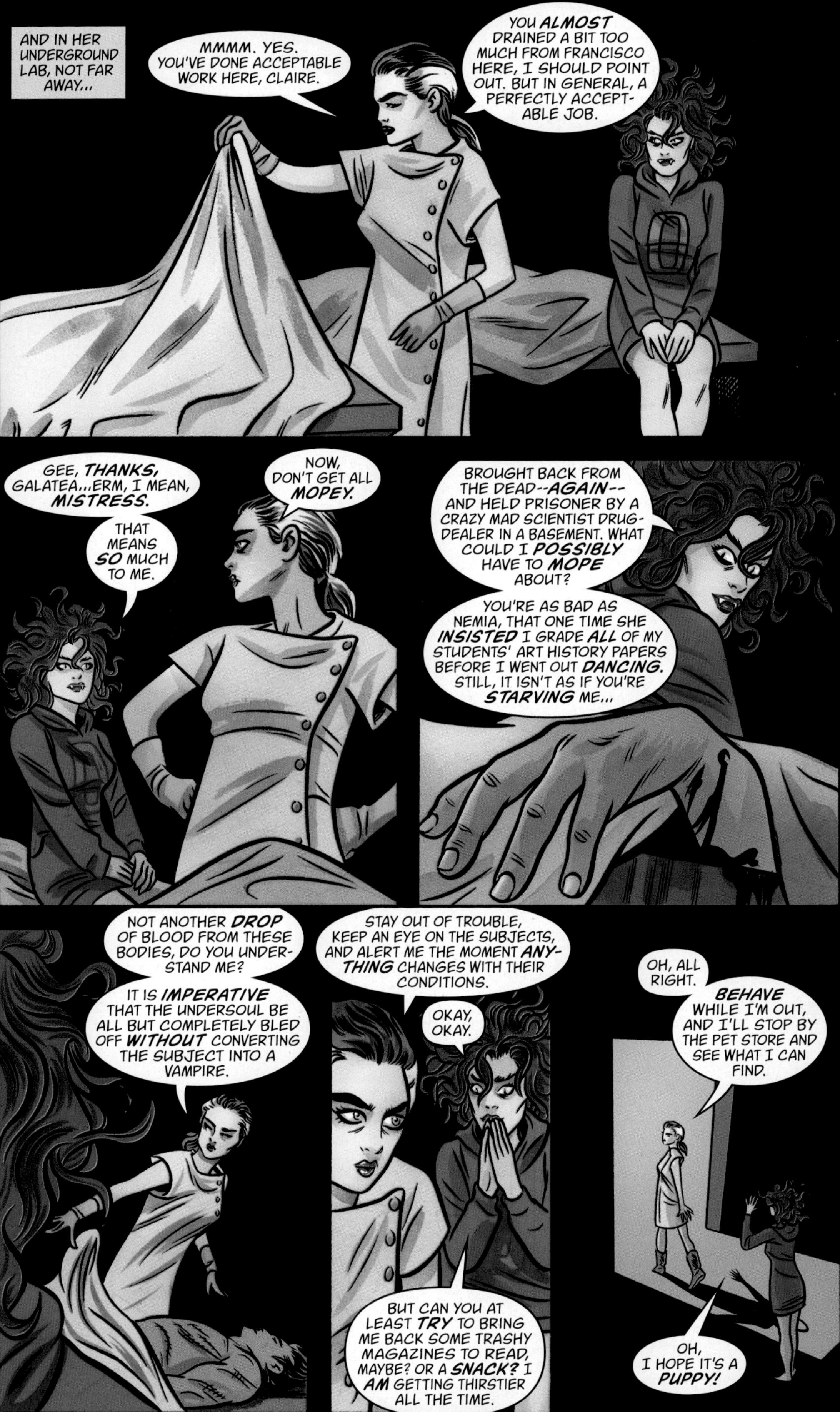

AND IN HER UNDERGROUND LAB, NOT FAR AWAY...
MMMM. YES. YOU'VE DONE ACCEPTABLE WORK HERE, CLAIRE.
YOU **ALMOST** DRAINED A BIT TOO MUCH FROM FRANCISCO HERE, I SHOULD POINT OUT. BUT IN GENERAL, A PERFECTLY ACCEPTABLE JOB.
GEE, **THANKS,** GALATEA...ERM, I MEAN, **MISTRESS.**
THAT MEANS **SO** MUCH TO ME.
NOW, DON'T GET ALL **MOPEY.**
BROUGHT BACK FROM THE DEAD--**AGAIN**--AND HELD PRISONER BY A CRAZY MAD SCIENTIST DRUG-DEALER IN A BASEMENT. WHAT COULD I **POSSIBLY** HAVE TO **MOPE** ABOUT?
YOU'RE AS BAD AS NEMIA, THAT ONE TIME SHE **INSISTED** I GRADE **ALL** OF MY STUDENTS' ART HISTORY PAPERS BEFORE I WENT OUT **DANCING.** STILL, IT ISN'T AS IF YOU'RE **STARVING** ME...
NOT ANOTHER **DROP** OF BLOOD FROM THESE BODIES, DO YOU UNDERSTAND ME?
IT IS **IMPERATIVE** THAT THE UNDERSOUL BE ALL BUT COMPLETELY BLED OFF **WITHOUT** CONVERTING THE SUBJECT INTO A VAMPIRE.
STAY OUT OF TROUBLE, KEEP AN EYE ON THE SUBJECTS, AND ALERT ME THE MOMENT **ANYTHING** CHANGES WITH THEIR CONDITIONS.
OKAY, OKAY.
BUT CAN YOU AT LEAST **TRY** TO BRING ME BACK SOME TRASHY MAGAZINES TO READ, MAYBE? OR A **SNACK?** I **AM** GETTING THIRSTIER ALL THE TIME.
OH, ALL RIGHT.
BEHAVE WHILE I'M OUT, AND I'LL STOP BY THE PET STORE AND SEE WHAT I CAN FIND.
OH, I HOPE IT'S A **PUPPY!**

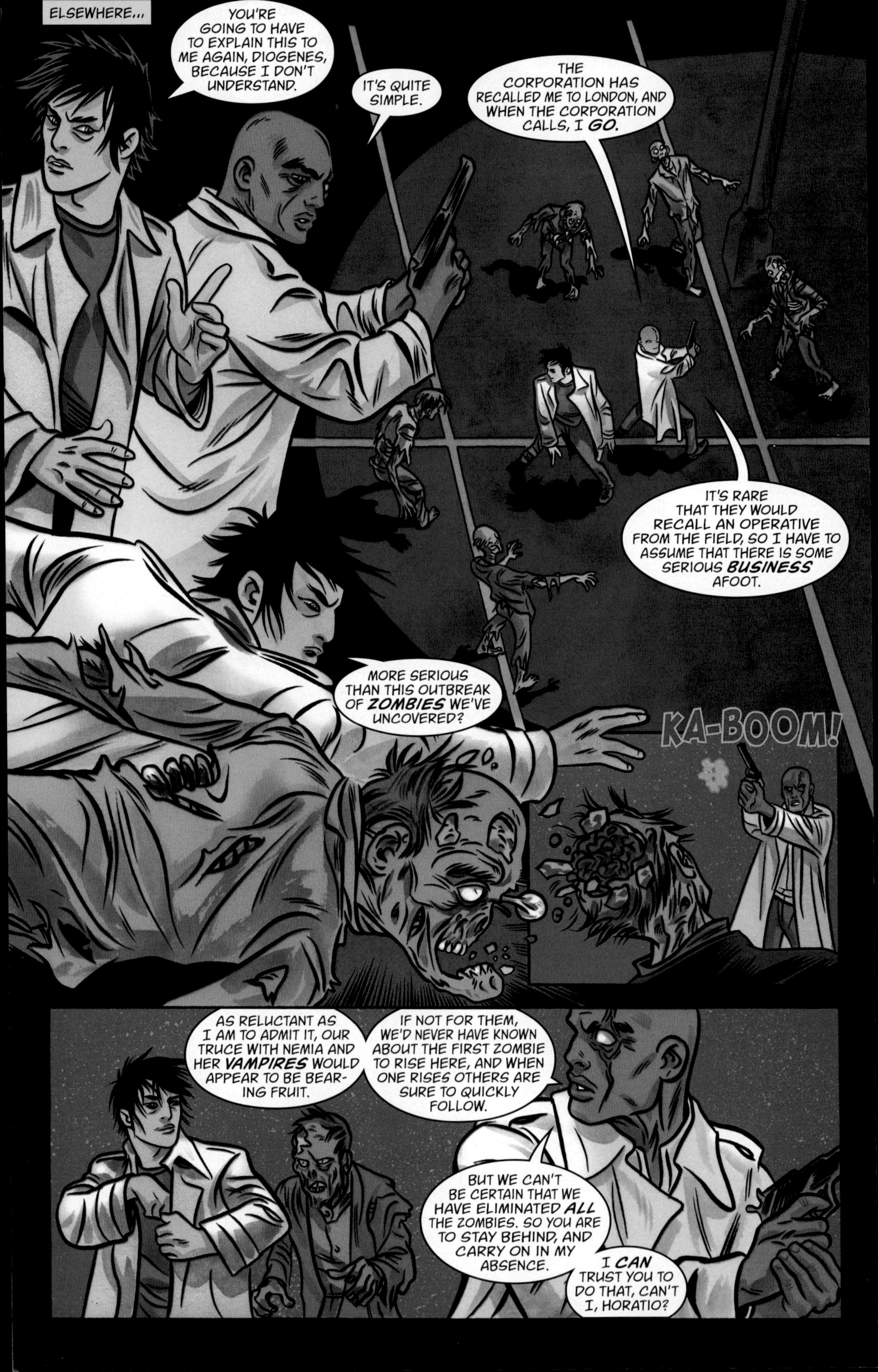
ELSEWHERE...
YOU'RE GOING TO HAVE TO EXPLAIN THIS TO ME AGAIN, DIOGENES, BECAUSE I DON'T UNDERSTAND.
IT'S QUITE SIMPLE.
THE CORPORATION HAS RECALLED ME TO LONDON, AND WHEN THE CORPORATION CALLS, I GO.
IT'S RARE THAT THEY WOULD RECALL AN OPERATIVE FROM THE FIELD, SO I HAVE TO ASSUME THAT THERE IS SOME SERIOUS BUSINESS AFOOT.
MORE SERIOUS THAN THIS OUTBREAK OF ZOMBIES WE'VE UNCOVERED?
KA-BOOM!
AS RELUCTANT AS I AM TO ADMIT IT, OUR TRUCE WITH NEMIA AND HER VAMPIRES WOULD APPEAR TO BE BEARING FRUIT.
IF NOT FOR THEM, WE'D NEVER HAVE KNOWN ABOUT THE FIRST ZOMBIE TO RISE HERE, AND WHEN ONE RISES OTHERS ARE SURE TO QUICKLY FOLLOW.
BUT WE CAN'T BE CERTAIN THAT WE HAVE ELIMINATED ALL THE ZOMBIES. SO YOU ARE TO STAY BEHIND, AND CARRY ON IN MY ABSENCE.
I CAN TRUST YOU TO DO THAT, CAN'T I, HORATIO?

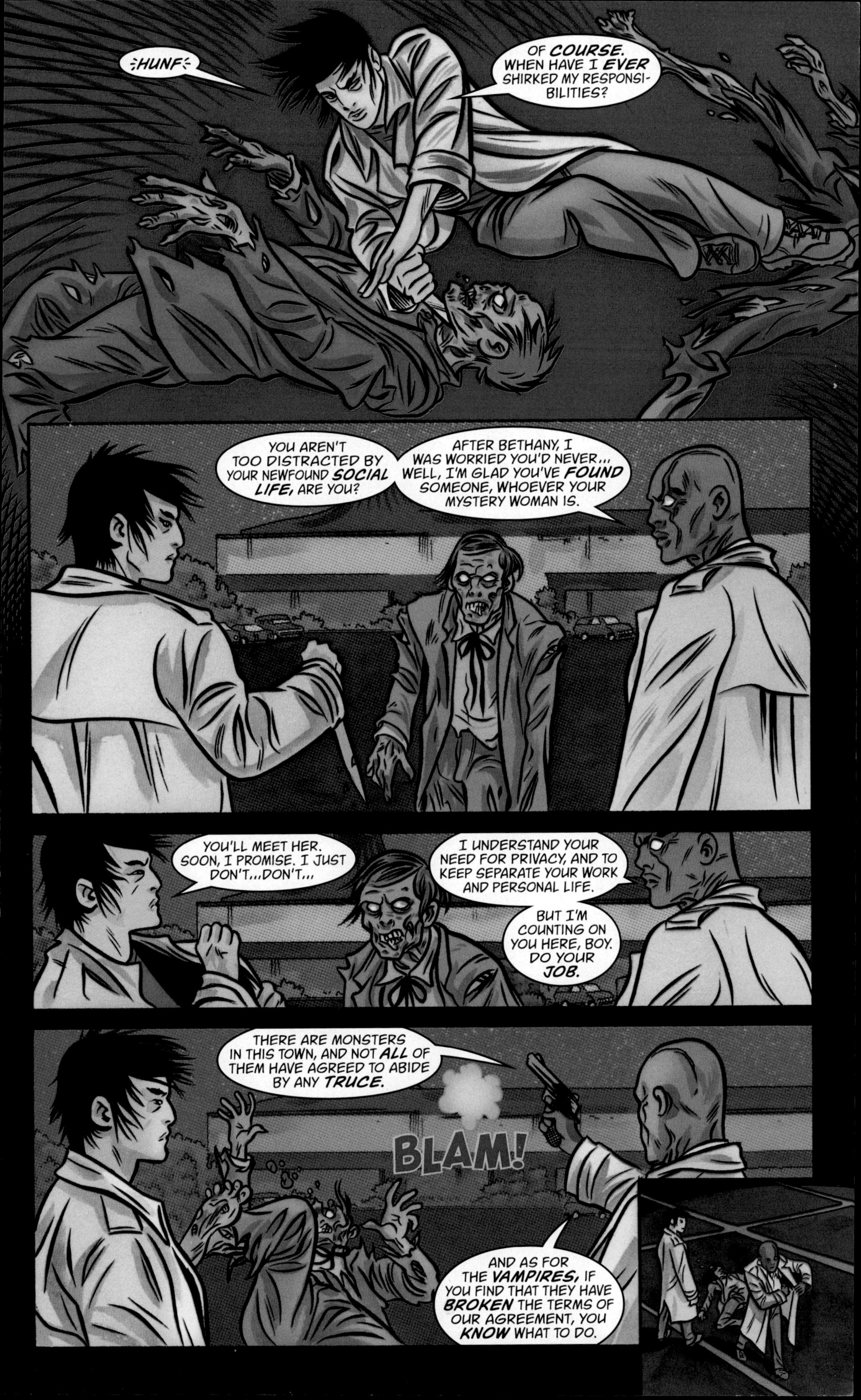
HUNF
OF COURSE. WHEN HAVE I EVER SHIRKED MY RESPONSI-BILITIES?
YOU AREN'T TOO DISTRACTED BY YOUR NEWFOUND SOCIAL LIFE, ARE YOU?
AFTER BETHANY, I WAS WORRIED YOU'D NEVER... WELL, I'M GLAD YOU'VE FOUND SOMEONE, WHOEVER YOUR MYSTERY WOMAN IS.
YOU'LL MEET HER. SOON, I PROMISE. I JUST DON'T...DON'T...
I UNDERSTAND YOUR NEED FOR PRIVACY, AND TO KEEP SEPARATE YOUR WORK AND PERSONAL LIFE.
BUT I'M COUNTING ON YOU HERE, BOY. DO YOUR JOB.
THERE ARE MONSTERS IN THIS TOWN, AND NOT ALL OF THEM HAVE AGREED TO ABIDE BY ANY TRUCE.
BLAM!
AND AS FOR THE VAMPIRES, IF YOU FIND THAT THEY HAVE BROKEN THE TERMS OF OUR AGREEMENT, YOU KNOW WHAT TO DO.

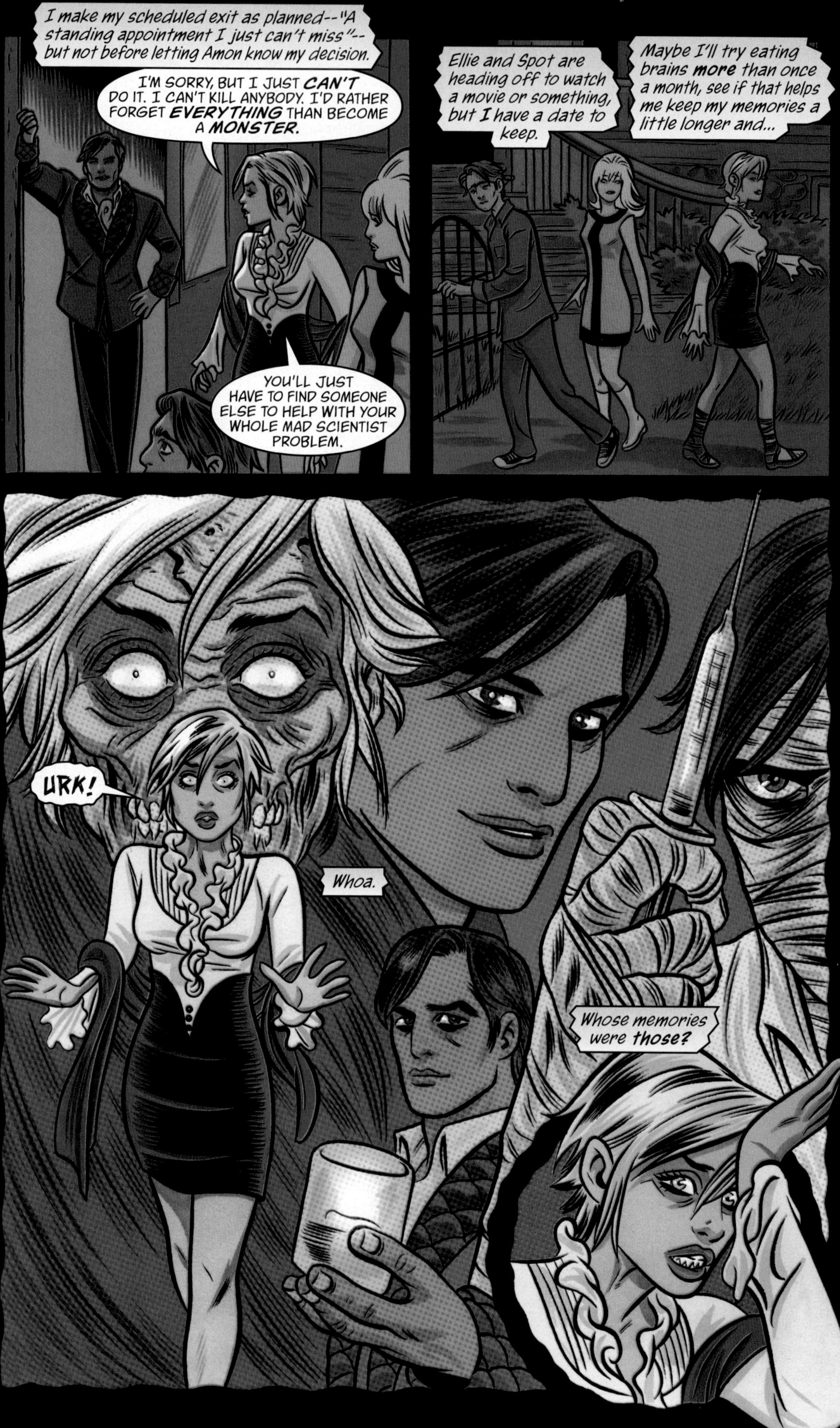
I make my scheduled exit as planned--"A standing appointment I just can't miss"--but not before letting Amon know my decision.
I'M SORRY, BUT I JUST CAN'T DO IT. I CAN'T KILL ANYBODY. I'D RATHER FORGET EVERYTHING THAN BECOME A MONSTER.
YOU'LL JUST HAVE TO FIND SOMEONE ELSE TO HELP WITH YOUR WHOLE MAD SCIENTIST PROBLEM.
Ellie and Spot are heading off to watch a movie or something, but I have a date to keep.
Maybe I'll try eating brains more than once a month, see if that helps me keep my memories a little longer and...
URK!
Whoa.
Whose memories were those?

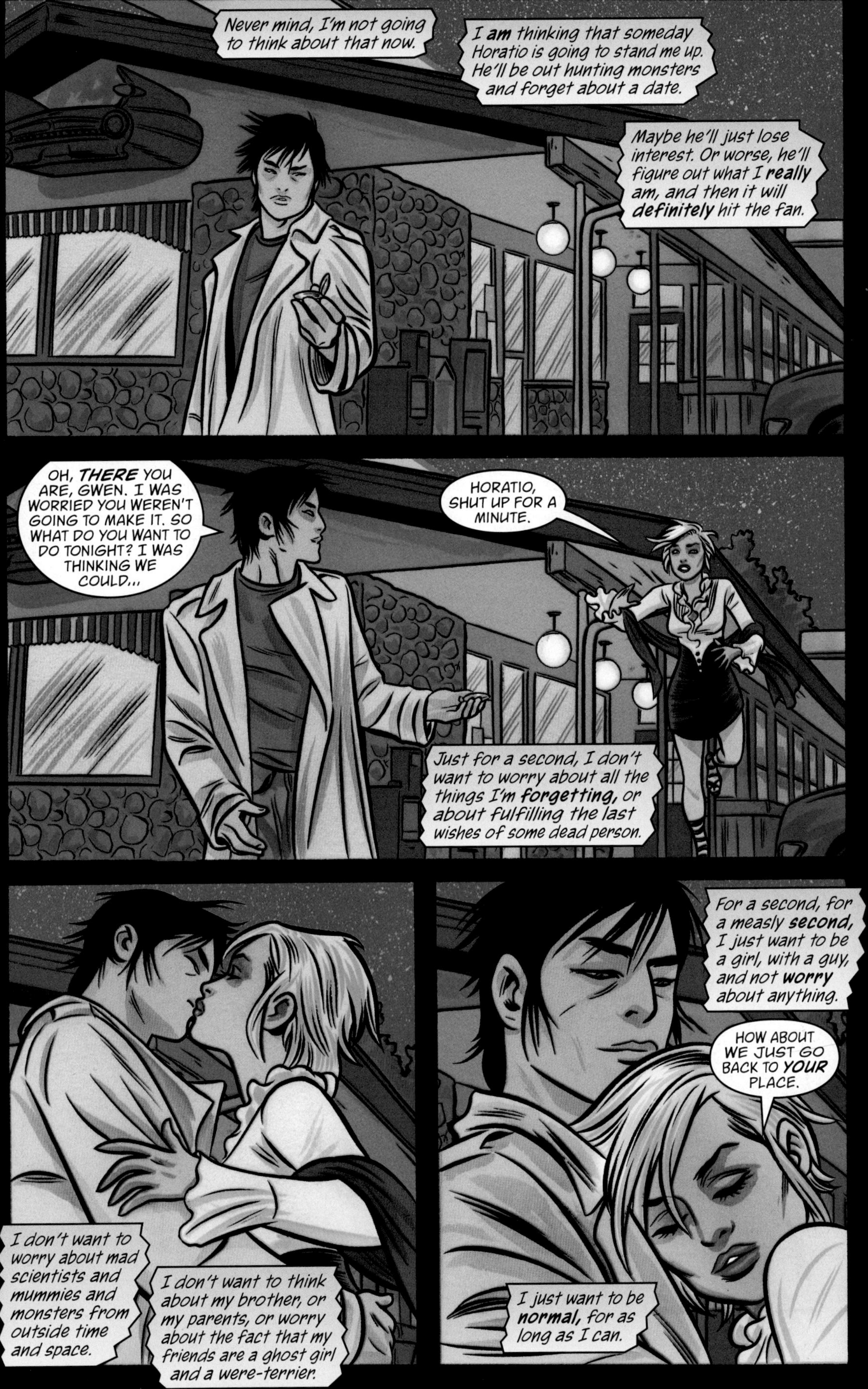

Never mind, I'm not going to think about that now.
I **am** thinking that someday Horatio is going to stand me up. He'll be out hunting monsters and forget about a date.
Maybe he'll just lose interest. Or worse, he'll figure out what I **really am**, and then it will **definitely** hit the fan.
OH, **THERE** YOU ARE, GWEN. I WAS WORRIED YOU WEREN'T GOING TO MAKE IT. SO WHAT DO YOU WANT TO DO TONIGHT? I WAS THINKING WE COULD...
HORATIO, SHUT UP FOR A MINUTE.
Just for a second, I don't want to worry about all the things I'm **forgetting**, or about fulfilling the last wishes of some dead person.
I don't want to worry about mad scientists and mummies and monsters from outside time and space.
I don't want to think about my brother, or my parents, or worry about the fact that my friends are a ghost girl and a were-terrier.
For a second, for a measly **second**, I just want to be a girl, with a guy, and not **worry** about anything.
HOW ABOUT WE JUST GO BACK TO ***YOUR*** PLACE.
I just want to be **normal**, for as long as I can.

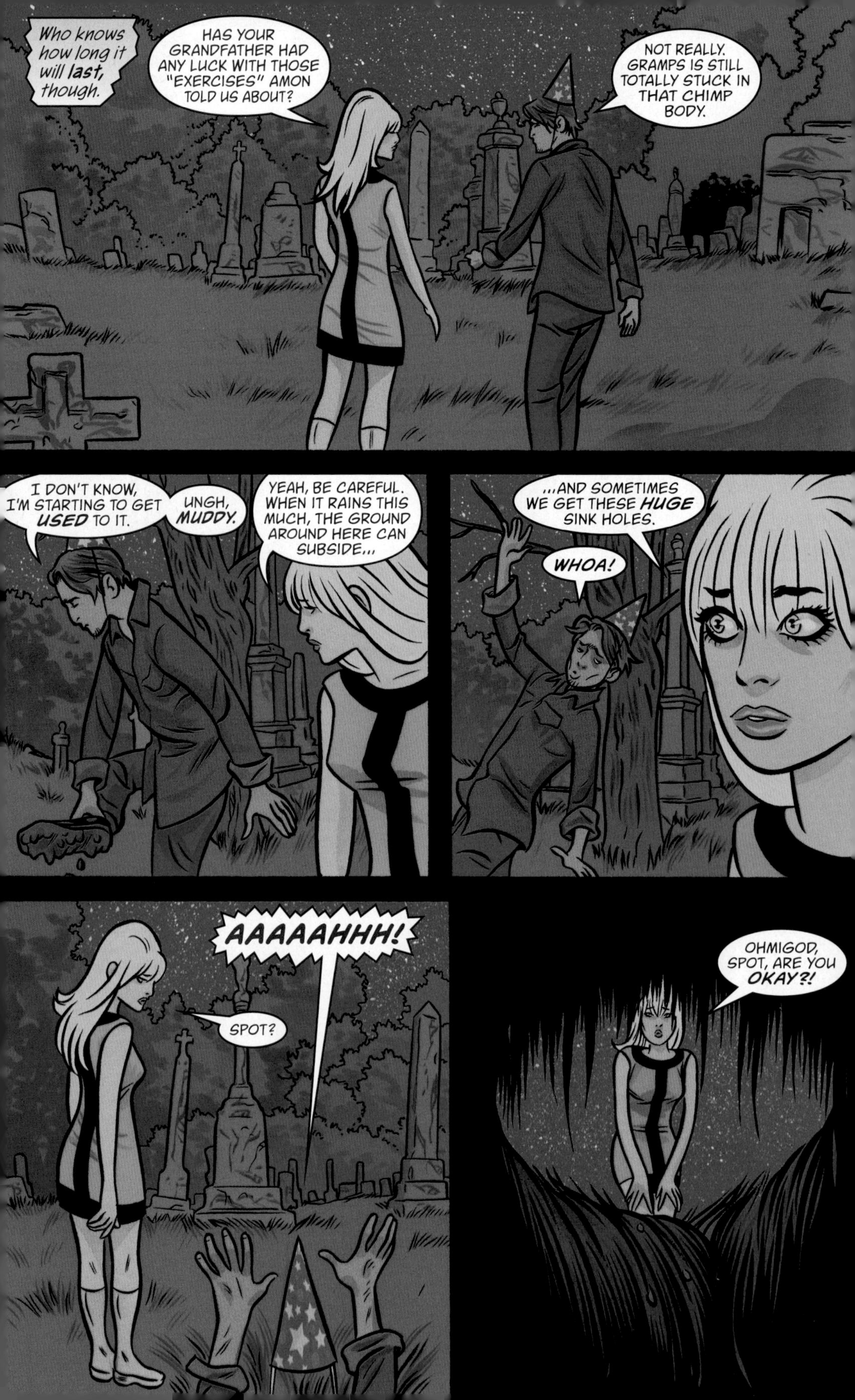
Who knows how long it will **last,** though.
HAS YOUR GRANDFATHER HAD ANY LUCK WITH THOSE "EXERCISES" AMON TOLD US ABOUT?
NOT REALLY. GRAMPS IS STILL TOTALLY STUCK IN THAT CHIMP BODY.
I DON'T KNOW, I'M STARTING TO GET **USED** TO IT.
UNGH, **MUDDY.**
YEAH, BE CAREFUL. WHEN IT RAINS THIS MUCH, THE GROUND AROUND HERE CAN SUBSIDE...
...AND SOMETIMES WE GET THESE **HUGE** SINK HOLES.
WHOA!
AAAAAHHH!
SPOT?
OHMIGOD, SPOT, ARE YOU **OKAY?!**

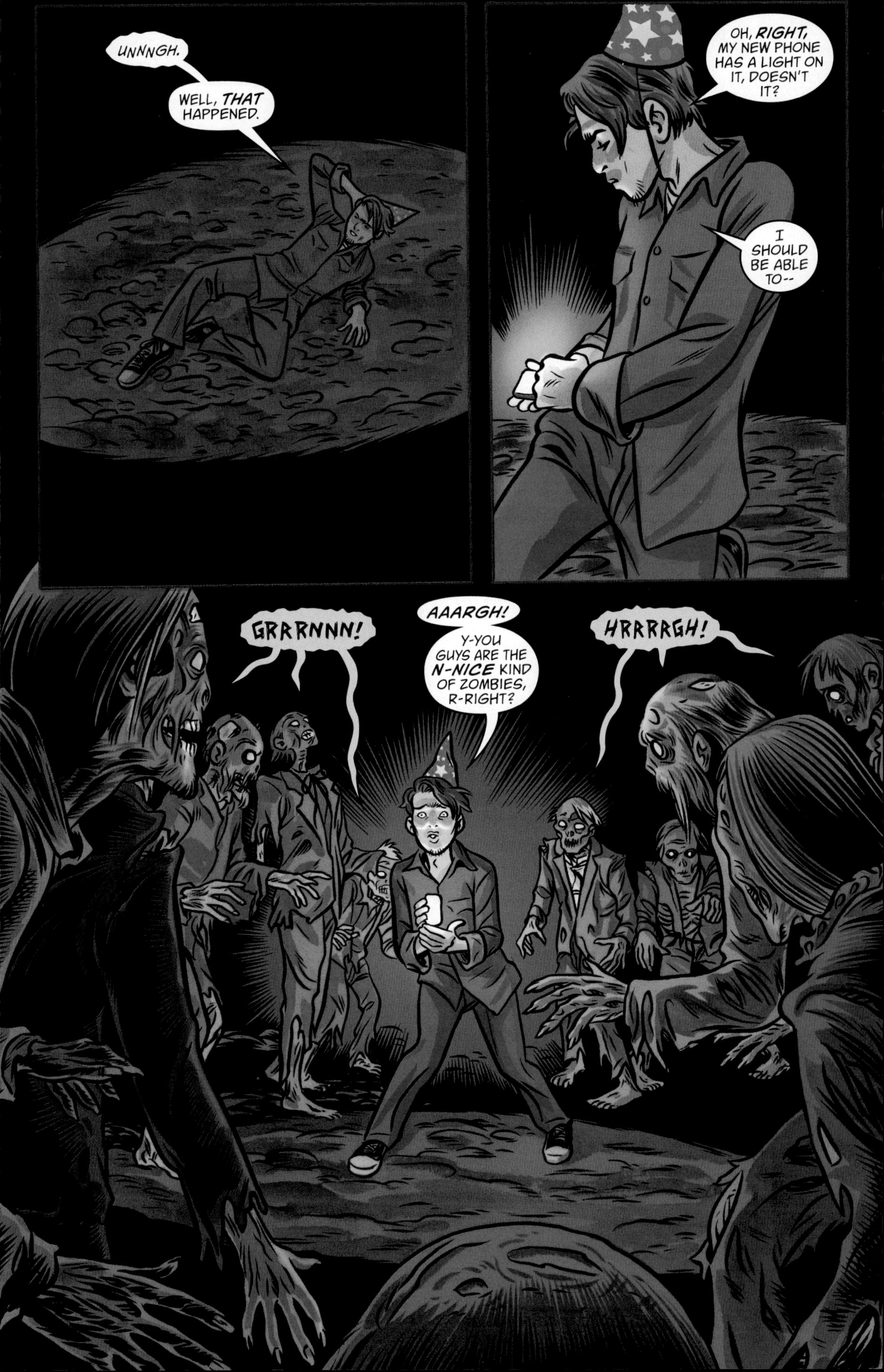
UNNNGH.
WELL, *THAT* HAPPENED.
OH, *RIGHT,* MY NEW PHONE HAS A LIGHT ON IT, DOESN'T IT?
I SHOULD BE ABLE TO--
GRRRNNN!
AAARGH!
Y-YOU GUYS ARE THE *N-NICE* KIND OF ZOMBIES, R-RIGHT?
HRRRRGH!

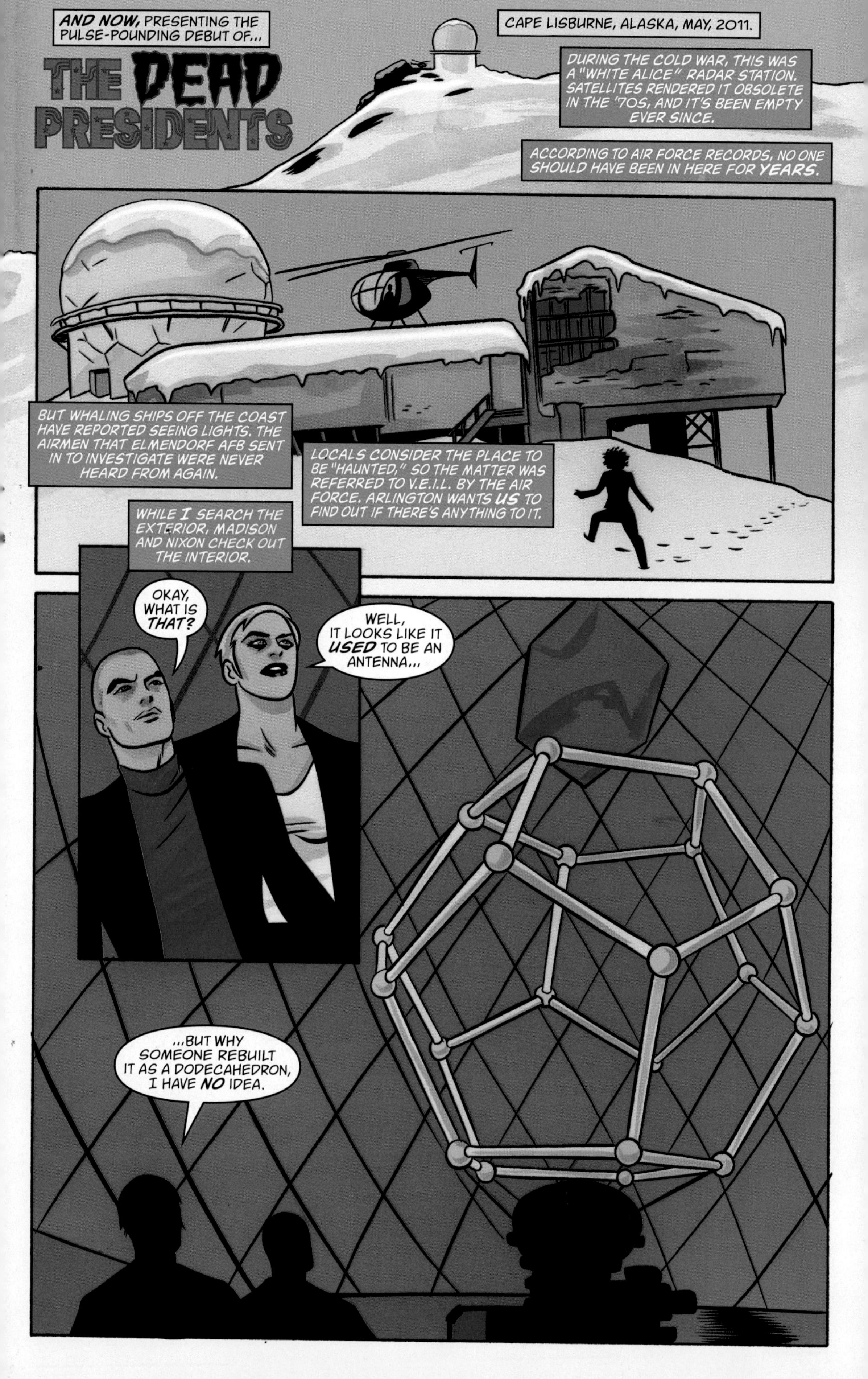
AND NOW, PRESENTING THE PULSE-POUNDING DEBUT OF...
THE DEAD PRESIDENTS
CAPE LISBURNE, ALASKA, MAY, 2011.
DURING THE COLD WAR, THIS WAS A "WHITE ALICE" RADAR STATION. SATELLITES RENDERED IT OBSOLETE IN THE '70S, AND IT'S BEEN EMPTY EVER SINCE.
ACCORDING TO AIR FORCE RECORDS, NO ONE SHOULD HAVE BEEN IN HERE FOR YEARS.
BUT WHALING SHIPS OFF THE COAST HAVE REPORTED SEEING LIGHTS. THE AIRMEN THAT ELMENDORF AFB SENT IN TO INVESTIGATE WERE NEVER HEARD FROM AGAIN.
LOCALS CONSIDER THE PLACE TO BE "HAUNTED," SO THE MATTER WAS REFERRED TO V.E.I.L. BY THE AIR FORCE. ARLINGTON WANTS US TO FIND OUT IF THERE'S ANYTHING TO IT.
WHILE I SEARCH THE EXTERIOR, MADISON AND NIXON CHECK OUT THE INTERIOR.
OKAY, WHAT IS THAT?
WELL, IT LOOKS LIKE IT USED TO BE AN ANTENNA...
...BUT WHY SOMEONE REBUILT IT AS A DODECAHEDRON, I HAVE NO IDEA.

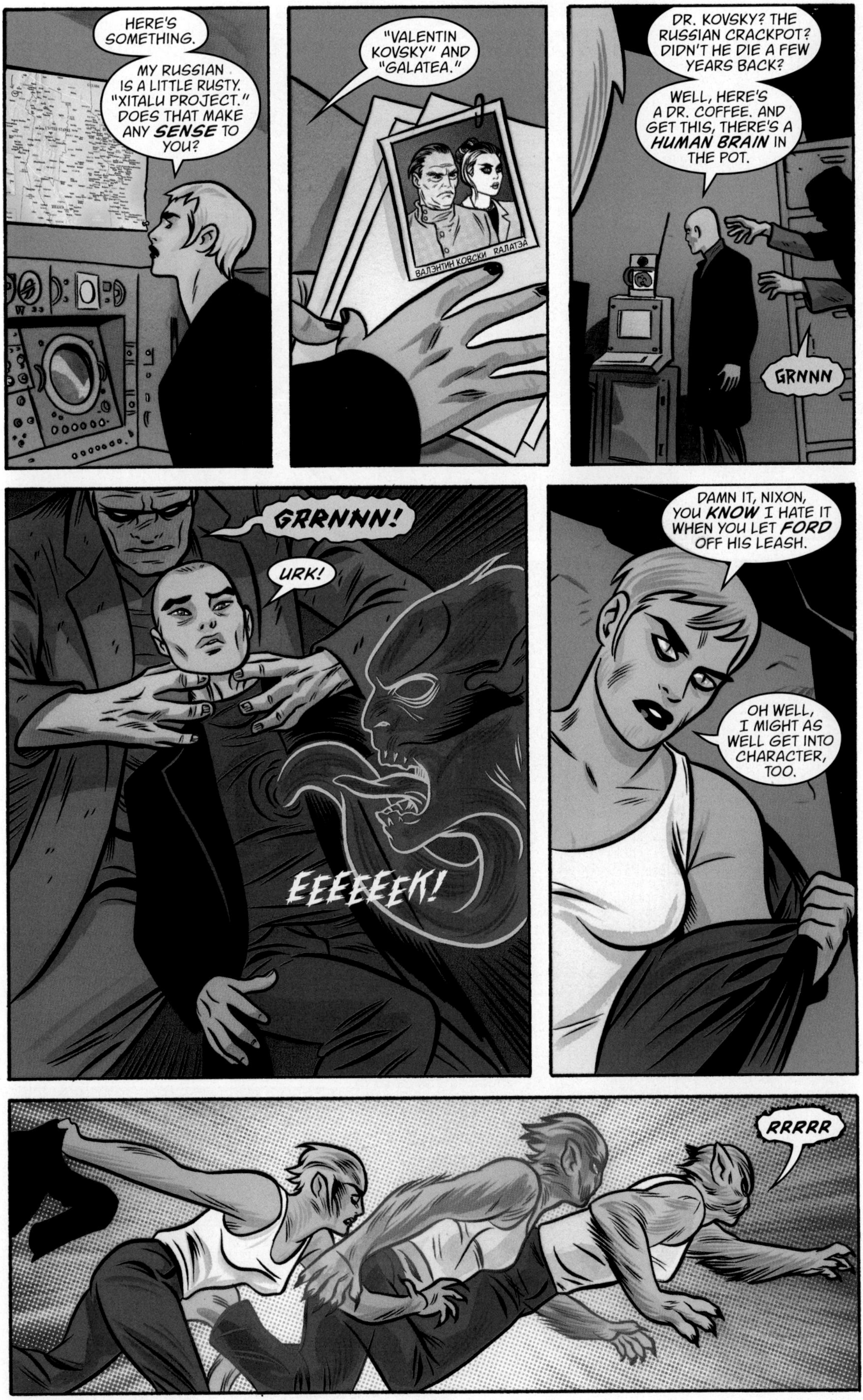
HERE'S SOMETHING.
MY RUSSIAN IS A LITTLE RUSTY. "XITALU PROJECT." DOES THAT MAKE ANY SENSE TO YOU?
"VALENTIN KOVSKY" AND "GALATEA."
ВАЛЭНТИН КОВСКИ ГАЛАТЭА
DR. KOVSKY? THE RUSSIAN CRACKPOT? DIDN'T HE DIE A FEW YEARS BACK?
WELL, HERE'S A DR. COFFEE. AND GET THIS, THERE'S A HUMAN BRAIN IN THE POT.
GRNNN
GRRNNN!
URK!
EEEEEEK!
DAMN IT, NIXON, YOU KNOW I HATE IT WHEN YOU LET FORD OFF HIS LEASH.
OH WELL, I MIGHT AS WELL GET INTO CHARACTER, TOO.
RRRRR

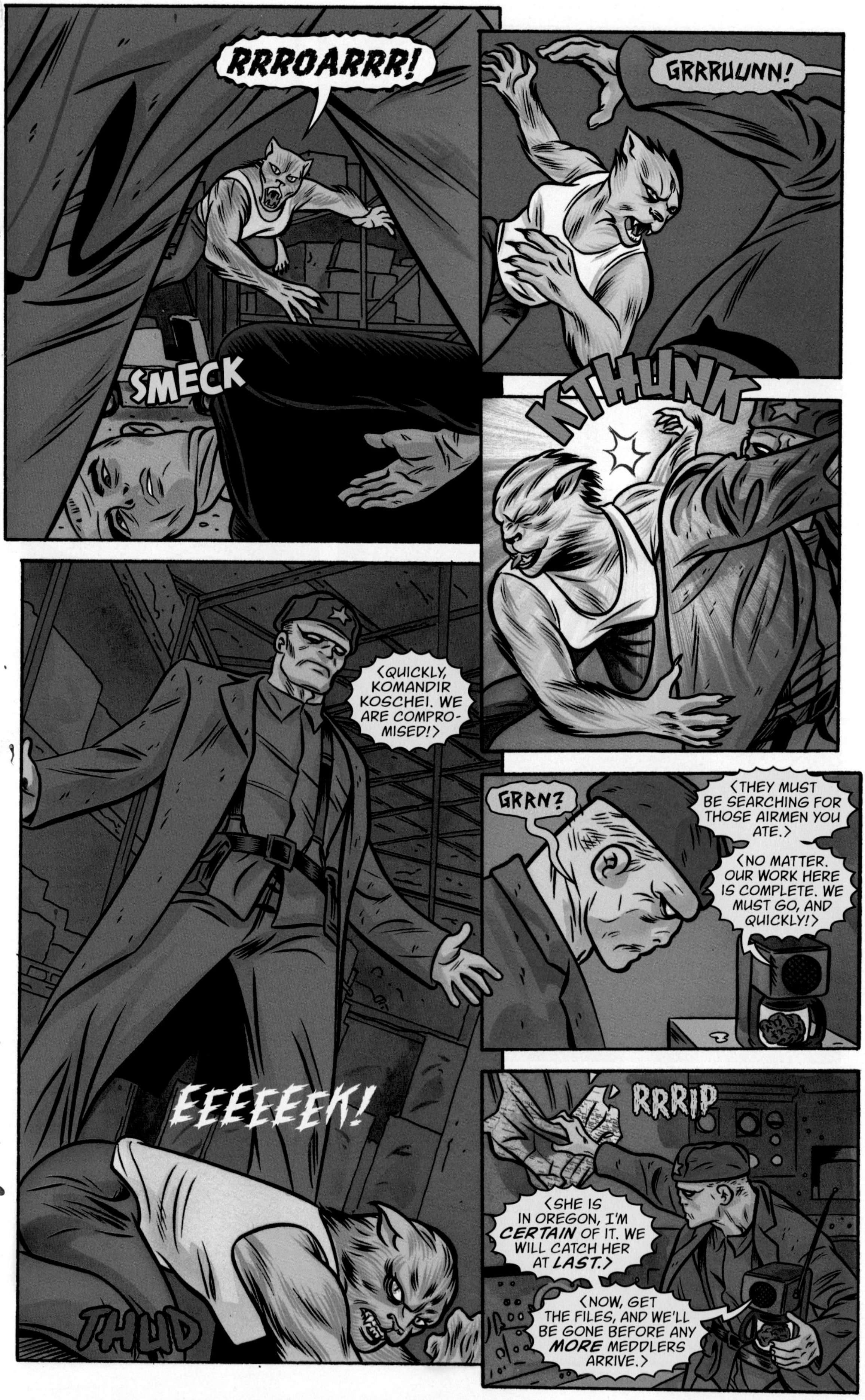
RRROARRR!
SMECK
GRRRUUNN!
KTHUNK
‹QUICKLY, KOMANDIR KOSCHEI. WE ARE COMPRO-MISED!›
EEEEEEK!
THUD
GRRN?
‹THEY MUST BE SEARCHING FOR THOSE AIRMEN YOU ATE.›
‹NO MATTER. OUR WORK HERE IS COMPLETE. WE MUST GO, AND QUICKLY!›
RRRIP
‹SHE IS IN OREGON, I'M ***CERTAIN*** OF IT. WE WILL CATCH HER AT ***LAST.***›
‹NOW, GET THE FILES, AND WE'LL BE GONE BEFORE ANY ***MORE*** MEDDLERS ARRIVE.›

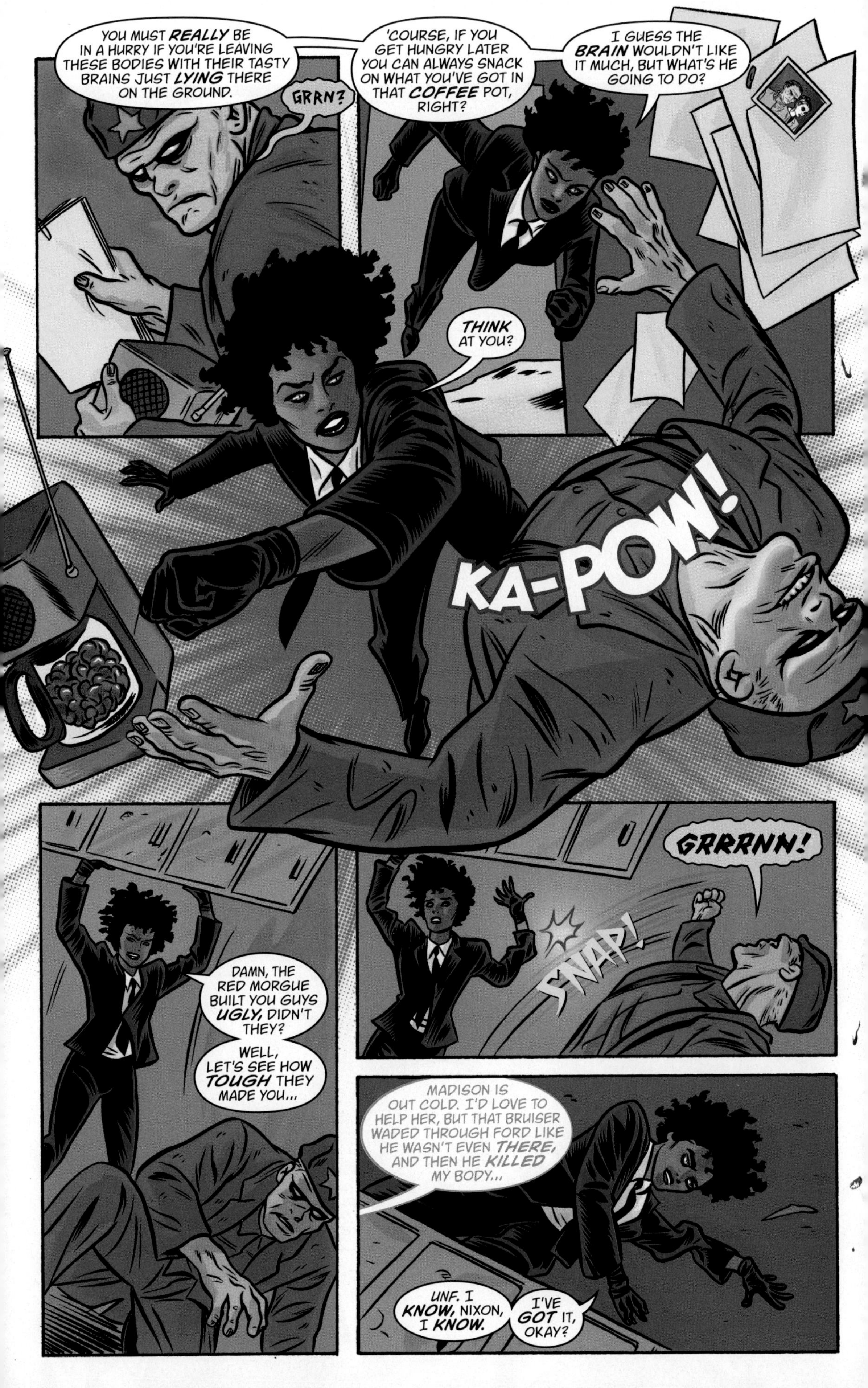

YOU MUST REALLY BE IN A HURRY IF YOU'RE LEAVING THESE BODIES WITH THEIR TASTY BRAINS JUST LYING THERE ON THE GROUND.
GRRN?
'COURSE, IF YOU GET HUNGRY LATER YOU CAN ALWAYS SNACK ON WHAT YOU'VE GOT IN THAT COFFEE POT, RIGHT?
I GUESS THE BRAIN WOULDN'T LIKE IT MUCH, BUT WHAT'S HE GOING TO DO?
THINK AT YOU?
KA-POW!
DAMN, THE RED MORGUE BUILT YOU GUYS UGLY, DIDN'T THEY?
WELL, LET'S SEE HOW TOUGH THEY MADE YOU...
GRRRNN!
SNAP!
MADISON IS OUT COLD. I'D LOVE TO HELP HER, BUT THAT BRUISER WADED THROUGH FORD LIKE HE WASN'T EVEN THERE, AND THEN HE KILLED MY BODY...
UNF. I KNOW, NIXON, I KNOW.
I'VE GOT IT, OKAY?

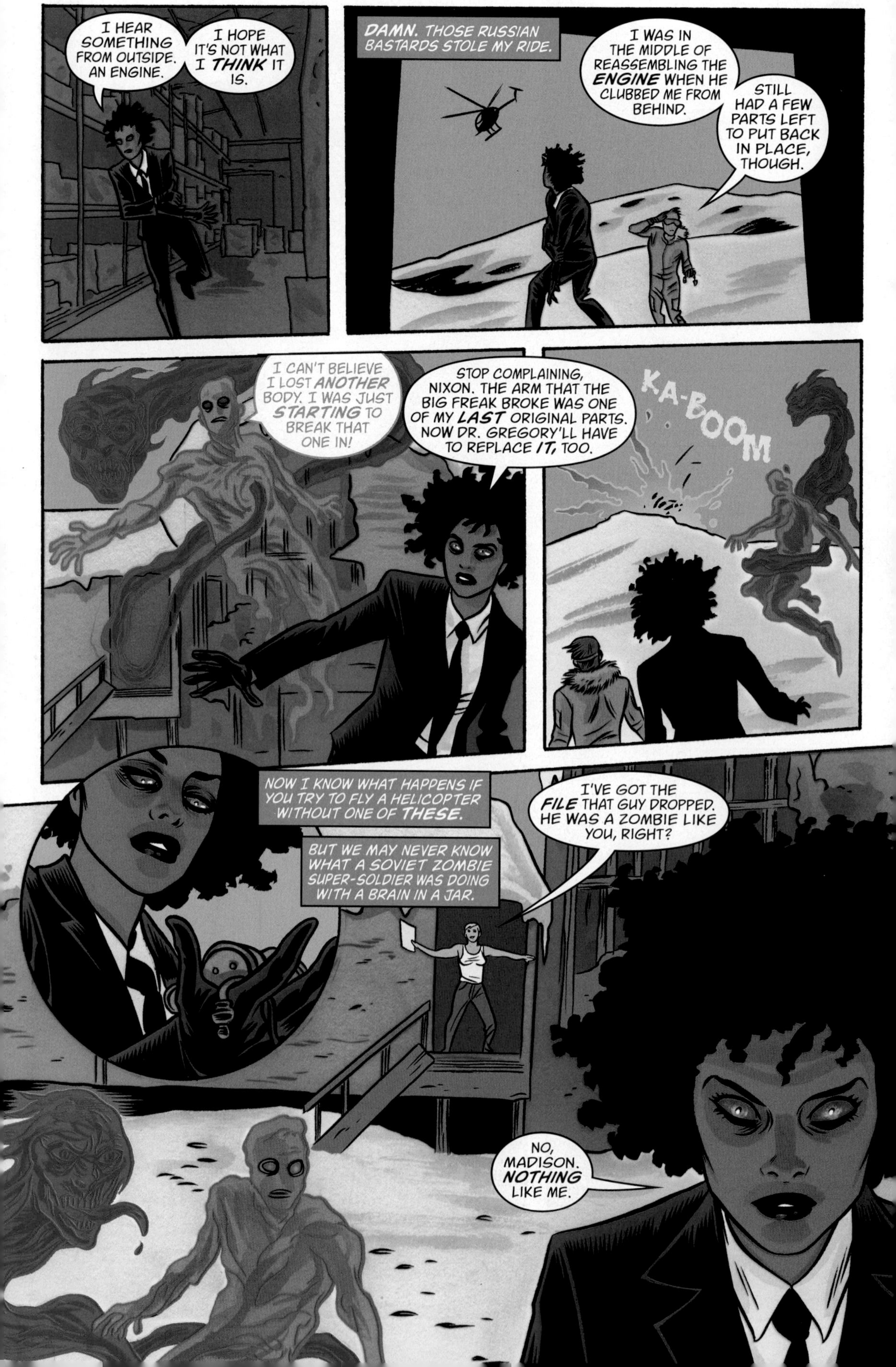
I HEAR SOMETHING FROM OUTSIDE. AN ENGINE.
I HOPE IT'S NOT WHAT I THINK IT IS.
DAMN. THOSE RUSSIAN BASTARDS STOLE MY RIDE.
I WAS IN THE MIDDLE OF REASSEMBLING THE ENGINE WHEN HE CLUBBED ME FROM BEHIND.
STILL HAD A FEW PARTS LEFT TO PUT BACK IN PLACE, THOUGH.
I CAN'T BELIEVE I LOST ANOTHER BODY. I WAS JUST STARTING TO BREAK THAT ONE IN!
STOP COMPLAINING, NIXON. THE ARM THAT THE BIG FREAK BROKE WAS ONE OF MY LAST ORIGINAL PARTS. NOW DR. GREGORY'LL HAVE TO REPLACE IT, TOO.
KA-BOOM
NOW I KNOW WHAT HAPPENS IF YOU TRY TO FLY A HELICOPTER WITHOUT ONE OF THESE.
BUT WE MAY NEVER KNOW WHAT A SOVIET ZOMBIE SUPER-SOLDIER WAS DOING WITH A BRAIN IN A JAR.
I'VE GOT THE FILE THAT GUY DROPPED. HE WAS A ZOMBIE LIKE YOU, RIGHT?
NO, MADISON. NOTHING LIKE ME.

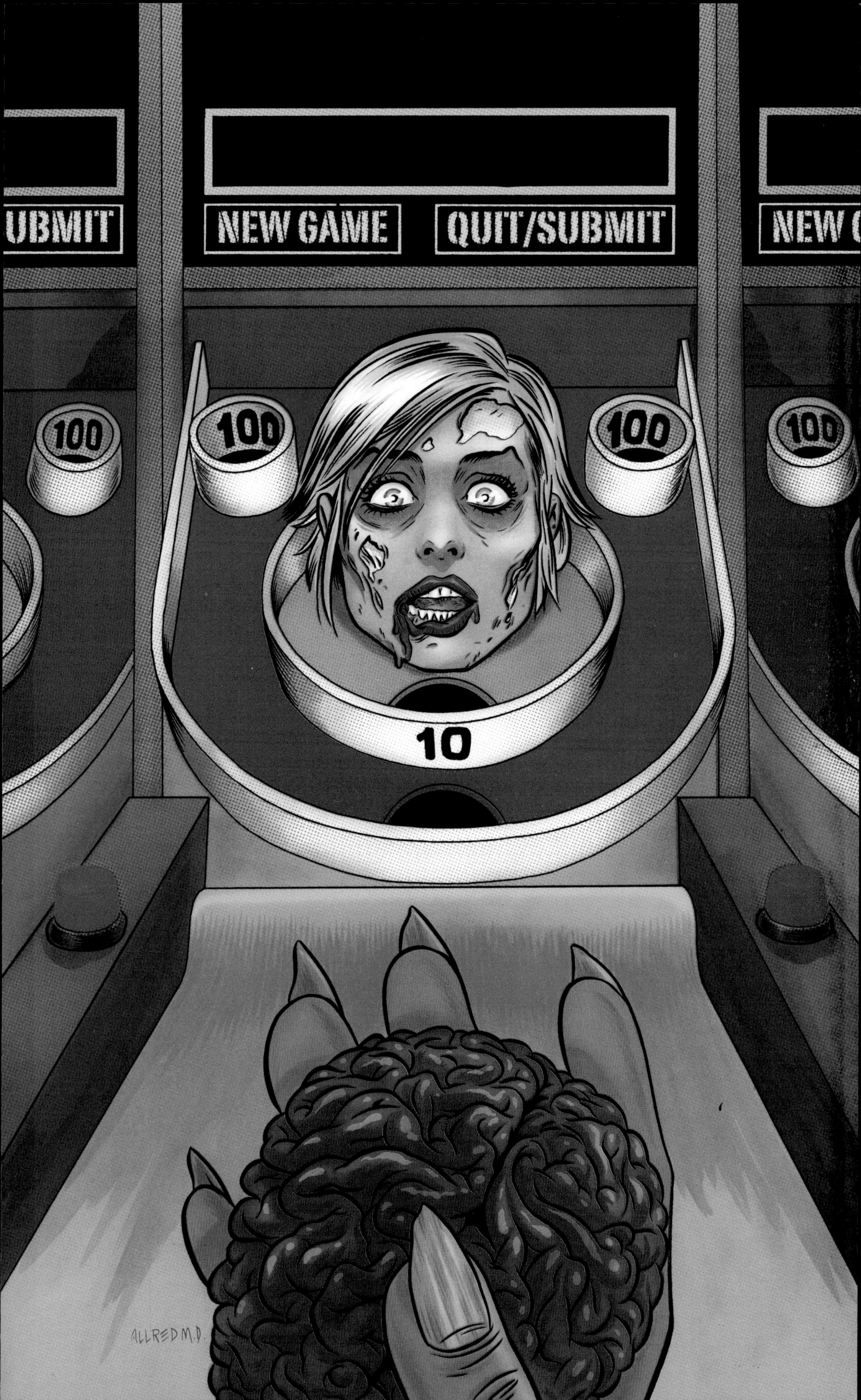
UBMIT
NEW GAME
QUIT/SUBMIT
NEW G
100
100
100
100
10
ALLRED M.D.

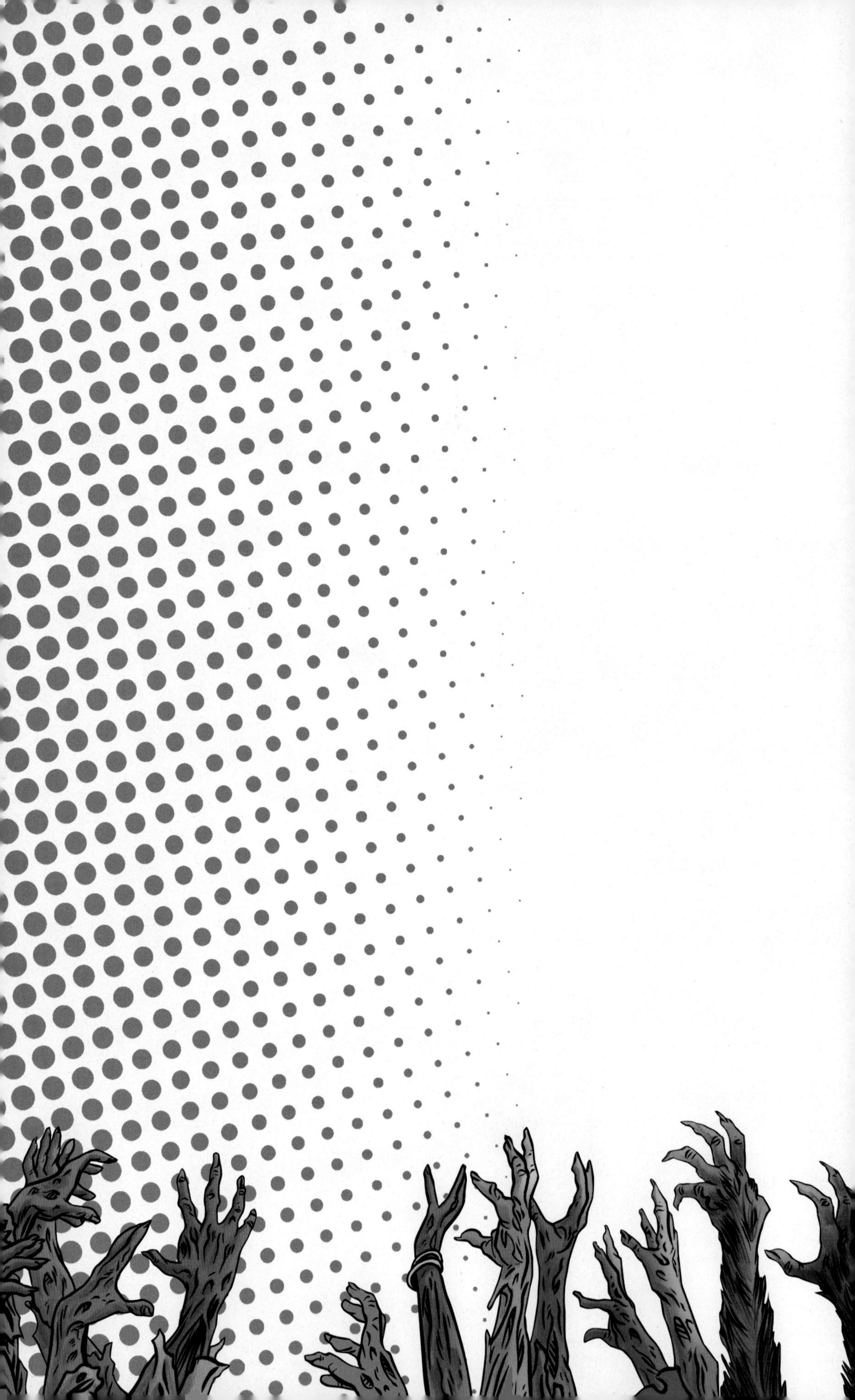

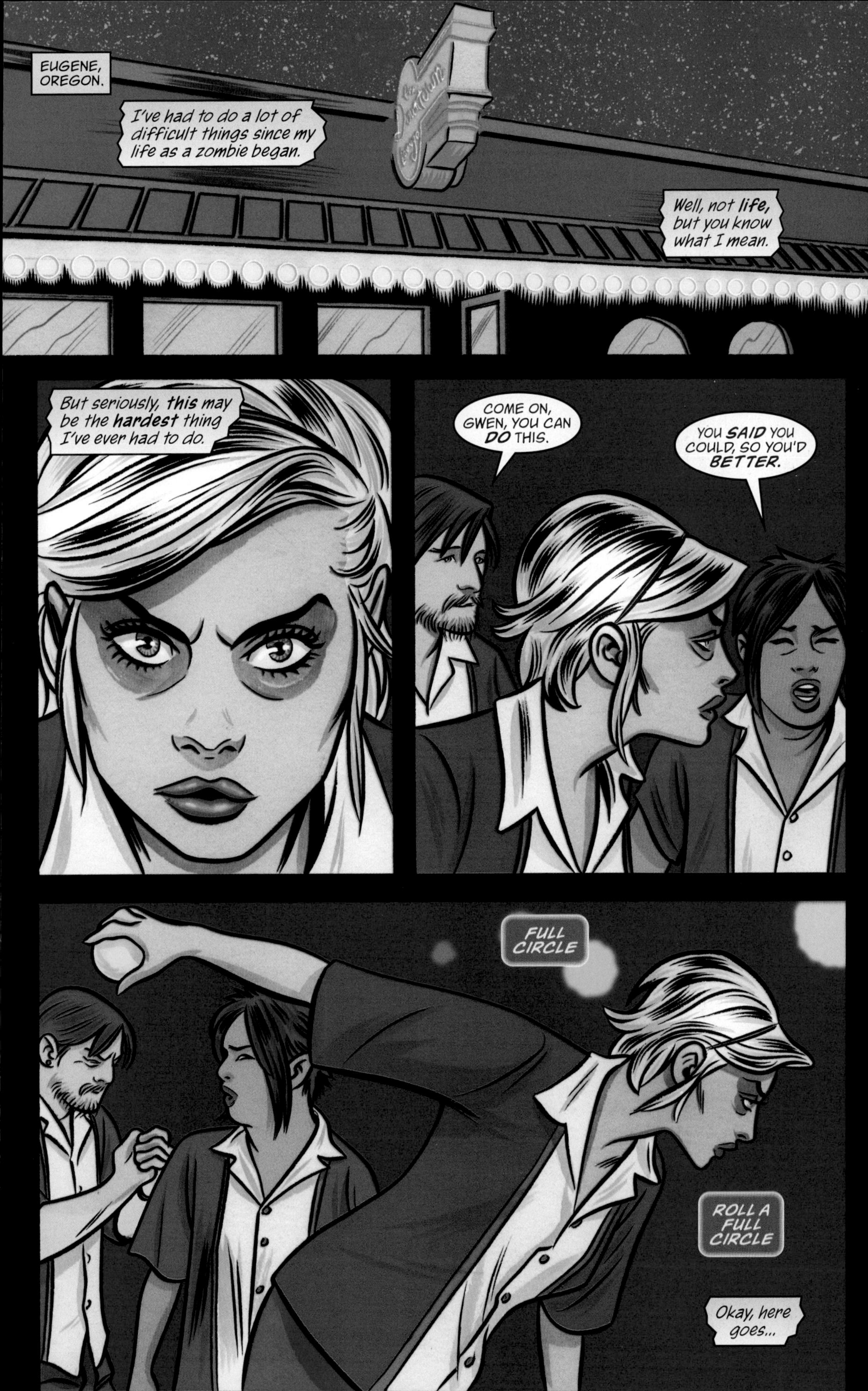
EUGENE, OREGON.
I've had to do a lot of difficult things since my life as a zombie began.
Well, not life, but you know what I mean.
But seriously, this may be the hardest thing I've ever had to do.
COME ON, GWEN, YOU CAN DO THIS.
YOU SAID YOU COULD, SO YOU'D BETTER.
FULL CIRCLE
ROLL A FULL CIRCLE
Okay, here goes...

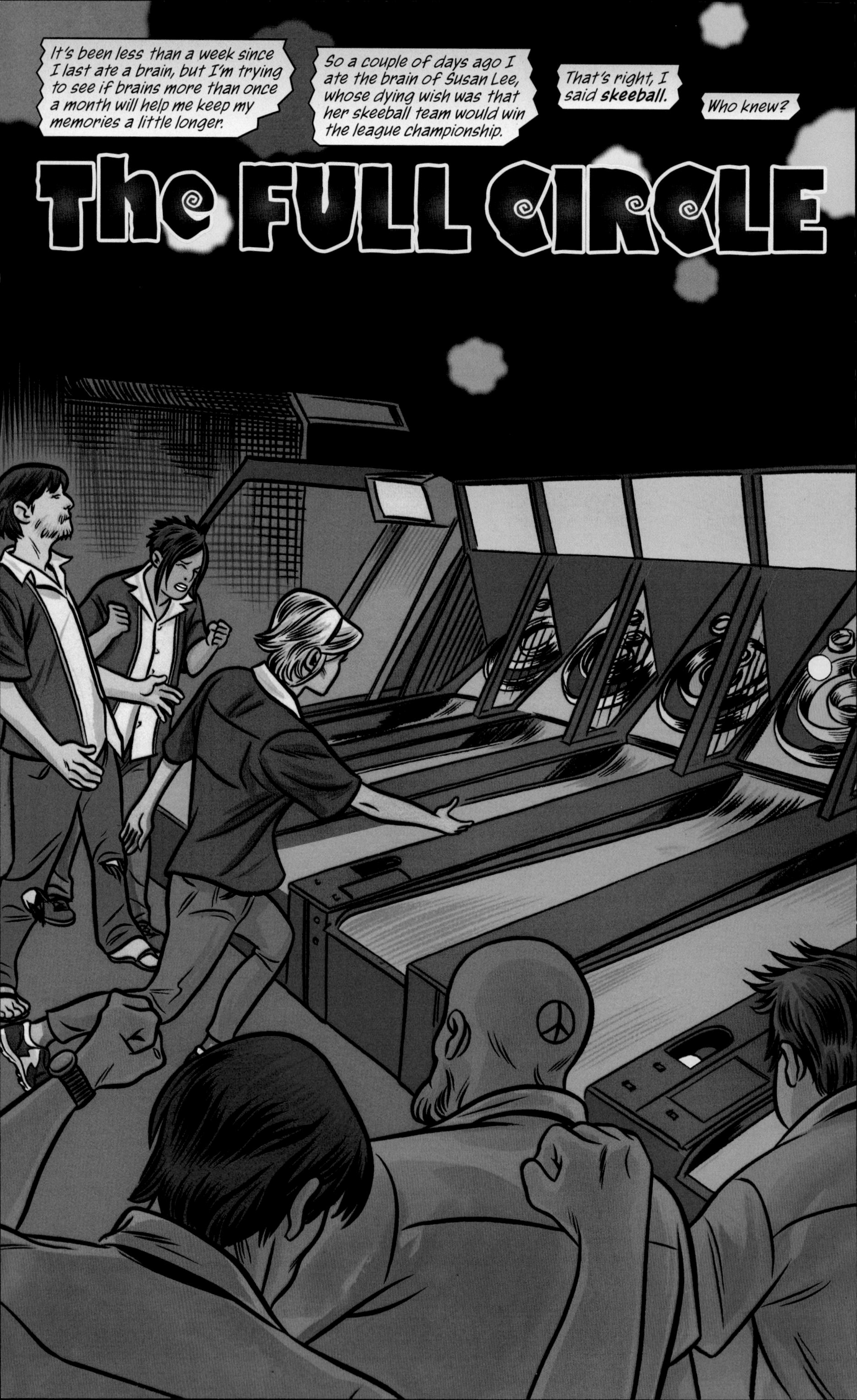
It's been less than a week since I last ate a brain, but I'm trying to see if brains more than once a month will help me keep my memories a little longer.
So a couple of days ago I ate the brain of Susan Lee, whose dying wish was that her skeeball team would win the league championship.
That's right, I said **skeeball**.
Who knew?
The FULL CIRCLE

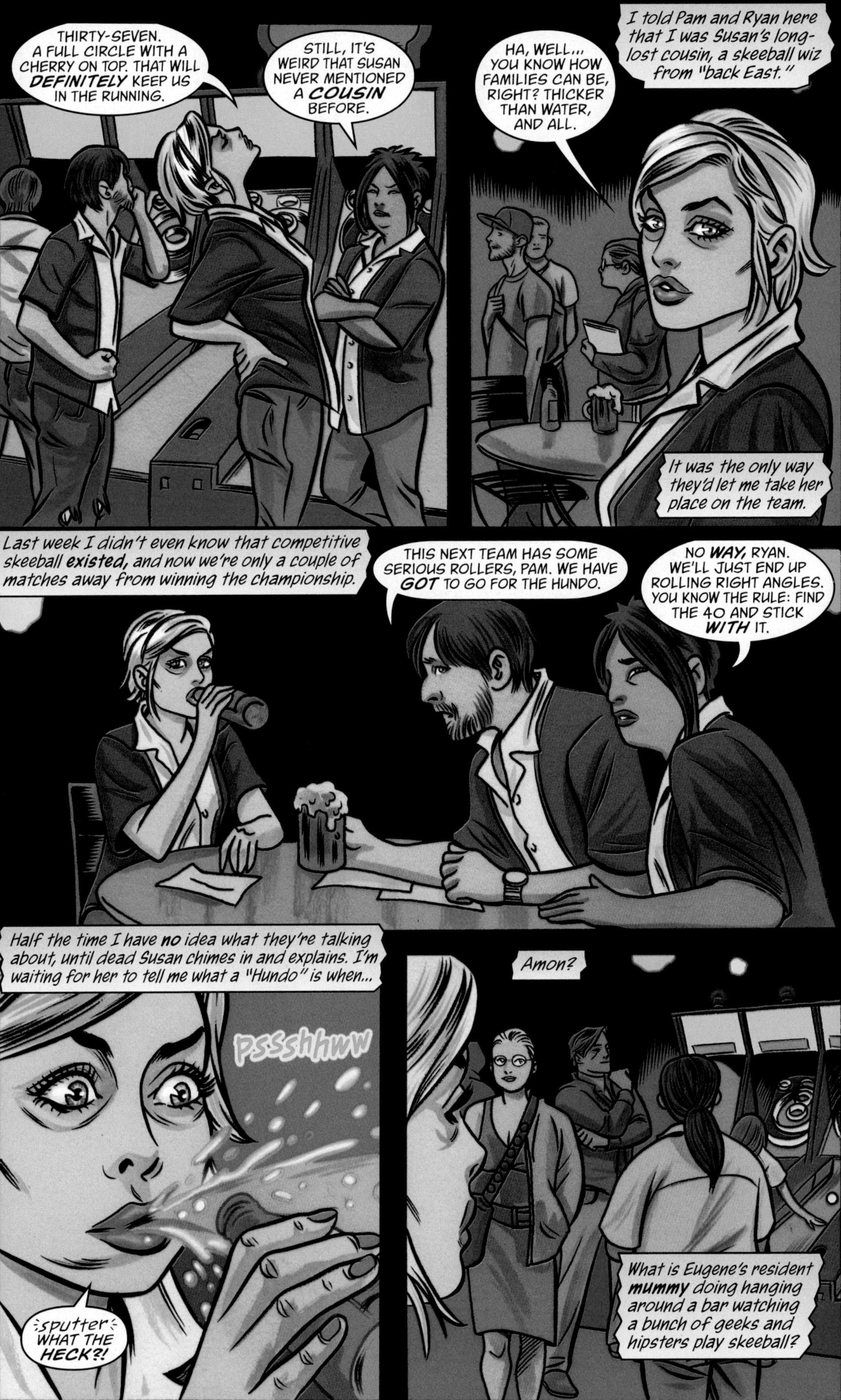
THIRTY-SEVEN. A FULL CIRCLE WITH A CHERRY ON TOP. THAT WILL DEFINITELY KEEP US IN THE RUNNING.
STILL, IT'S WEIRD THAT SUSAN NEVER MENTIONED A COUSIN BEFORE.
HA, WELL... YOU KNOW HOW FAMILIES CAN BE, RIGHT? THICKER THAN WATER, AND ALL.
I told Pam and Ryan here that I was Susan's long-lost cousin, a skeeball wiz from "back East."
It was the only way they'd let me take her place on the team.
Last week I didn't even know that competitive skeeball existed, and now we're only a couple of matches away from winning the championship.
THIS NEXT TEAM HAS SOME SERIOUS ROLLERS, PAM. WE HAVE GOT TO GO FOR THE HUNDO.
NO WAY, RYAN. WE'LL JUST END UP ROLLING RIGHT ANGLES. YOU KNOW THE RULE: FIND THE 40 AND STICK WITH IT.
Half the time I have no idea what they're talking about, until dead Susan chimes in and explains. I'm waiting for her to tell me what a "Hundo" is when...
PSSSHHWW
sputter WHAT THE HECK?!
Amon?
What is Eugene's resident mummy doing hanging around a bar watching a bunch of geeks and hipsters play skeeball?

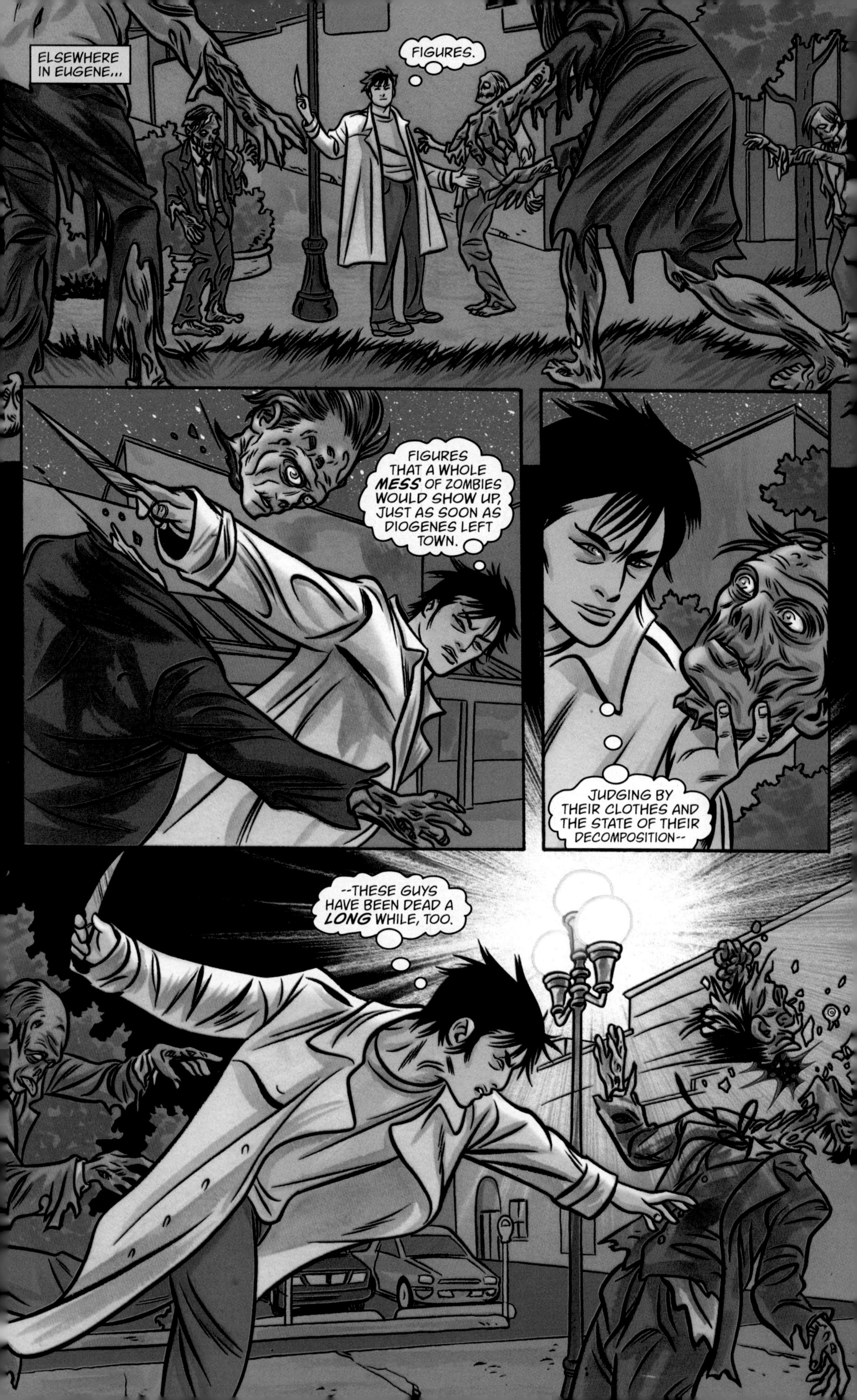
ELSEWHERE IN EUGENE...
FIGURES.
FIGURES THAT A WHOLE MESS OF ZOMBIES WOULD SHOW UP, JUST AS SOON AS DIOGENES LEFT TOWN.
JUDGING BY THEIR CLOTHES AND THE STATE OF THEIR DECOMPOSITION--
--THESE GUYS HAVE BEEN DEAD A LONG WHILE, TOO.

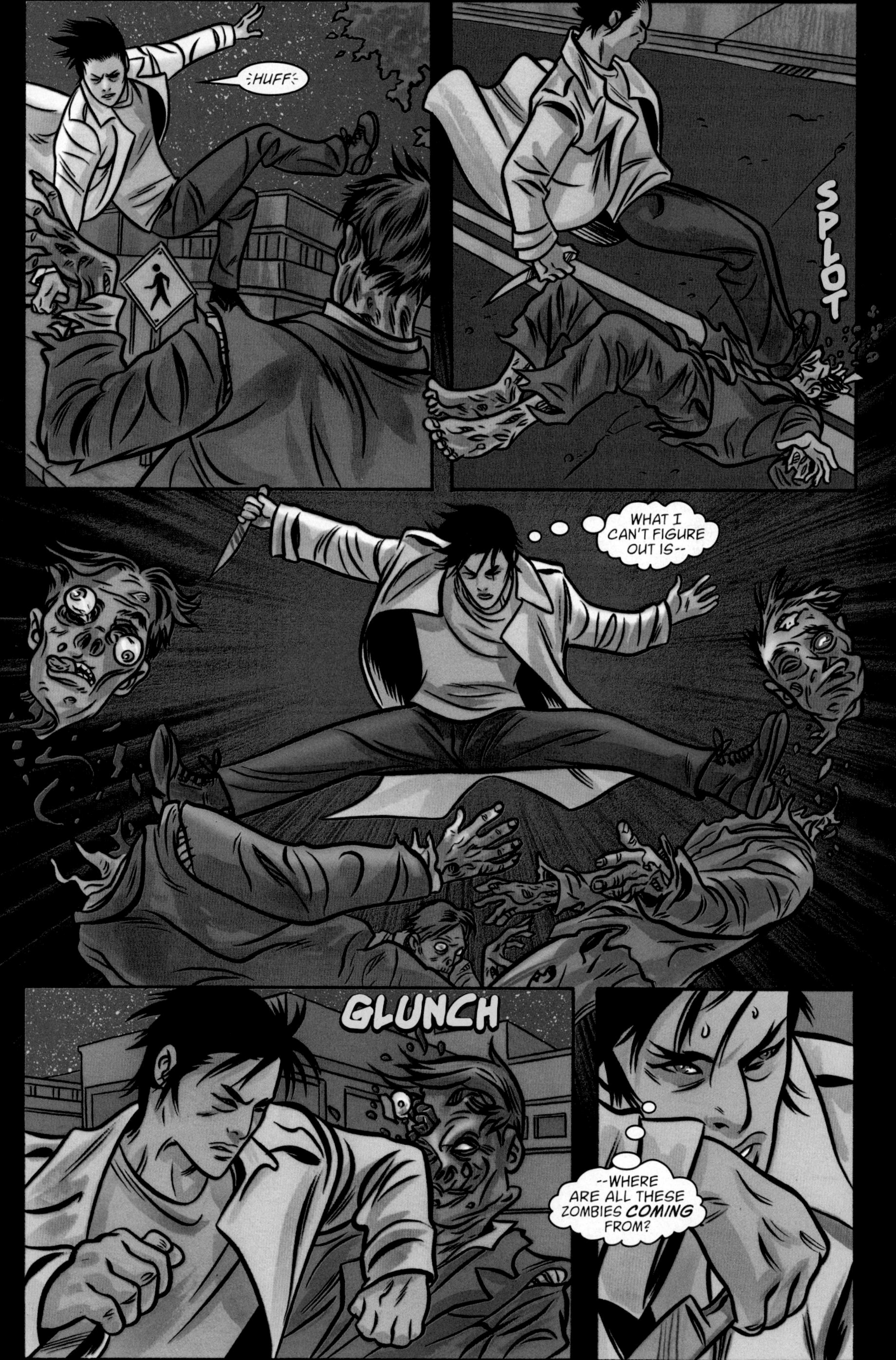
HUFF
SPLOT
WHAT I CAN'T FIGURE OUT IS--
GLUNCH
--WHERE ARE ALL THESE ZOMBIES **COMING** FROM?

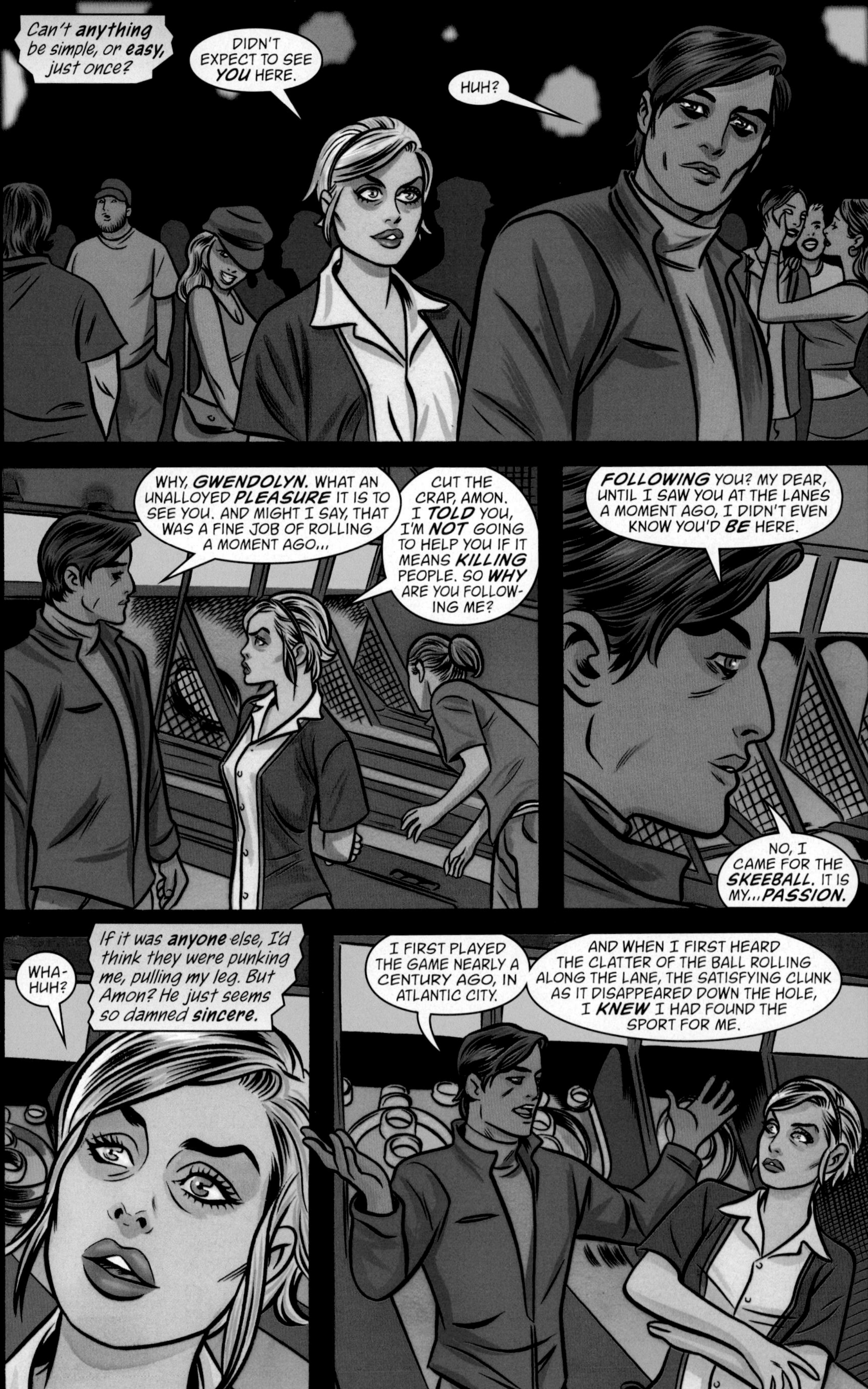
Can't anything be simple, or easy, just once?
DIDN'T EXPECT TO SEE YOU HERE.
HUH?
WHY, GWENDOLYN. WHAT AN UNALLOYED PLEASURE IT IS TO SEE YOU. AND MIGHT I SAY, THAT WAS A FINE JOB OF ROLLING A MOMENT AGO...
CUT THE CRAP, AMON. I TOLD YOU, I'M NOT GOING TO HELP YOU IF IT MEANS KILLING PEOPLE. SO WHY ARE YOU FOLLOW-ING ME?
FOLLOWING YOU? MY DEAR, UNTIL I SAW YOU AT THE LANES A MOMENT AGO, I DIDN'T EVEN KNOW YOU'D BE HERE.
NO, I CAME FOR THE SKEEBALL. IT IS MY...PASSION.
WHA-HUH?
If it was anyone else, I'd think they were punking me, pulling my leg. But Amon? He just seems so damned sincere.
I FIRST PLAYED THE GAME NEARLY A CENTURY AGO, IN ATLANTIC CITY.
AND WHEN I FIRST HEARD THE CLATTER OF THE BALL ROLLING ALONG THE LANE, THE SATISFYING CLUNK AS IT DISAPPEARED DOWN THE HOLE, I KNEW I HAD FOUND THE SPORT FOR ME.

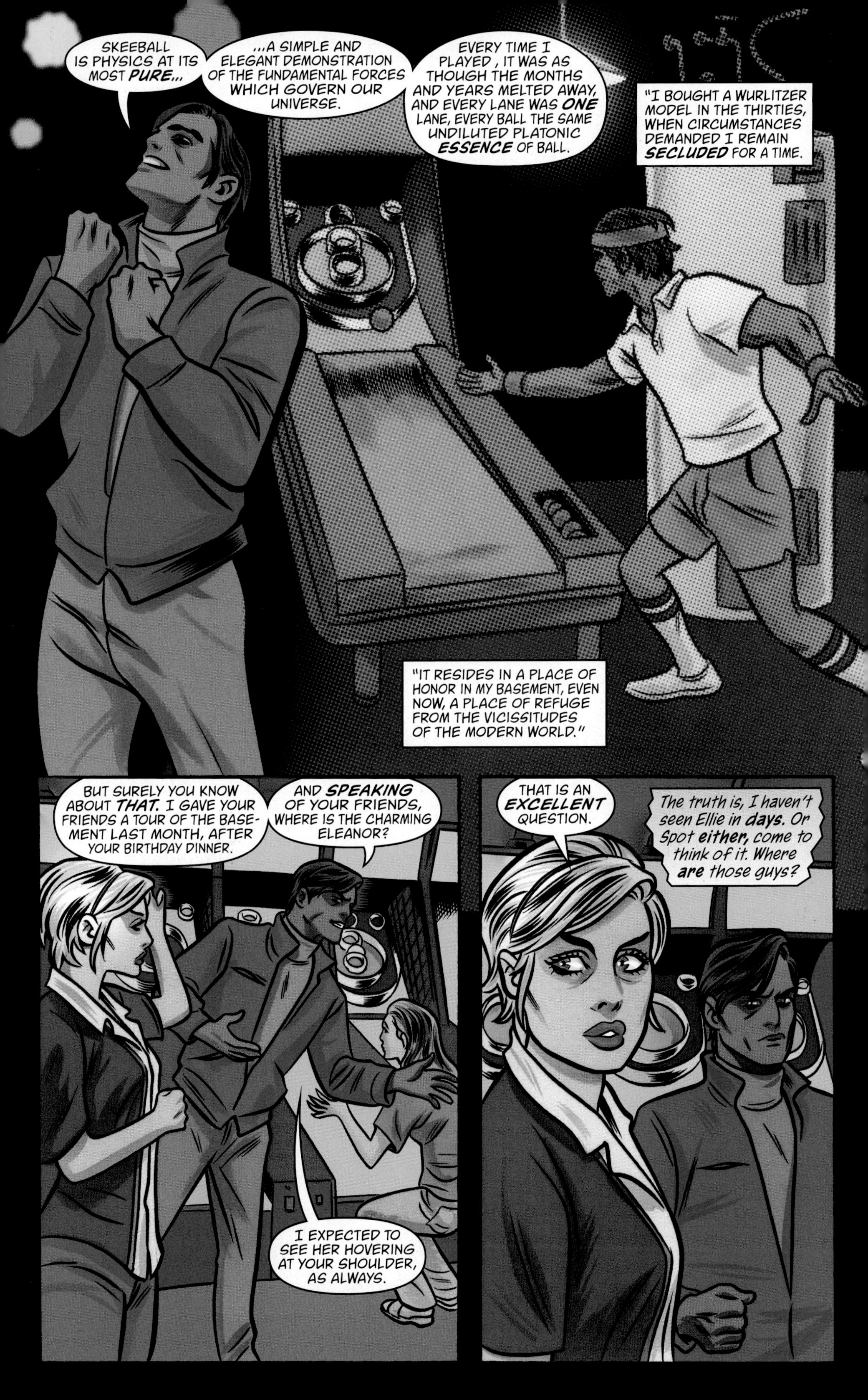
SKEEBALL IS PHYSICS AT ITS MOST PURE...
...A SIMPLE AND ELEGANT DEMONSTRATION OF THE FUNDAMENTAL FORCES WHICH GOVERN OUR UNIVERSE.
EVERY TIME I PLAYED, IT WAS AS THOUGH THE MONTHS AND YEARS MELTED AWAY, AND EVERY LANE WAS ONE LANE, EVERY BALL THE SAME UNDILUTED PLATONIC ESSENCE OF BALL.
"I BOUGHT A WURLITZER MODEL IN THE THIRTIES, WHEN CIRCUMSTANCES DEMANDED I REMAIN SECLUDED FOR A TIME.
"IT RESIDES IN A PLACE OF HONOR IN MY BASEMENT, EVEN NOW, A PLACE OF REFUGE FROM THE VICISSITUDES OF THE MODERN WORLD."
BUT SURELY YOU KNOW ABOUT THAT. I GAVE YOUR FRIENDS A TOUR OF THE BASEMENT LAST MONTH, AFTER YOUR BIRTHDAY DINNER.
AND SPEAKING OF YOUR FRIENDS, WHERE IS THE CHARMING ELEANOR?
I EXPECTED TO SEE HER HOVERING AT YOUR SHOULDER, AS ALWAYS.
THAT IS AN EXCELLENT QUESTION.
The truth is, I haven't seen Ellie in days. Or Spot either, come to think of it. Where are those guys?

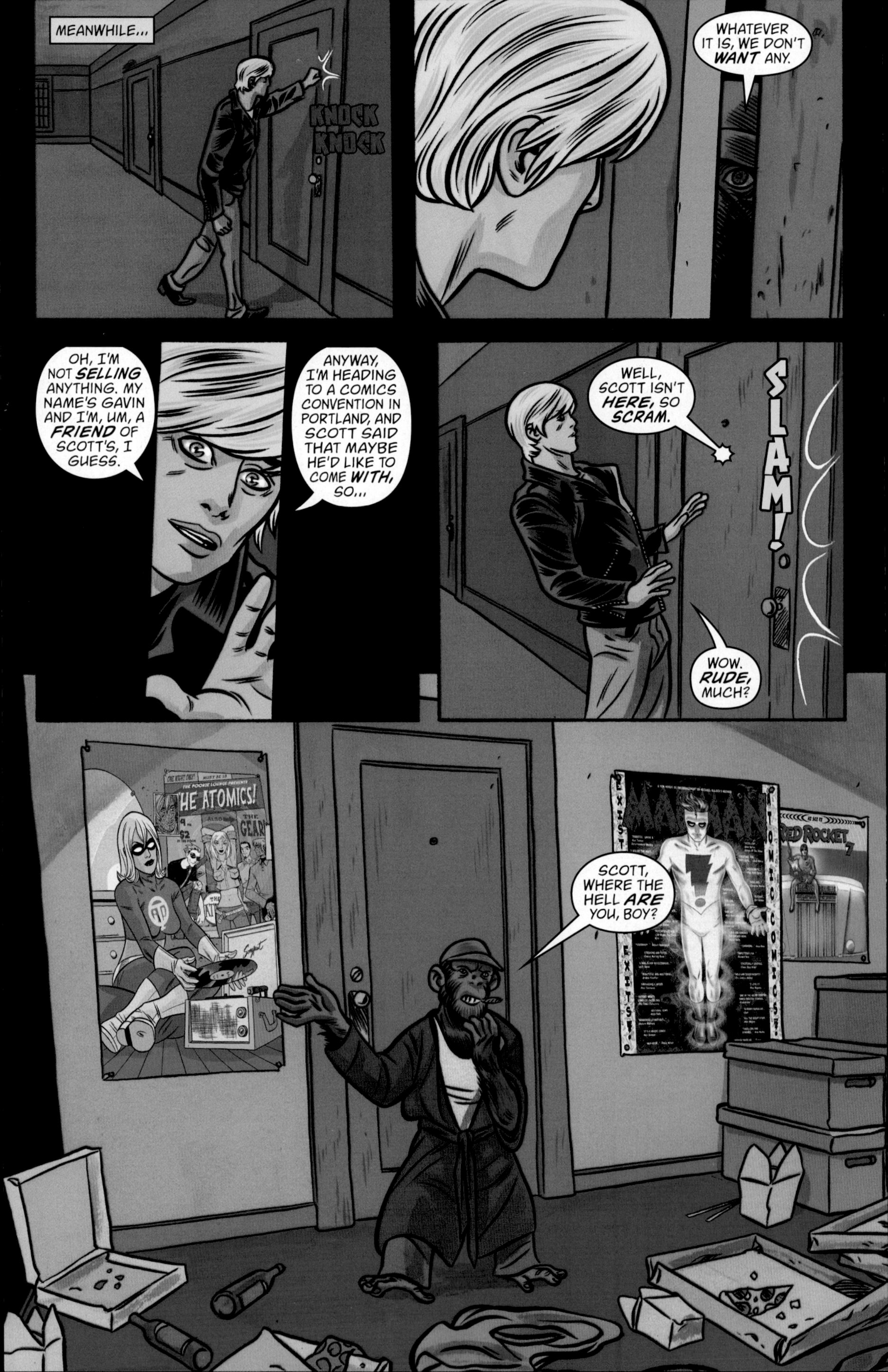

MEANWHILE...
KNOCK KNOCK
WHATEVER IT IS, WE DON'T WANT ANY.
OH, I'M NOT SELLING ANYTHING. MY NAME'S GAVIN AND I'M, UM, A FRIEND OF SCOTT'S, I GUESS.
ANYWAY, I'M HEADING TO A COMICS CONVENTION IN PORTLAND, AND SCOTT SAID THAT MAYBE HE'D LIKE TO COME WITH, SO...
WELL, SCOTT ISN'T HERE, SO SCRAM.
SLAM!
WOW. RUDE, MUCH?
THE POOKIE LOUNGE PRESENTS
THE ATOMICS!
RED ROCKET 7
SCOTT, WHERE THE HELL ARE YOU, BOY?

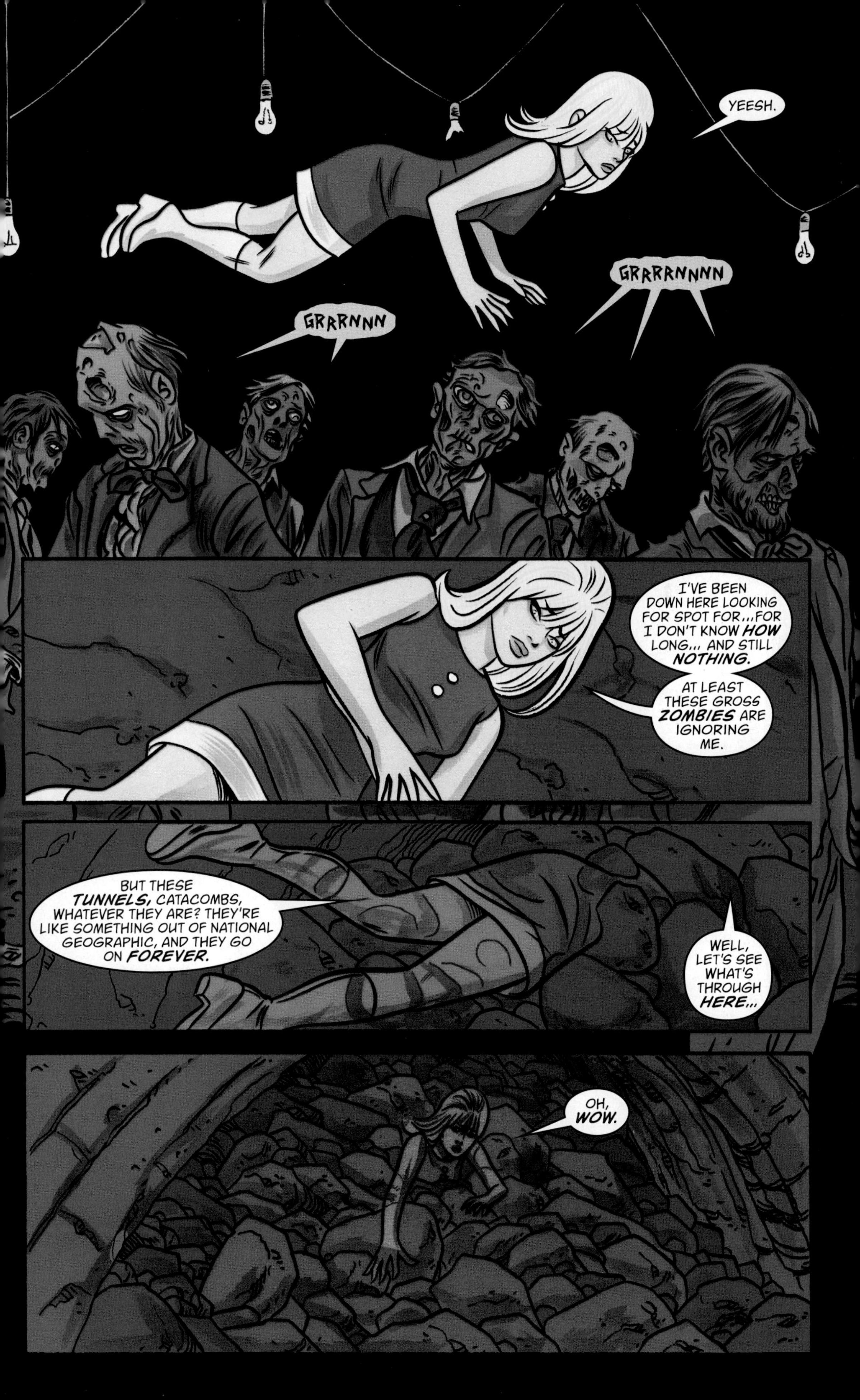
YEESH.
GRRRNNN
GRRRRNNNN
I'VE BEEN DOWN HERE LOOKING FOR SPOT FOR... FOR I DON'T KNOW HOW LONG... AND STILL NOTHING.
AT LEAST THESE GROSS ZOMBIES ARE IGNORING ME.
BUT THESE TUNNELS, CATACOMBS, WHATEVER THEY ARE? THEY'RE LIKE SOMETHING OUT OF NATIONAL GEOGRAPHIC, AND THEY GO ON FOREVER.
WELL, LET'S SEE WHAT'S THROUGH HERE...
OH, WOW.

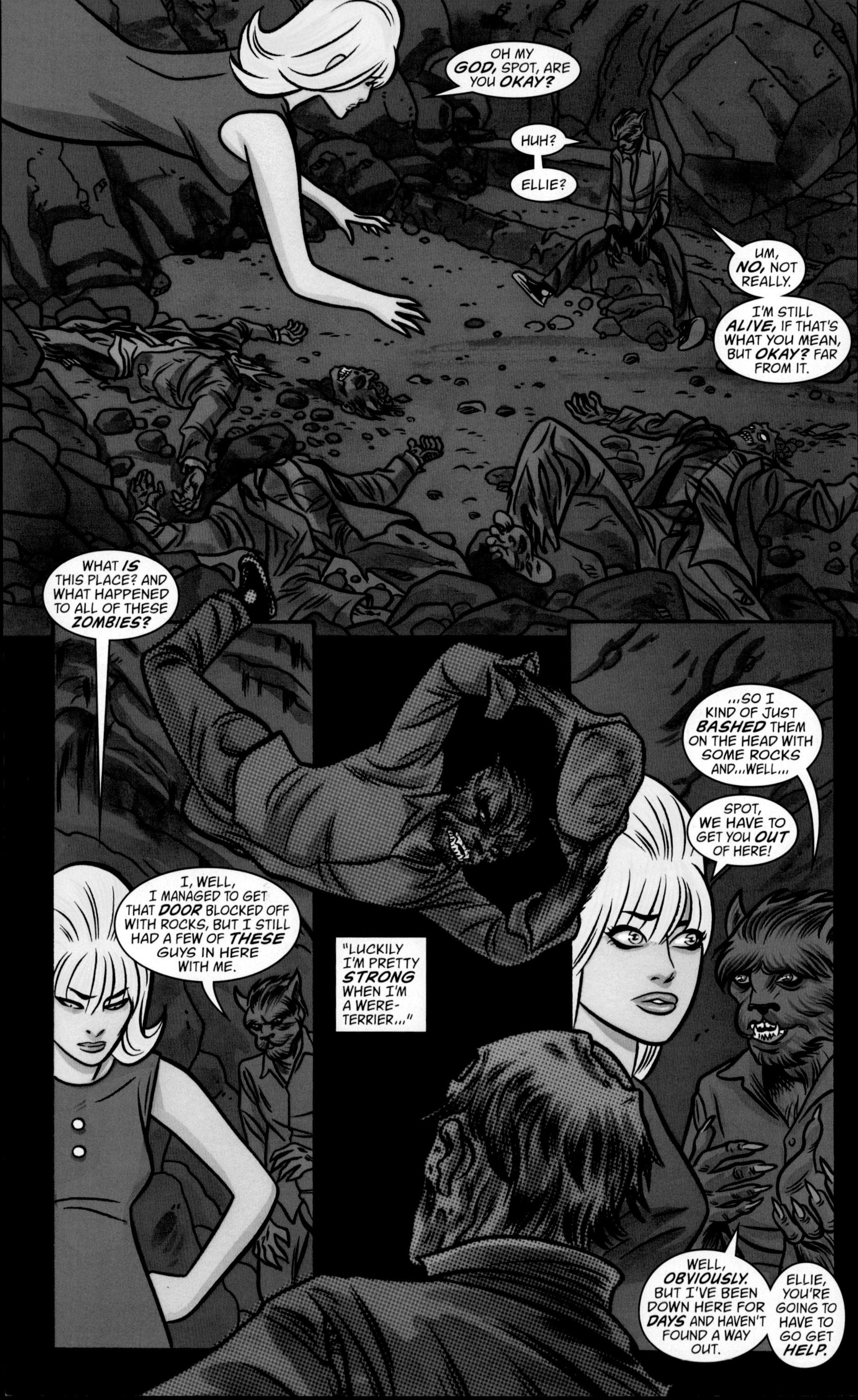
OH MY GOD, SPOT, ARE YOU OKAY?
HUH?
ELLIE?
UM, NO, NOT REALLY.
I'M STILL ALIVE, IF THAT'S WHAT YOU MEAN, BUT OKAY? FAR FROM IT.
WHAT IS THIS PLACE? AND WHAT HAPPENED TO ALL OF THESE ZOMBIES?
I, WELL, I MANAGED TO GET THAT DOOR BLOCKED OFF WITH ROCKS, BUT I STILL HAD A FEW OF THESE GUYS IN HERE WITH ME.
"LUCKILY I'M PRETTY STRONG WHEN I'M A WERE-TERRIER..."
...SO I KIND OF JUST BASHED THEM ON THE HEAD WITH SOME ROCKS AND...WELL...
SPOT, WE HAVE TO GET YOU OUT OF HERE!
WELL, OBVIOUSLY. BUT I'VE BEEN DOWN HERE FOR DAYS AND HAVEN'T FOUND A WAY OUT.
ELLIE, YOU'RE GOING TO HAVE TO GO GET HELP.

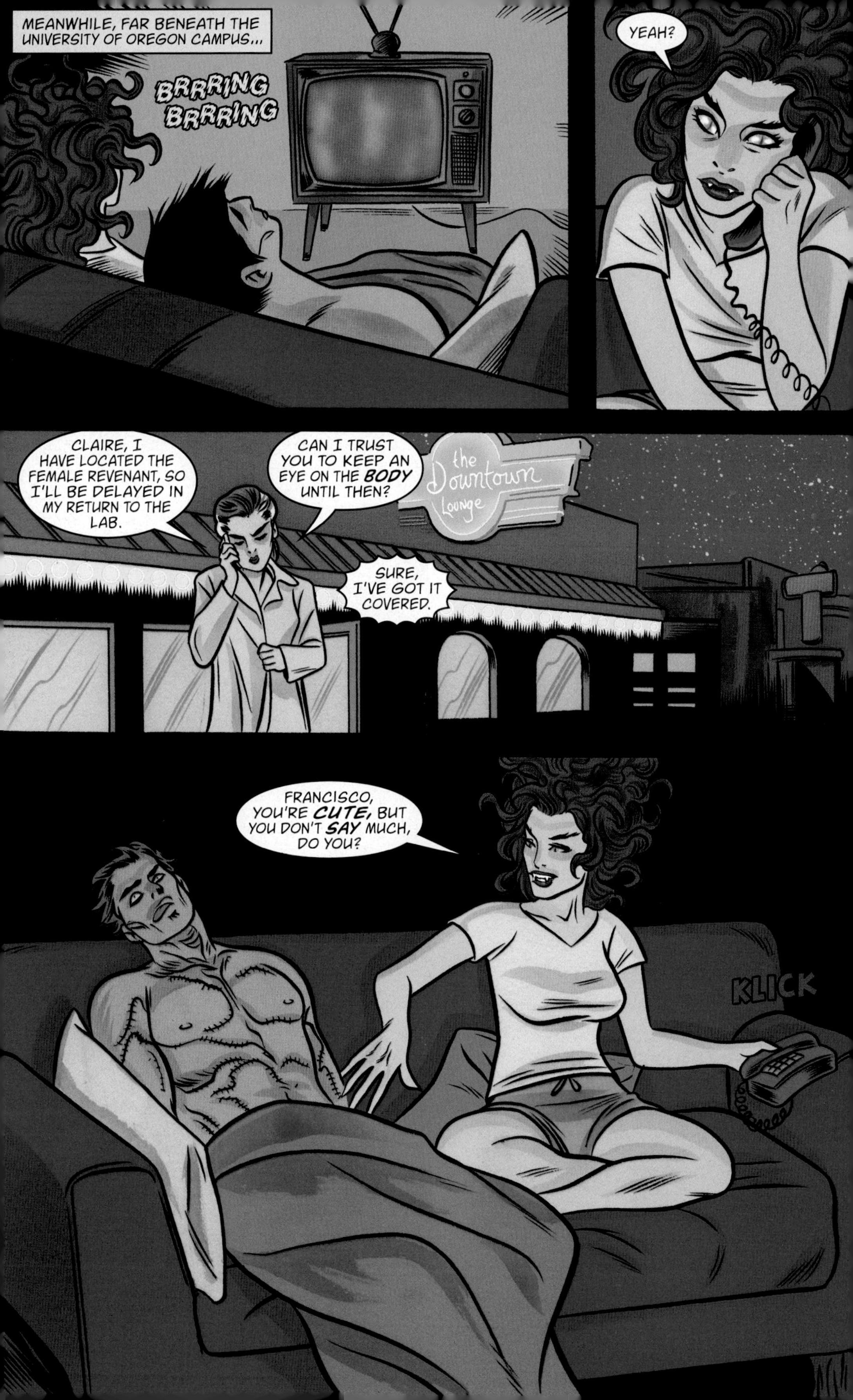
MEANWHILE, FAR BENEATH THE UNIVERSITY OF OREGON CAMPUS...
BRRRING BRRRING
YEAH?
CLAIRE, I HAVE LOCATED THE FEMALE REVENANT, SO I'LL BE DELAYED IN MY RETURN TO THE LAB.
CAN I TRUST YOU TO KEEP AN EYE ON THE BODY UNTIL THEN?
the Downtown Lounge
SURE, I'VE GOT IT COVERED.
FRANCISCO, YOU'RE CUTE, BUT YOU DON'T SAY MUCH, DO YOU?
KLICK

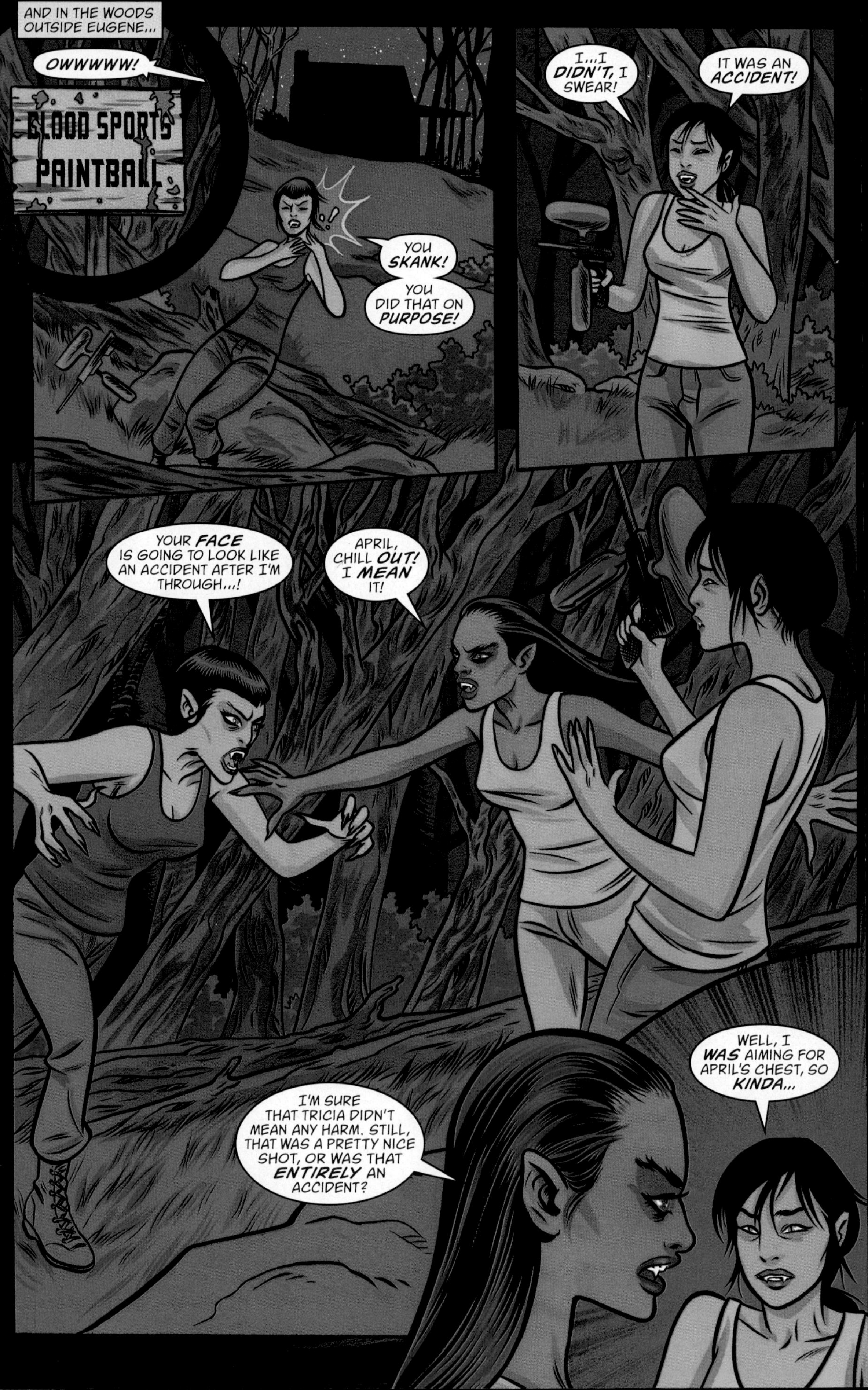
AND IN THE WOODS OUTSIDE EUGENE...
OWWWWW!
BLOOD SPORTS PAINTBALL
YOU SKANK!
YOU DID THAT ON PURPOSE!
I...I DIDN'T, I SWEAR!
IT WAS AN ACCIDENT!
YOUR FACE IS GOING TO LOOK LIKE AN ACCIDENT AFTER I'M THROUGH...!
APRIL, CHILL OUT! I MEAN IT!
I'M SURE THAT TRICIA DIDN'T MEAN ANY HARM. STILL, THAT WAS A PRETTY NICE SHOT, OR WAS THAT ENTIRELY AN ACCIDENT?
WELL, I WAS AIMING FOR APRIL'S CHEST, SO KINDA...

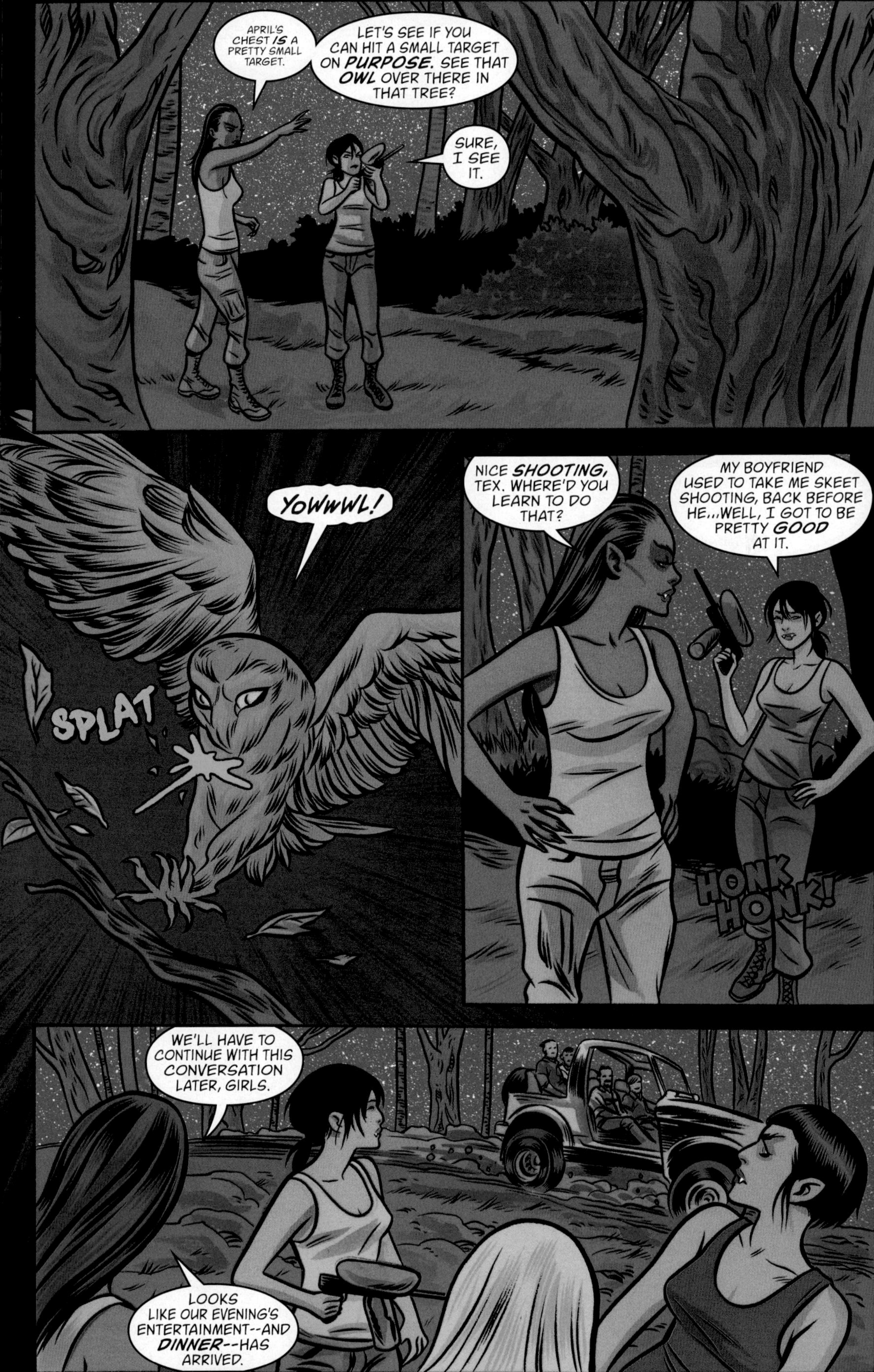
APRIL'S CHEST IS A PRETTY SMALL TARGET.
LET'S SEE IF YOU CAN HIT A SMALL TARGET ON PURPOSE. SEE THAT OWL OVER THERE IN THAT TREE?
SURE, I SEE IT.
YOWWWL!
SPLAT
NICE SHOOTING, TEX. WHERE'D YOU LEARN TO DO THAT?
MY BOYFRIEND USED TO TAKE ME SKEET SHOOTING, BACK BEFORE HE...WELL, I GOT TO BE PRETTY GOOD AT IT.
HONK HONK!
WE'LL HAVE TO CONTINUE WITH THIS CONVERSATION LATER, GIRLS.
LOOKS LIKE OUR EVENING'S ENTERTAINMENT--AND DINNER--HAS ARRIVED.

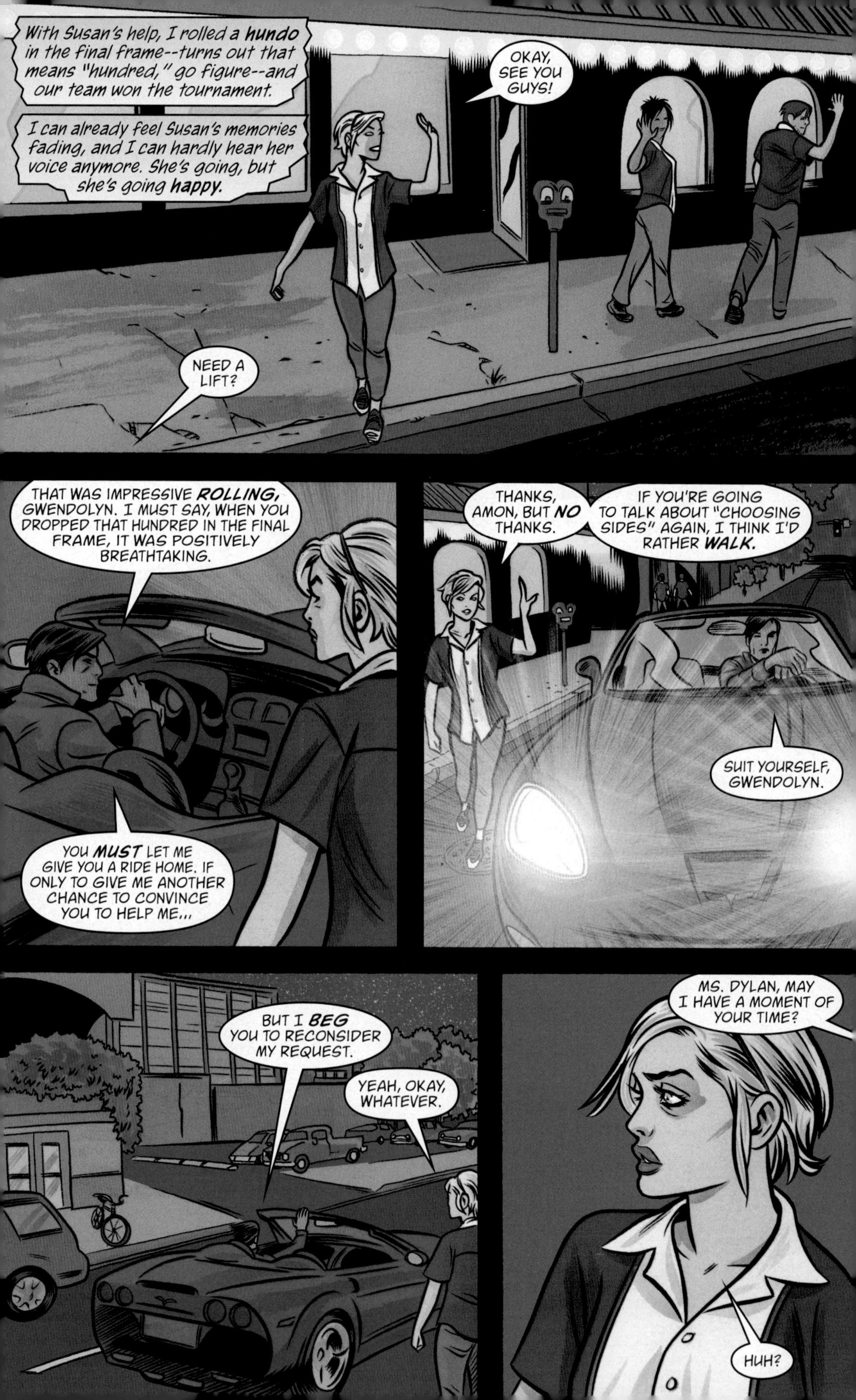
With Susan's help, I rolled a **hundo** in the final frame--turns out that means "hundred," go figure--and our team won the tournament.
I can already feel Susan's memories fading, and I can hardly hear her voice anymore. She's going, but she's going **happy.**
OKAY, SEE YOU GUYS!
NEED A LIFT?
THAT WAS IMPRESSIVE ***ROLLING,*** GWENDOLYN. I MUST SAY, WHEN YOU DROPPED THAT HUNDRED IN THE FINAL FRAME, IT WAS POSITIVELY BREATHTAKING.
YOU ***MUST*** LET ME GIVE YOU A RIDE HOME. IF ONLY TO GIVE ME ANOTHER CHANCE TO CONVINCE YOU TO HELP ME...
THANKS, AMON, BUT ***NO*** THANKS.
IF YOU'RE GOING TO TALK ABOUT "CHOOSING SIDES" AGAIN, I THINK I'D RATHER ***WALK.***
SUIT YOURSELF, GWENDOLYN.
BUT I ***BEG*** YOU TO RECONSIDER MY REQUEST.
YEAH, OKAY, WHATEVER.
MS. DYLAN, MAY I HAVE A MOMENT OF YOUR TIME?
HUH?

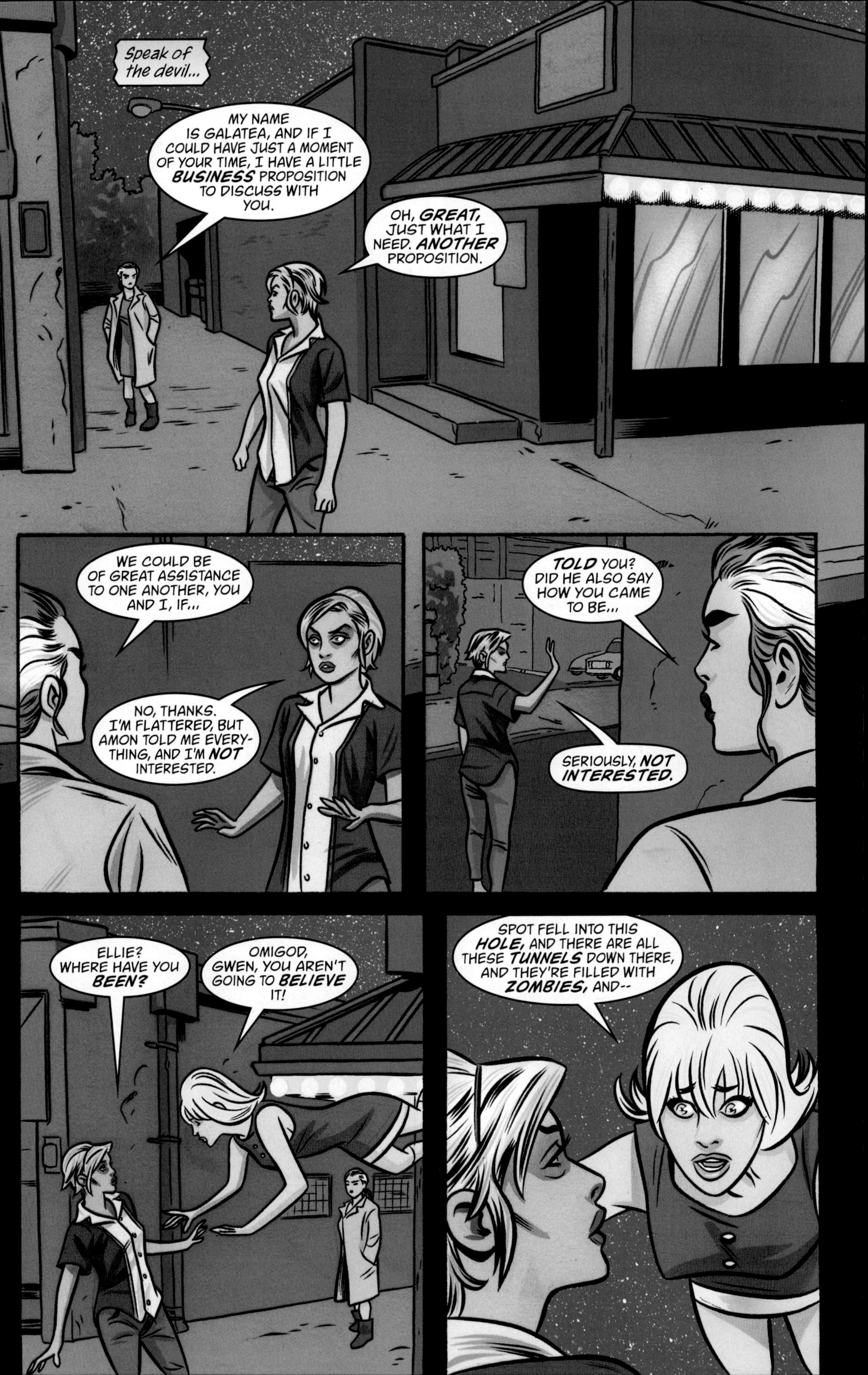
Speak of the devil...
MY NAME IS GALATEA, AND IF I COULD HAVE JUST A MOMENT OF YOUR TIME, I HAVE A LITTLE BUSINESS PROPOSITION TO DISCUSS WITH YOU.
OH, GREAT, JUST WHAT I NEED. ANOTHER PROPOSITION.
WE COULD BE OF GREAT ASSISTANCE TO ONE ANOTHER, YOU AND I, IF...
NO, THANKS. I'M FLATTERED, BUT AMON TOLD ME EVERY-THING, AND I'M NOT INTERESTED.
TOLD YOU? DID HE ALSO SAY HOW YOU CAME TO BE...
SERIOUSLY, NOT INTERESTED.
ELLIE? WHERE HAVE YOU BEEN?
OMIGOD, GWEN, YOU AREN'T GOING TO BELIEVE IT!
SPOT FELL INTO THIS HOLE, AND THERE ARE ALL THESE TUNNELS DOWN THERE, AND THEY'RE FILLED WITH ZOMBIES, AND--

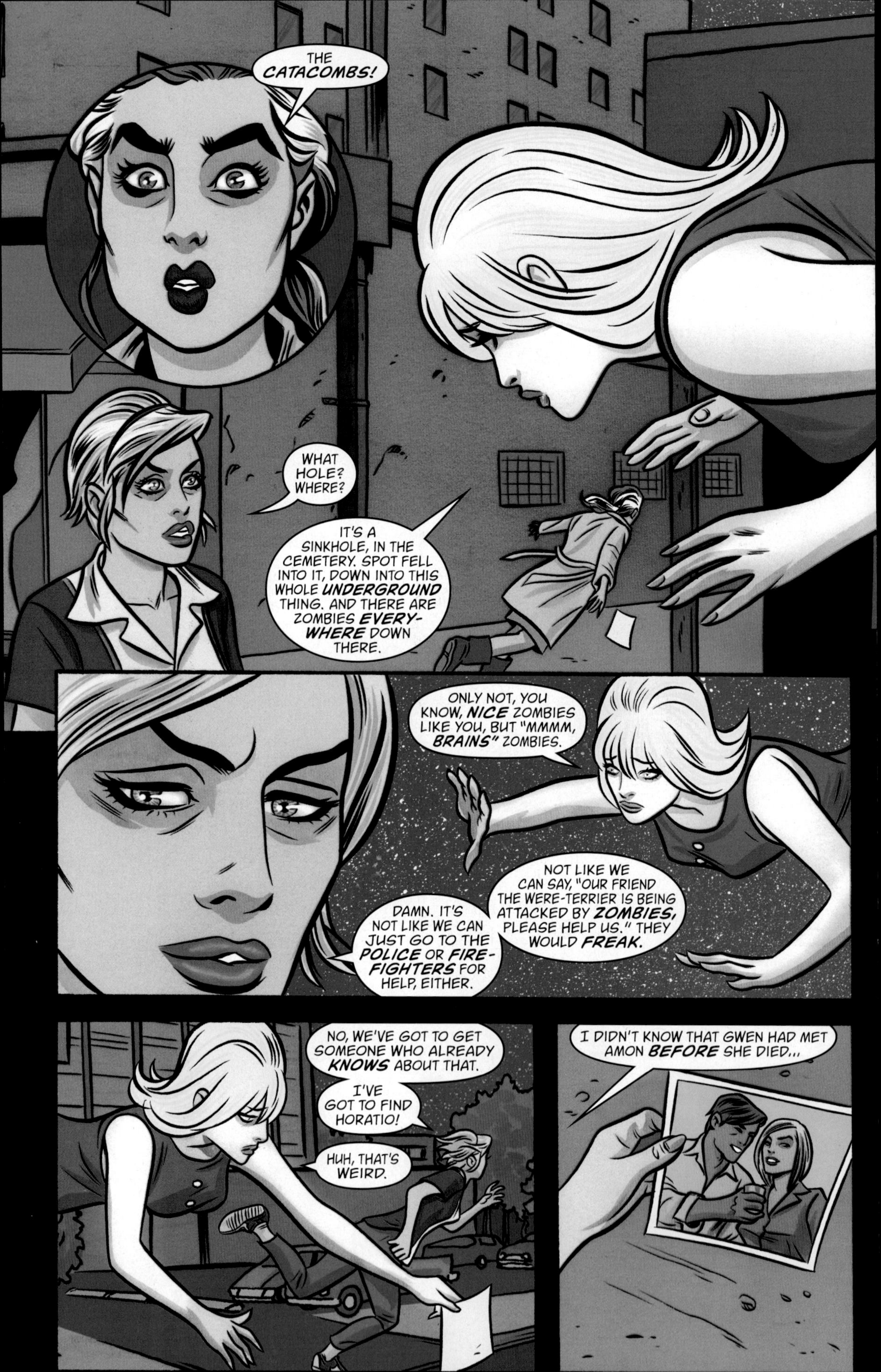
THE CATACOMBS!
WHAT HOLE? WHERE?
IT'S A SINKHOLE, IN THE CEMETERY. SPOT FELL INTO IT, DOWN INTO THIS WHOLE UNDERGROUND THING. AND THERE ARE ZOMBIES EVERY-WHERE DOWN THERE.
ONLY NOT, YOU KNOW, NICE ZOMBIES LIKE YOU, BUT "MMMM, BRAINS" ZOMBIES.
DAMN. IT'S NOT LIKE WE CAN JUST GO TO THE POLICE OR FIRE-FIGHTERS FOR HELP, EITHER.
NOT LIKE WE CAN SAY, "OUR FRIEND THE WERE-TERRIER IS BEING ATTACKED BY ZOMBIES, PLEASE HELP US." THEY WOULD FREAK.
NO, WE'VE GOT TO GET SOMEONE WHO ALREADY KNOWS ABOUT THAT.
I'VE GOT TO FIND HORATIO!
HUH, THAT'S WEIRD.
I DIDN'T KNOW THAT GWEN HAD MET AMON BEFORE SHE DIED...

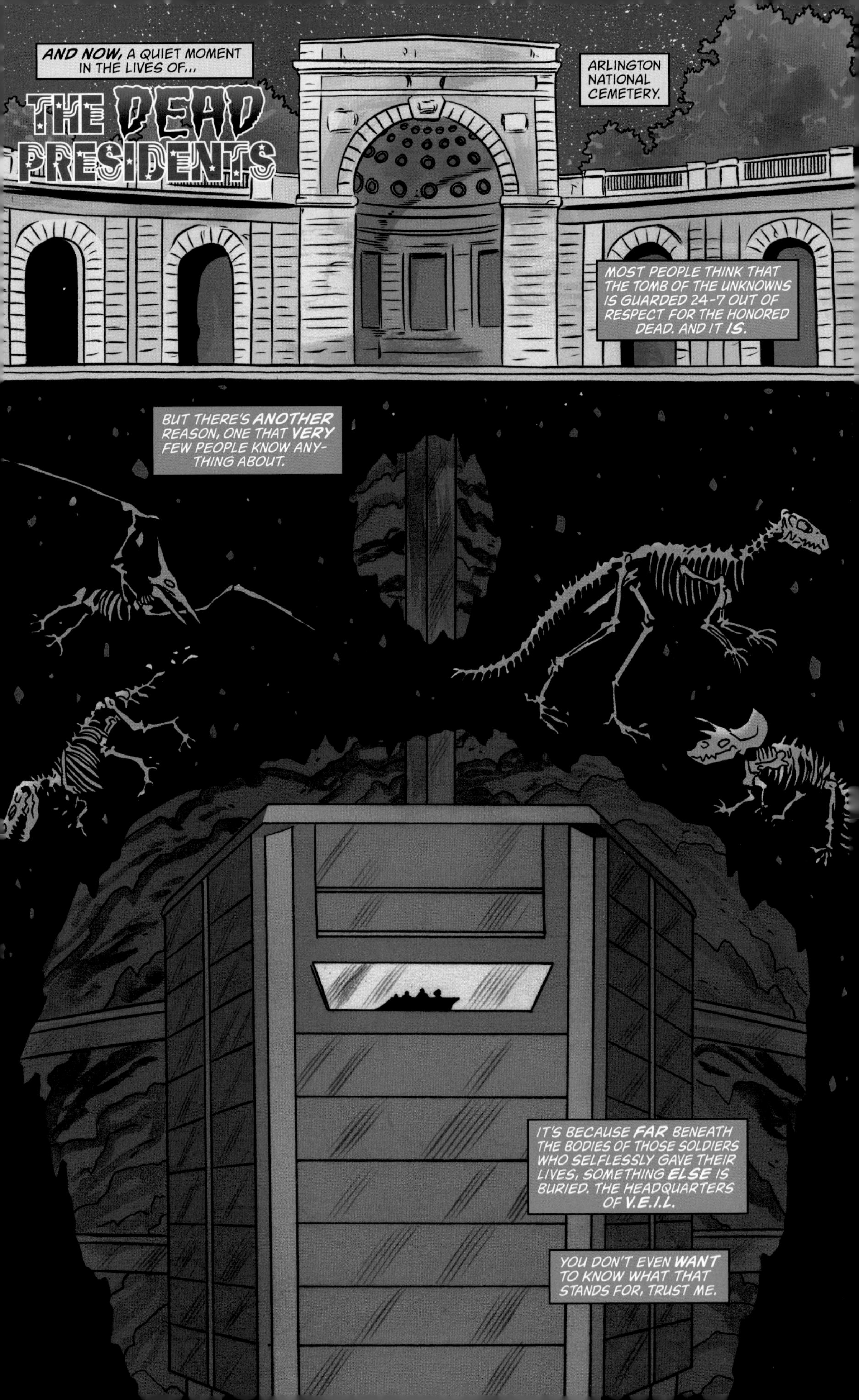
AND NOW, A QUIET MOMENT IN THE LIVES OF...
THE DEAD PRESIDENTS
ARLINGTON NATIONAL CEMETERY.
MOST PEOPLE THINK THAT THE TOMB OF THE UNKNOWNS IS GUARDED 24-7 OUT OF RESPECT FOR THE HONORED DEAD. AND IT IS.
BUT THERE'S ANOTHER REASON, ONE THAT VERY FEW PEOPLE KNOW ANY-THING ABOUT.
IT'S BECAUSE FAR BENEATH THE BODIES OF THOSE SOLDIERS WHO SELFLESSLY GAVE THEIR LIVES, SOMETHING ELSE IS BURIED. THE HEADQUARTERS OF V.E.I.L.
YOU DON'T EVEN WANT TO KNOW WHAT THAT STANDS FOR, TRUST ME.

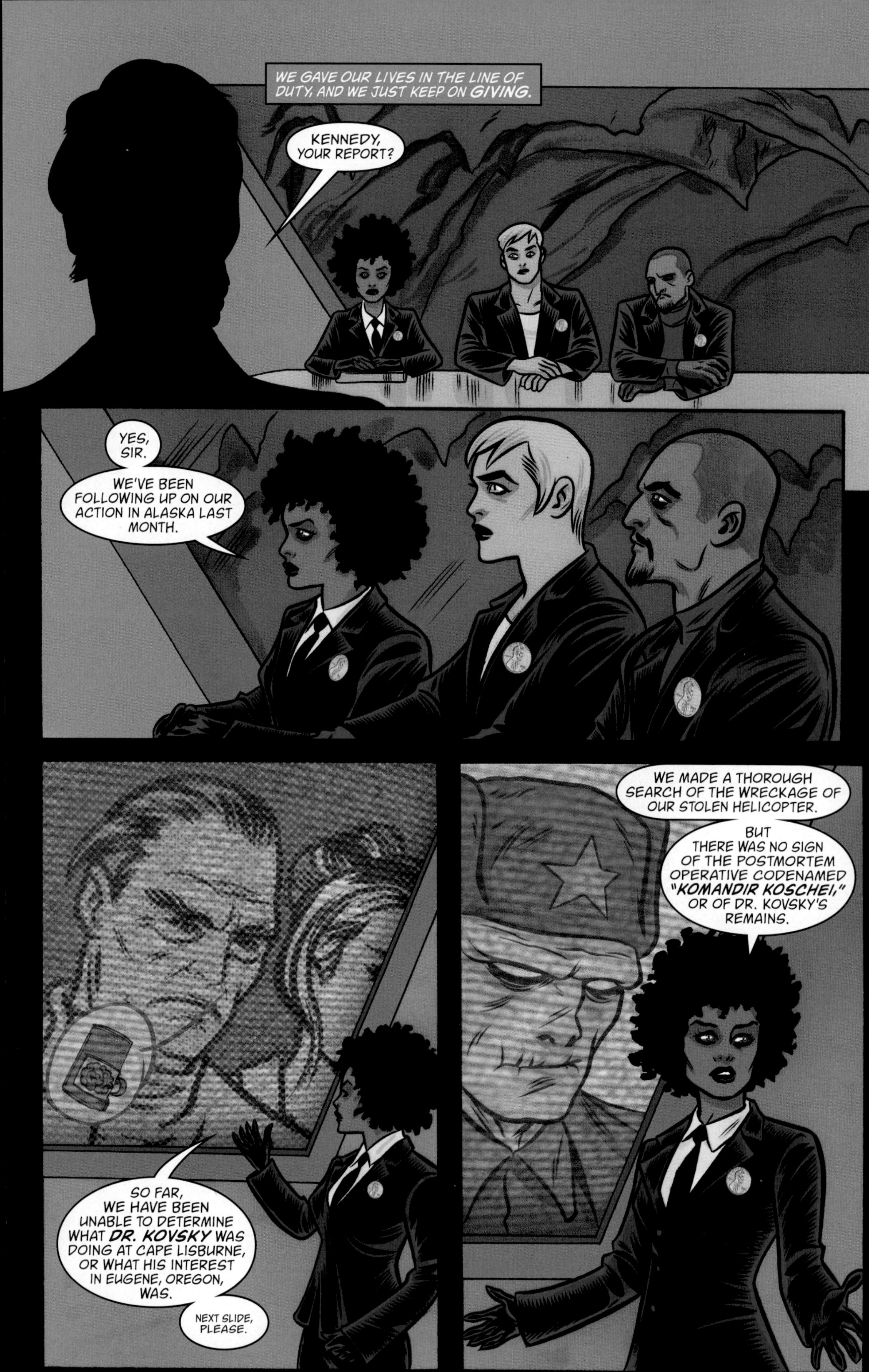

WE GAVE OUR LIVES IN THE LINE OF DUTY, AND WE JUST KEEP ON GIVING.
KENNEDY, YOUR REPORT?
YES, SIR.
WE'VE BEEN FOLLOWING UP ON OUR ACTION IN ALASKA LAST MONTH.
SO FAR, WE HAVE BEEN UNABLE TO DETERMINE WHAT DR. KOVSKY WAS DOING AT CAPE LISBURNE, OR WHAT HIS INTEREST IN EUGENE, OREGON, WAS.
NEXT SLIDE, PLEASE.
WE MADE A THOROUGH SEARCH OF THE WRECKAGE OF OUR STOLEN HELICOPTER.
BUT THERE WAS NO SIGN OF THE POSTMORTEM OPERATIVE CODENAMED "KOMANDIR KOSCHEI," OR OF DR. KOVSKY'S REMAINS.

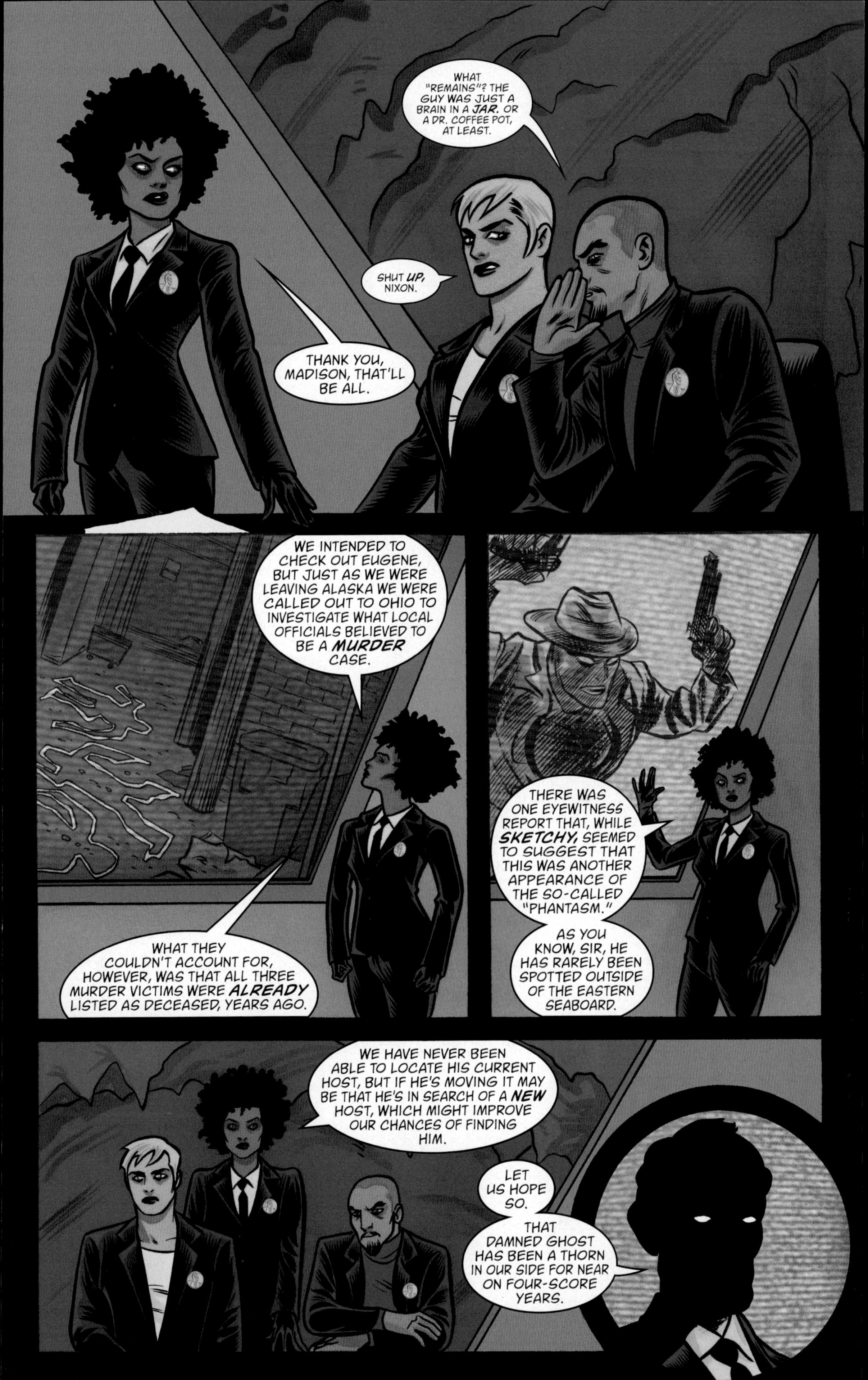
WHAT "REMAINS"? THE GUY WAS JUST A BRAIN IN A JAR. OR A DR. COFFEE POT, AT LEAST.
SHUT UP, NIXON.
THANK YOU, MADISON, THAT'LL BE ALL.
WE INTENDED TO CHECK OUT EUGENE, BUT JUST AS WE WERE LEAVING ALASKA WE WERE CALLED OUT TO OHIO TO INVESTIGATE WHAT LOCAL OFFICIALS BELIEVED TO BE A MURDER CASE.
WHAT THEY COULDN'T ACCOUNT FOR, HOWEVER, WAS THAT ALL THREE MURDER VICTIMS WERE ALREADY LISTED AS DECEASED, YEARS AGO.
THERE WAS ONE EYEWITNESS REPORT THAT, WHILE SKETCHY, SEEMED TO SUGGEST THAT THIS WAS ANOTHER APPEARANCE OF THE SO-CALLED "PHANTASM."
AS YOU KNOW, SIR, HE HAS RARELY BEEN SPOTTED OUTSIDE OF THE EASTERN SEABOARD.
WE HAVE NEVER BEEN ABLE TO LOCATE HIS CURRENT HOST, BUT IF HE'S MOVING IT MAY BE THAT HE'S IN SEARCH OF A NEW HOST, WHICH MIGHT IMPROVE OUR CHANCES OF FINDING HIM.
LET US HOPE SO.
THAT DAMNED GHOST HAS BEEN A THORN IN OUR SIDE FOR NEAR ON FOUR-SCORE YEARS.

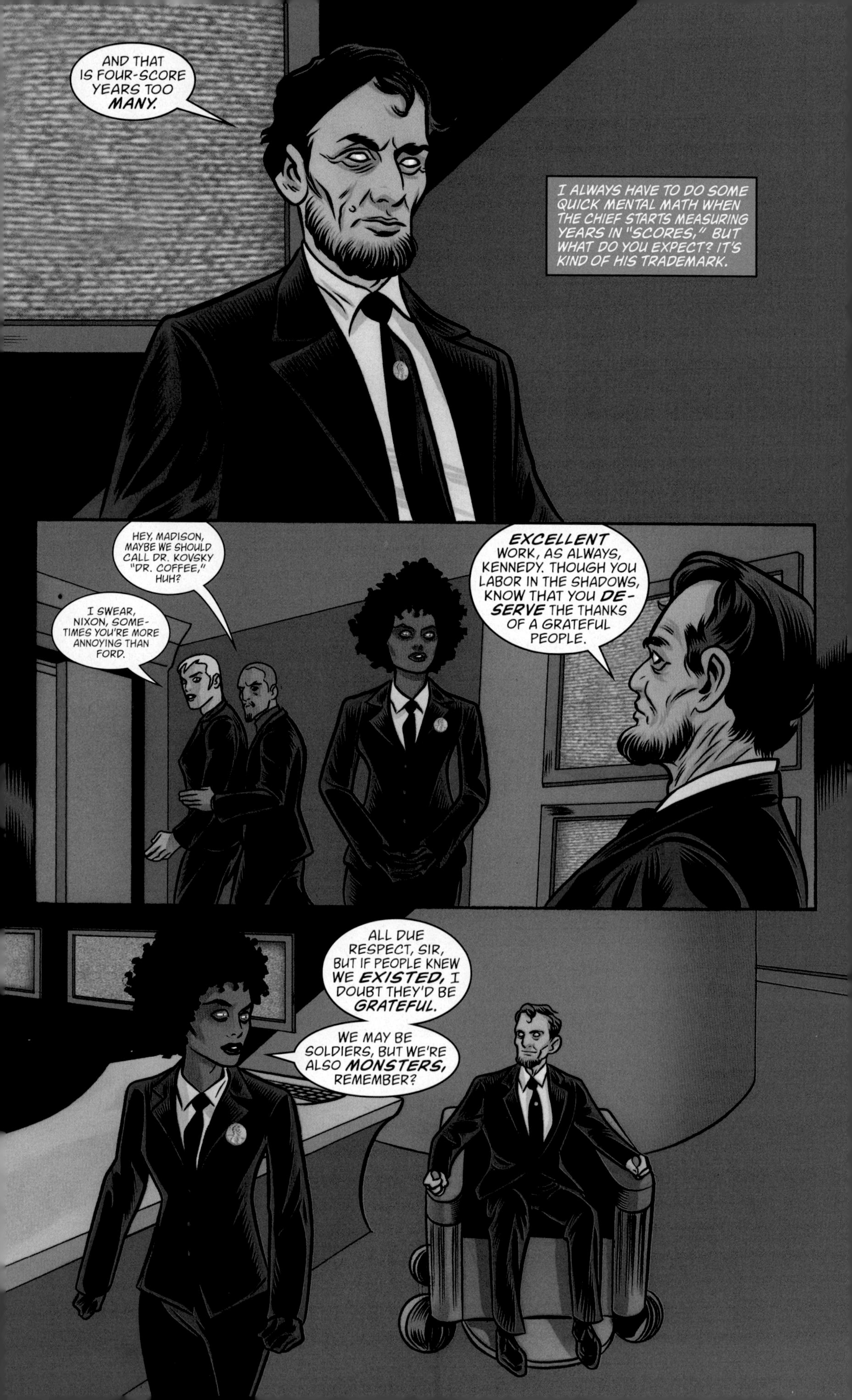
AND THAT IS FOUR-SCORE YEARS TOO MANY.
I ALWAYS HAVE TO DO SOME QUICK MENTAL MATH WHEN THE CHIEF STARTS MEASURING YEARS IN "SCORES," BUT WHAT DO YOU EXPECT? IT'S KIND OF HIS TRADEMARK.
HEY, MADISON, MAYBE WE SHOULD CALL DR. KOVSKY "DR. COFFEE," HUH?
I SWEAR, NIXON, SOMETIMES YOU'RE MORE ANNOYING THAN FORD.
EXCELLENT WORK, AS ALWAYS, KENNEDY. THOUGH YOU LABOR IN THE SHADOWS, KNOW THAT YOU DESERVE THE THANKS OF A GRATEFUL PEOPLE.
ALL DUE RESPECT, SIR, BUT IF PEOPLE KNEW WE EXISTED, I DOUBT THEY'D BE GRATEFUL.
WE MAY BE SOLDIERS, BUT WE'RE ALSO MONSTERS, REMEMBER?

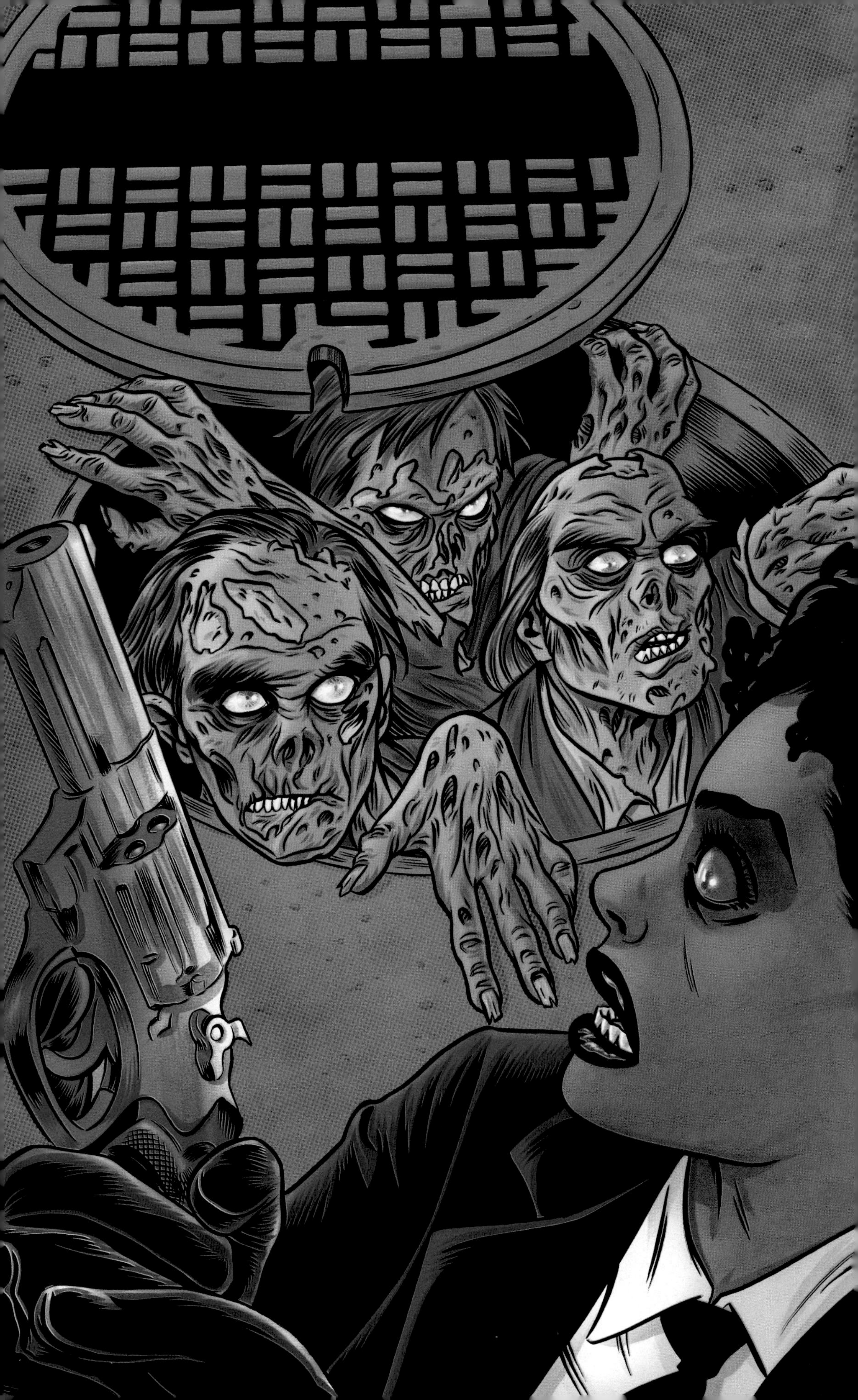

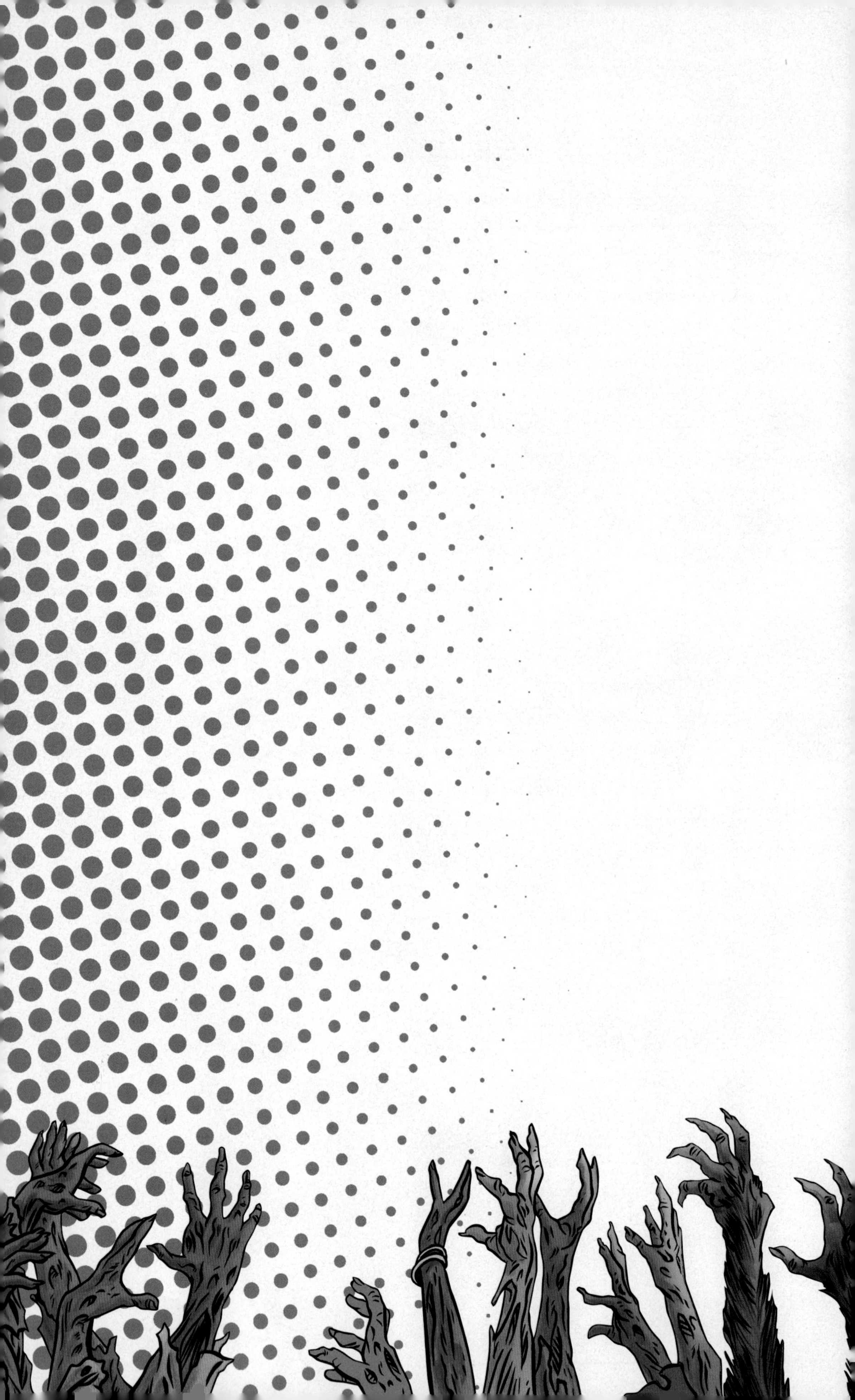

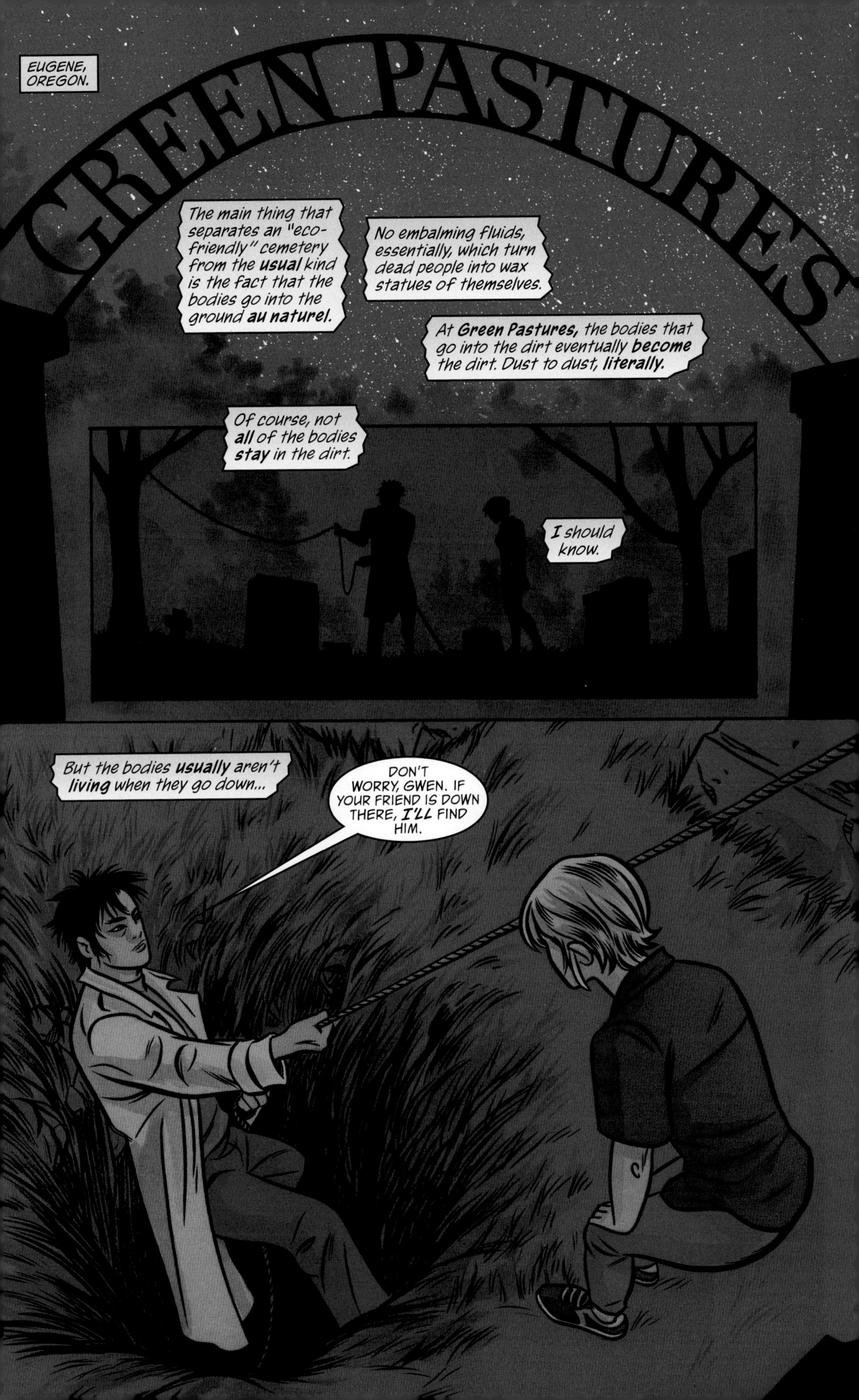
EUGENE, OREGON.
GREEN PASTURES
The main thing that separates an "eco-friendly" cemetery from the **usual** kind is the fact that the bodies go into the ground **au naturel.**
No embalming fluids, essentially, which turn dead people into wax statues of themselves.
At **Green Pastures,** the bodies that go into the dirt eventually **become** the dirt. Dust to dust, **literally.**
Of course, not **all** of the bodies **stay** in the dirt.
I should know.
But the bodies **usually** aren't **living** when they go down...
DON'T WORRY, GWEN. IF YOUR FRIEND IS DOWN THERE, ***I'LL*** FIND HIM.

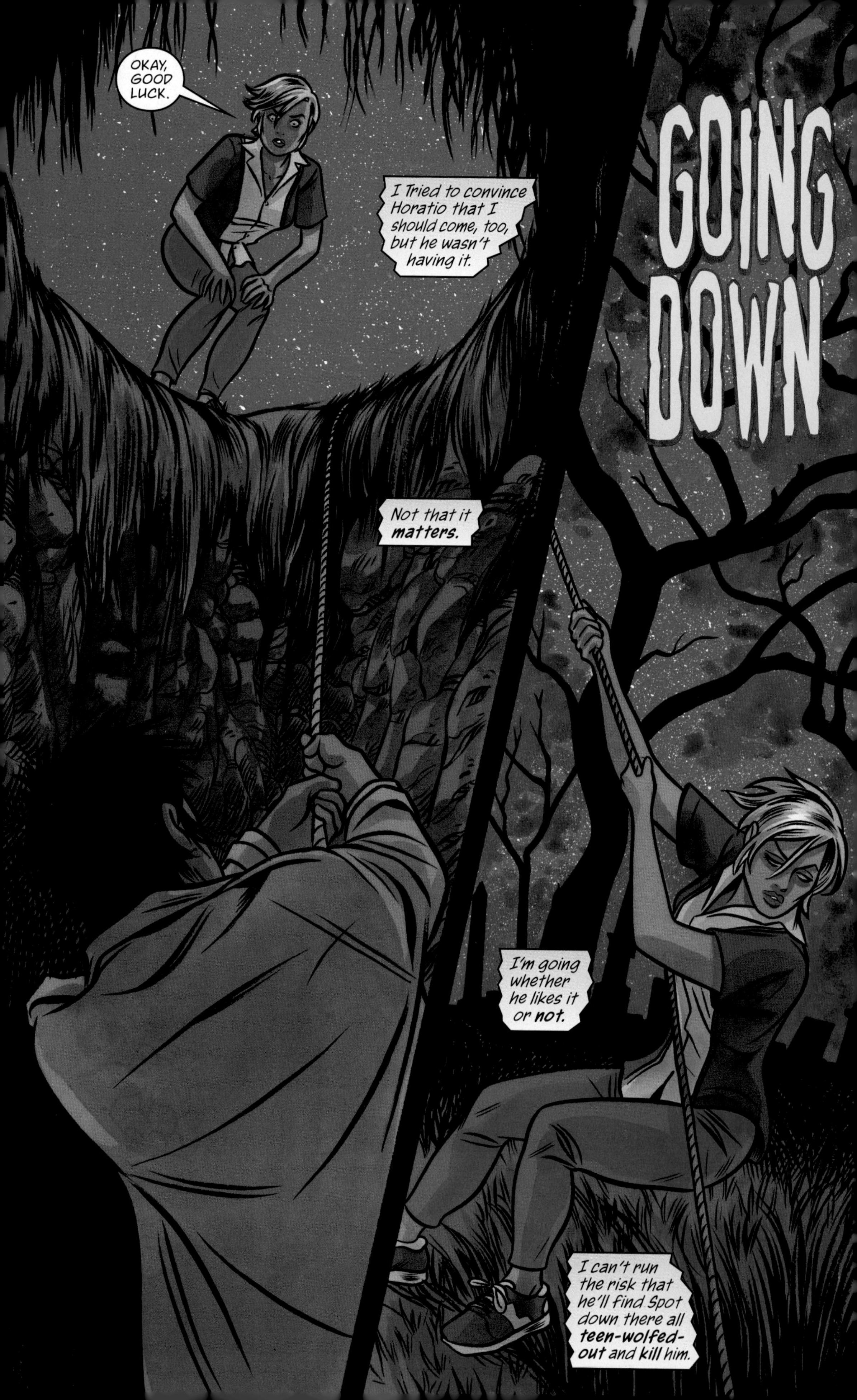
OKAY, GOOD LUCK.
GOING DOWN
I Tried to convince Horatio that I should come, too, but he wasn't having it.
Not that it **matters.**
I'm going whether he likes it or **not.**
I can't run the risk that he'll find Spot down there all **teen-wolfed-out** and **kill** him.

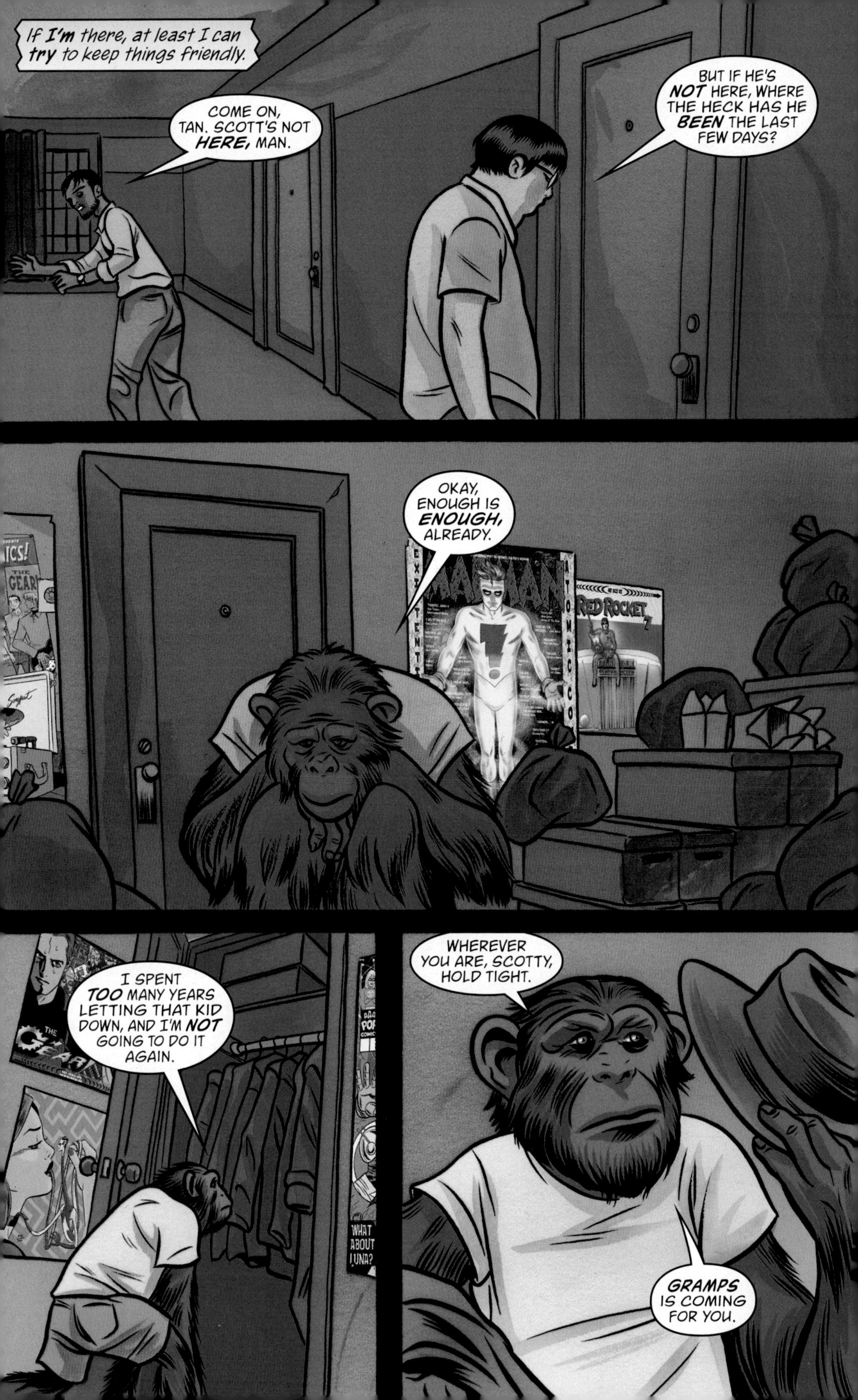
If **I'm** there, at least I can **try** to keep things friendly.
COME ON, TAN. SCOTT'S NOT **HERE,** MAN.
BUT IF HE'S **NOT** HERE, WHERE THE HECK HAS HE **BEEN** THE LAST FEW DAYS?
OKAY, ENOUGH IS **ENOUGH,** ALREADY.
RED ROCKET 7
I SPENT **TOO** MANY YEARS LETTING THAT KID DOWN, AND I'M **NOT** GOING TO DO IT AGAIN.
WHEREVER YOU ARE, SCOTTY, HOLD TIGHT.
GRAMPS IS COMING FOR YOU.

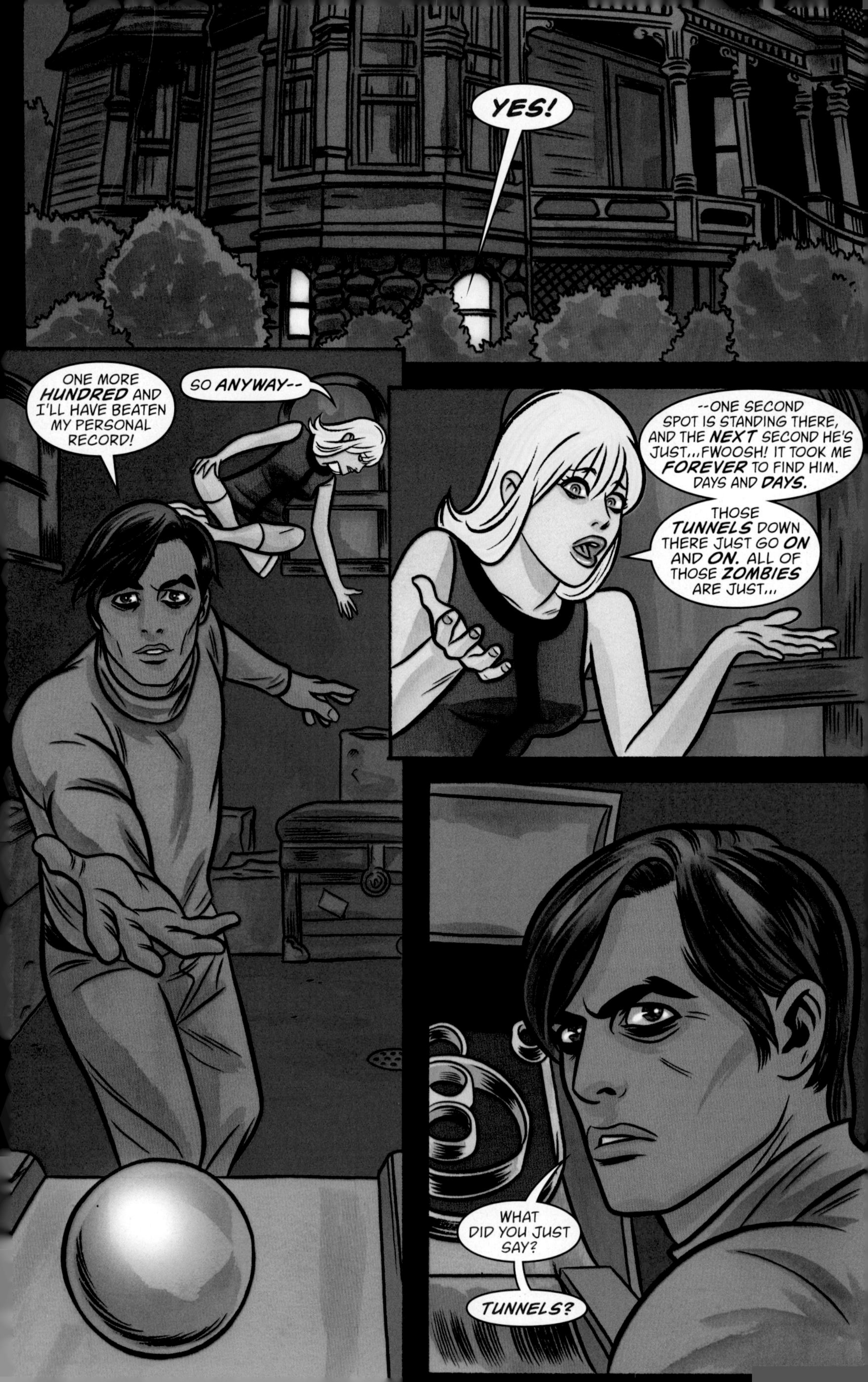
YES!
ONE MORE HUNDRED AND I'LL HAVE BEATEN MY PERSONAL RECORD!
SO ANYWAY--
--ONE SECOND SPOT IS STANDING THERE, AND THE NEXT SECOND HE'S JUST...FWOOSH! IT TOOK ME FOREVER TO FIND HIM. DAYS AND DAYS.
THOSE TUNNELS DOWN THERE JUST GO ON AND ON. ALL OF THOSE ZOMBIES ARE JUST...
WHAT DID YOU JUST SAY?
TUNNELS?

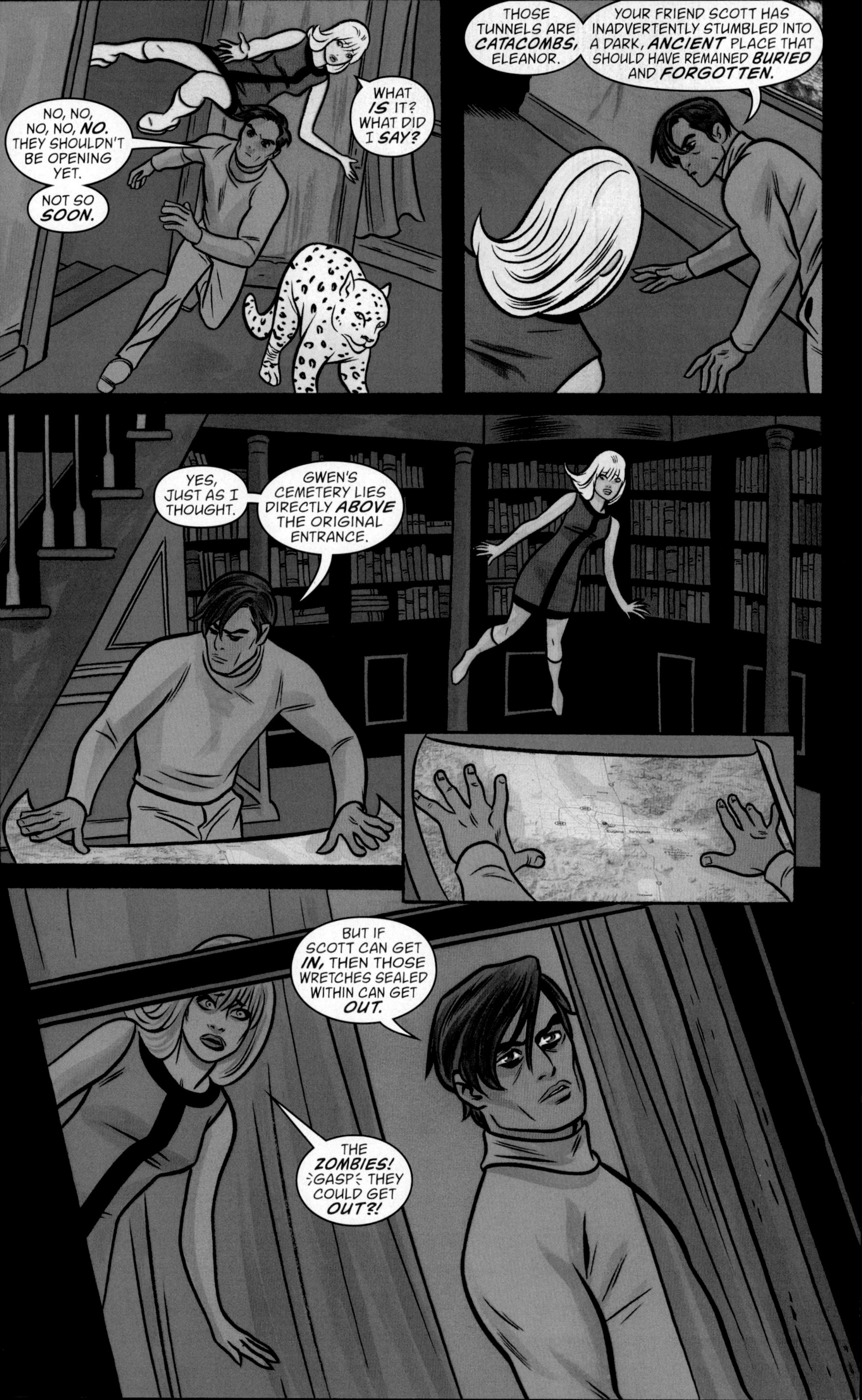
NO, NO, NO, NO, **NO.** THEY SHOULDN'T BE OPENING YET.
NOT SO **SOON.**
WHAT **IS** IT? WHAT DID I **SAY?**
THOSE TUNNELS ARE **CATACOMBS,** ELEANOR.
YOUR FRIEND SCOTT HAS INADVERTENTLY STUMBLED INTO A DARK, **ANCIENT** PLACE THAT SHOULD HAVE REMAINED **BURIED** AND **FORGOTTEN.**
YES, JUST AS I THOUGHT.
GWEN'S CEMETERY LIES DIRECTLY **ABOVE** THE ORIGINAL ENTRANCE.
BUT IF SCOTT CAN GET **IN,** THEN THOSE WRETCHES SEALED WITHIN CAN GET **OUT.**
THE **ZOMBIES!** GASP THEY COULD GET **OUT?!**

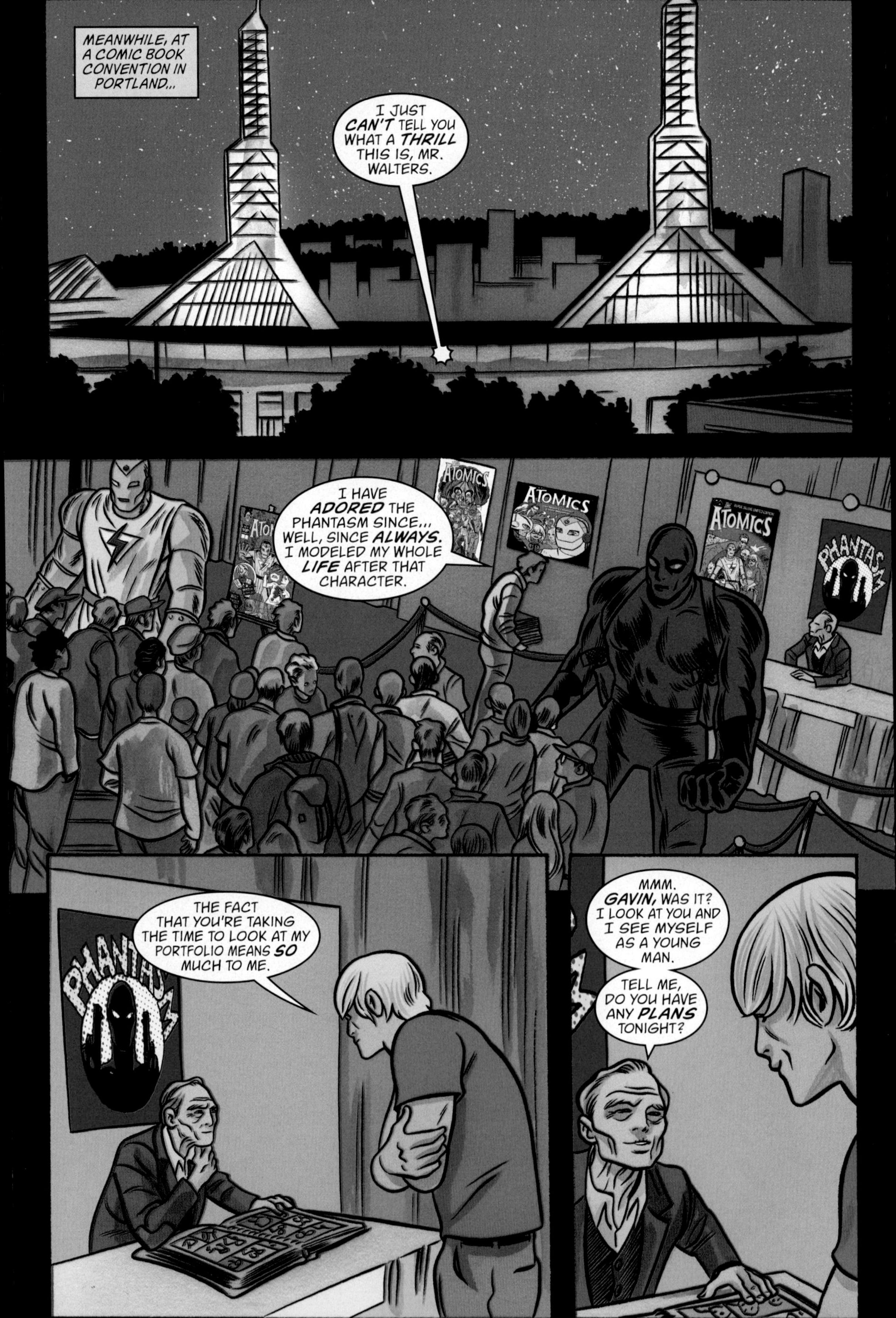
MEANWHILE, AT A COMIC BOOK CONVENTION IN PORTLAND...
I JUST CAN'T TELL YOU WHAT A THRILL THIS IS, MR. WALTERS.
ATOMICS
ATOMICS
ATOMICS
PHANTASM
I HAVE ADORED THE PHANTASM SINCE... WELL, SINCE ALWAYS. I MODELED MY WHOLE LIFE AFTER THAT CHARACTER.
PHANTASM
THE FACT THAT YOU'RE TAKING THE TIME TO LOOK AT MY PORTFOLIO MEANS SO MUCH TO ME.
MMM. GAVIN, WAS IT? I LOOK AT YOU AND I SEE MYSELF AS A YOUNG MAN.
TELL ME, DO YOU HAVE ANY PLANS TONIGHT?

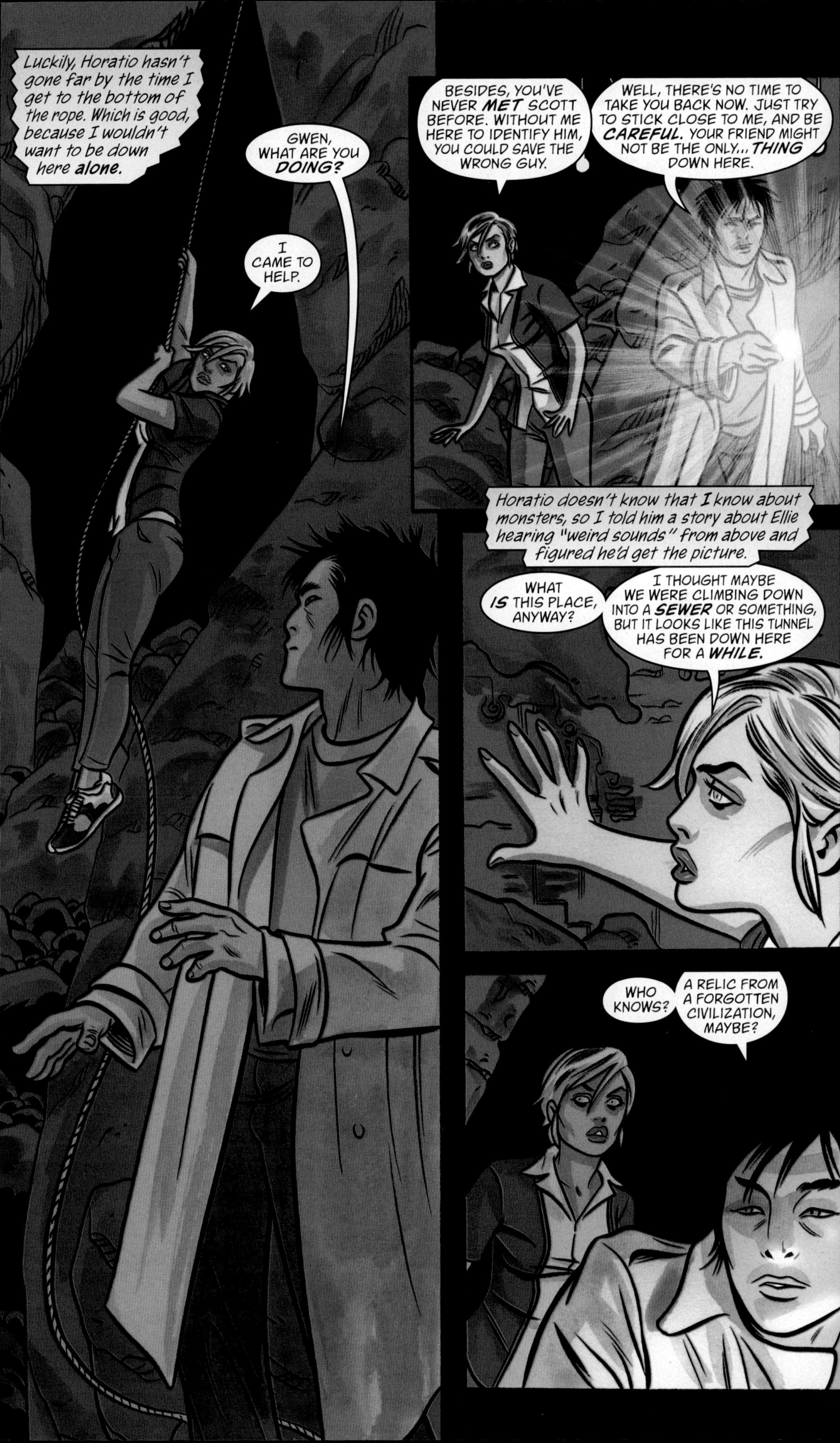
Luckily, Horatio hasn't gone far by the time I get to the bottom of the rope. Which is good, because I wouldn't want to be down here alone.
GWEN, WHAT ARE YOU DOING?
I CAME TO HELP.
BESIDES, YOU'VE NEVER MET SCOTT BEFORE. WITHOUT ME HERE TO IDENTIFY HIM, YOU COULD SAVE THE WRONG GUY.
WELL, THERE'S NO TIME TO TAKE YOU BACK NOW. JUST TRY TO STICK CLOSE TO ME, AND BE CAREFUL. YOUR FRIEND MIGHT NOT BE THE ONLY... THING DOWN HERE.
Horatio doesn't know that I know about monsters, so I told him a story about Ellie hearing "weird sounds" from above and figured he'd get the picture.
WHAT IS THIS PLACE, ANYWAY?
I THOUGHT MAYBE WE WERE CLIMBING DOWN INTO A SEWER OR SOMETHING, BUT IT LOOKS LIKE THIS TUNNEL HAS BEEN DOWN HERE FOR A WHILE.
WHO KNOWS?
A RELIC FROM A FORGOTTEN CIVILIZATION, MAYBE?

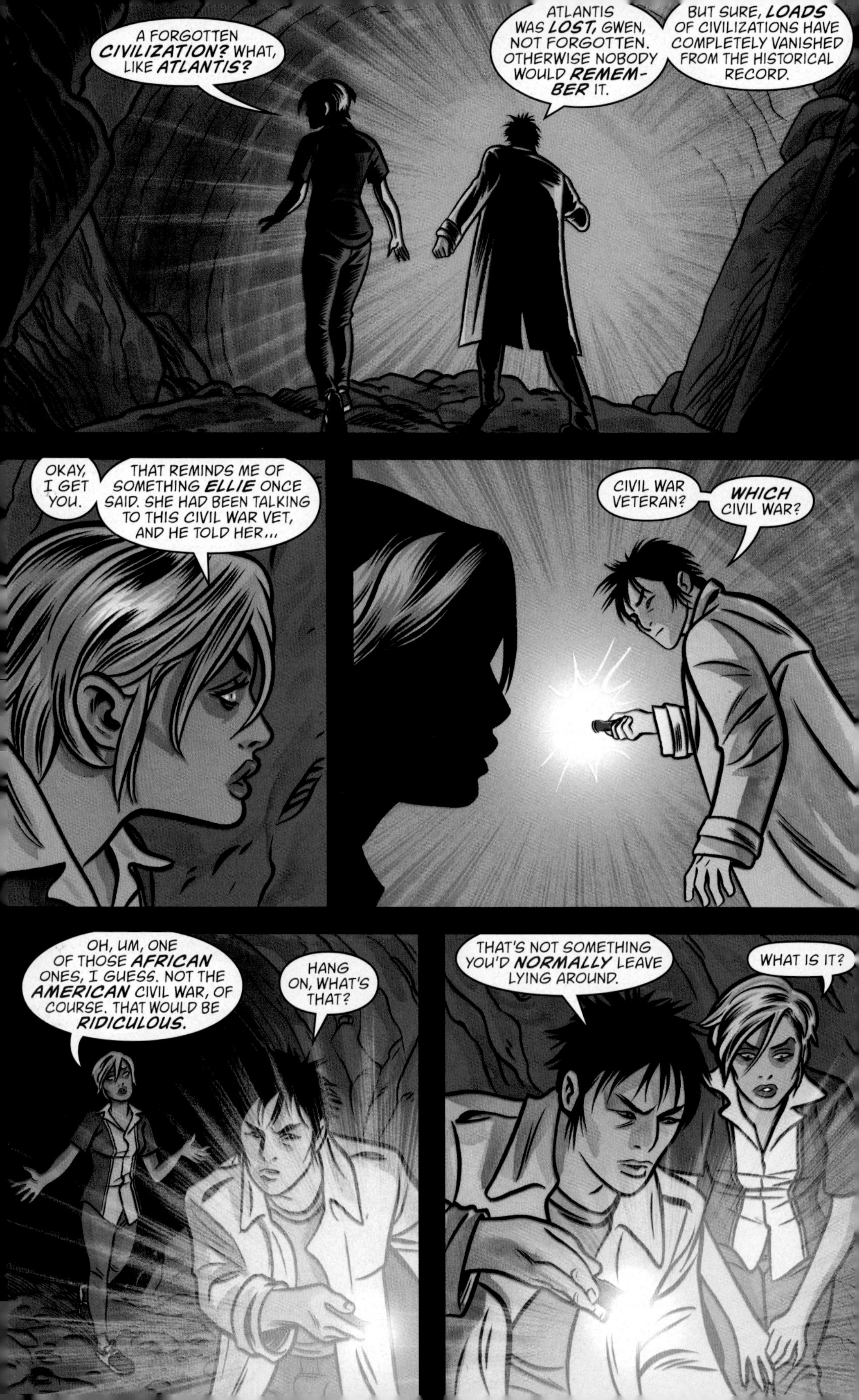
A FORGOTTEN CIVILIZATION? WHAT, LIKE ATLANTIS?
ATLANTIS WAS LOST, GWEN, NOT FORGOTTEN. OTHERWISE NOBODY WOULD REMEMBER IT.
BUT SURE, LOADS OF CIVILIZATIONS HAVE COMPLETELY VANISHED FROM THE HISTORICAL RECORD.
OKAY, I GET YOU.
THAT REMINDS ME OF SOMETHING ELLIE ONCE SAID. SHE HAD BEEN TALKING TO THIS CIVIL WAR VET, AND HE TOLD HER...
CIVIL WAR VETERAN?
WHICH CIVIL WAR?
OH, UM, ONE OF THOSE AFRICAN ONES, I GUESS. NOT THE AMERICAN CIVIL WAR, OF COURSE. THAT WOULD BE RIDICULOUS.
HANG ON, WHAT'S THAT?
THAT'S NOT SOMETHING YOU'D NORMALLY LEAVE LYING AROUND.
WHAT IS IT?

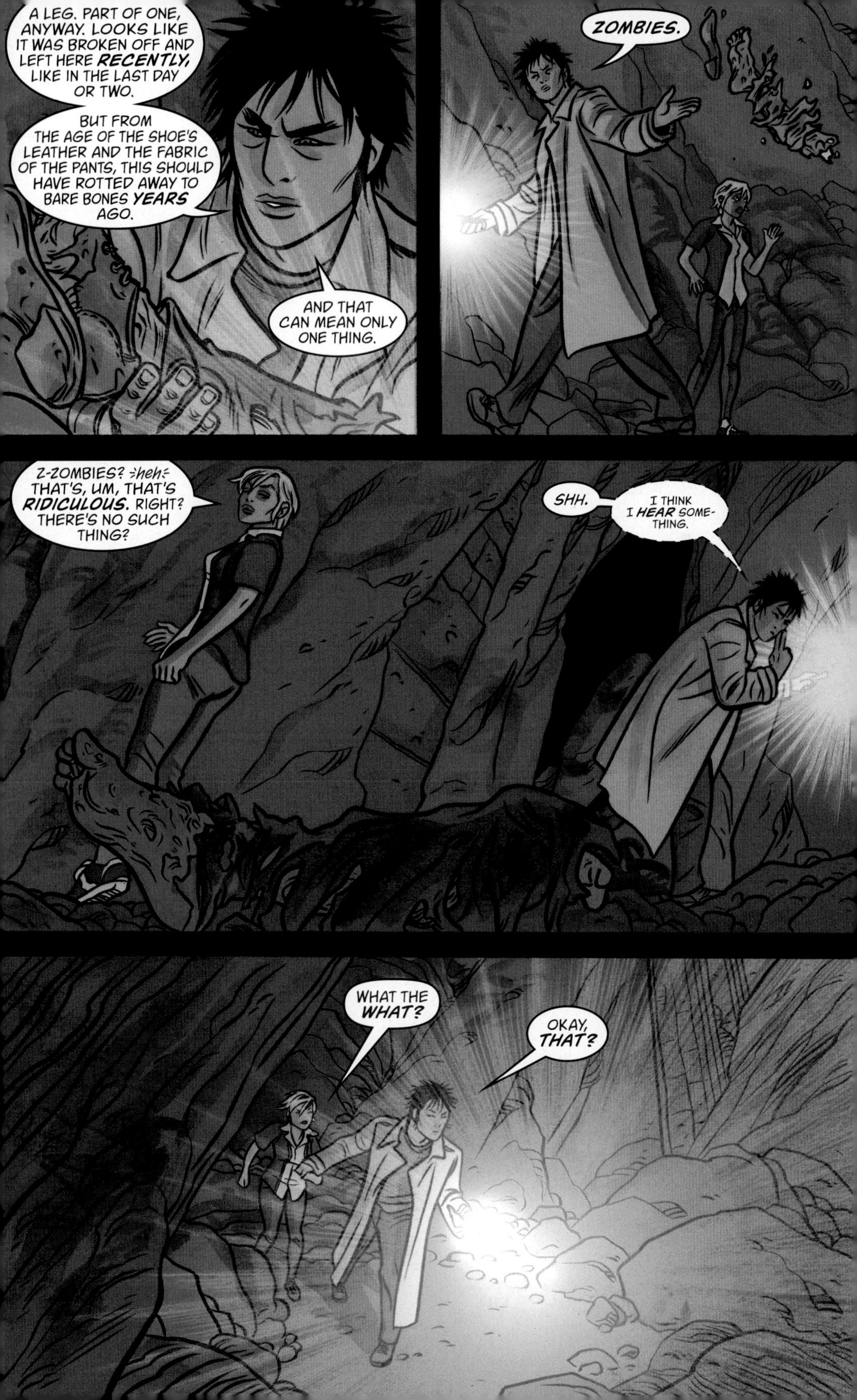
A LEG. PART OF ONE, ANYWAY. LOOKS LIKE IT WAS BROKEN OFF AND LEFT HERE RECENTLY, LIKE IN THE LAST DAY OR TWO.
BUT FROM THE AGE OF THE SHOE'S LEATHER AND THE FABRIC OF THE PANTS, THIS SHOULD HAVE ROTTED AWAY TO BARE BONES YEARS AGO.
AND THAT CAN MEAN ONLY ONE THING.
ZOMBIES.
Z-ZOMBIES? =heh= THAT'S, UM, THAT'S RIDICULOUS. RIGHT? THERE'S NO SUCH THING?
SHH.
I THINK I HEAR SOME-THING.
WHAT THE WHAT?
OKAY, THAT?

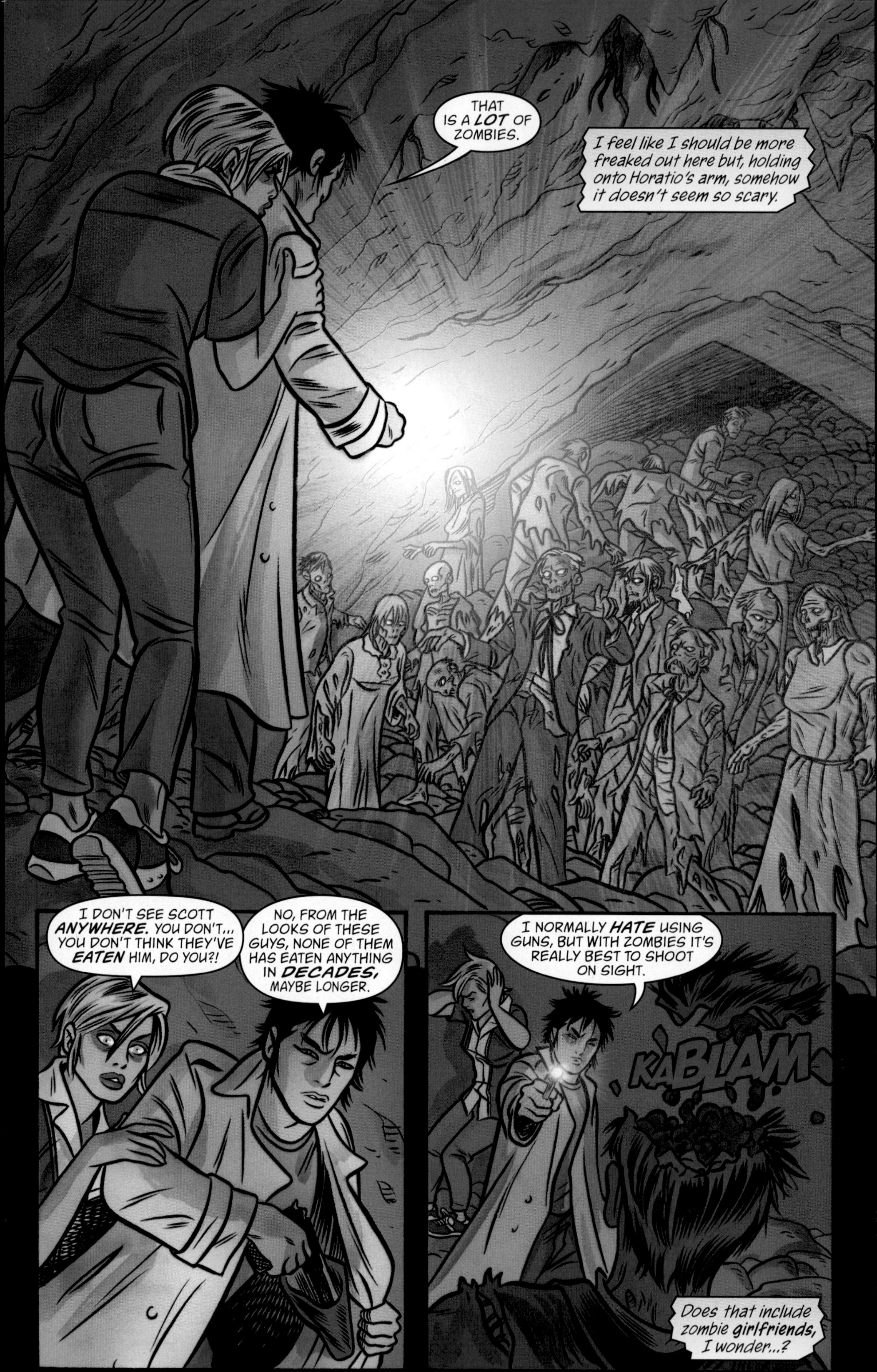
THAT IS A LOT OF ZOMBIES.
I feel like I should be more freaked out here but, holding onto Horatio's arm, somehow it doesn't seem so scary.
I DON'T SEE SCOTT ANYWHERE. YOU DON'T... YOU DON'T THINK THEY'VE EATEN HIM, DO YOU?!
NO, FROM THE LOOKS OF THESE GUYS, NONE OF THEM HAS EATEN ANYTHING IN DECADES, MAYBE LONGER.
I NORMALLY HATE USING GUNS, BUT WITH ZOMBIES IT'S REALLY BEST TO SHOOT ON SIGHT.
KABLAM
Does that include zombie girlfriends, I wonder...?

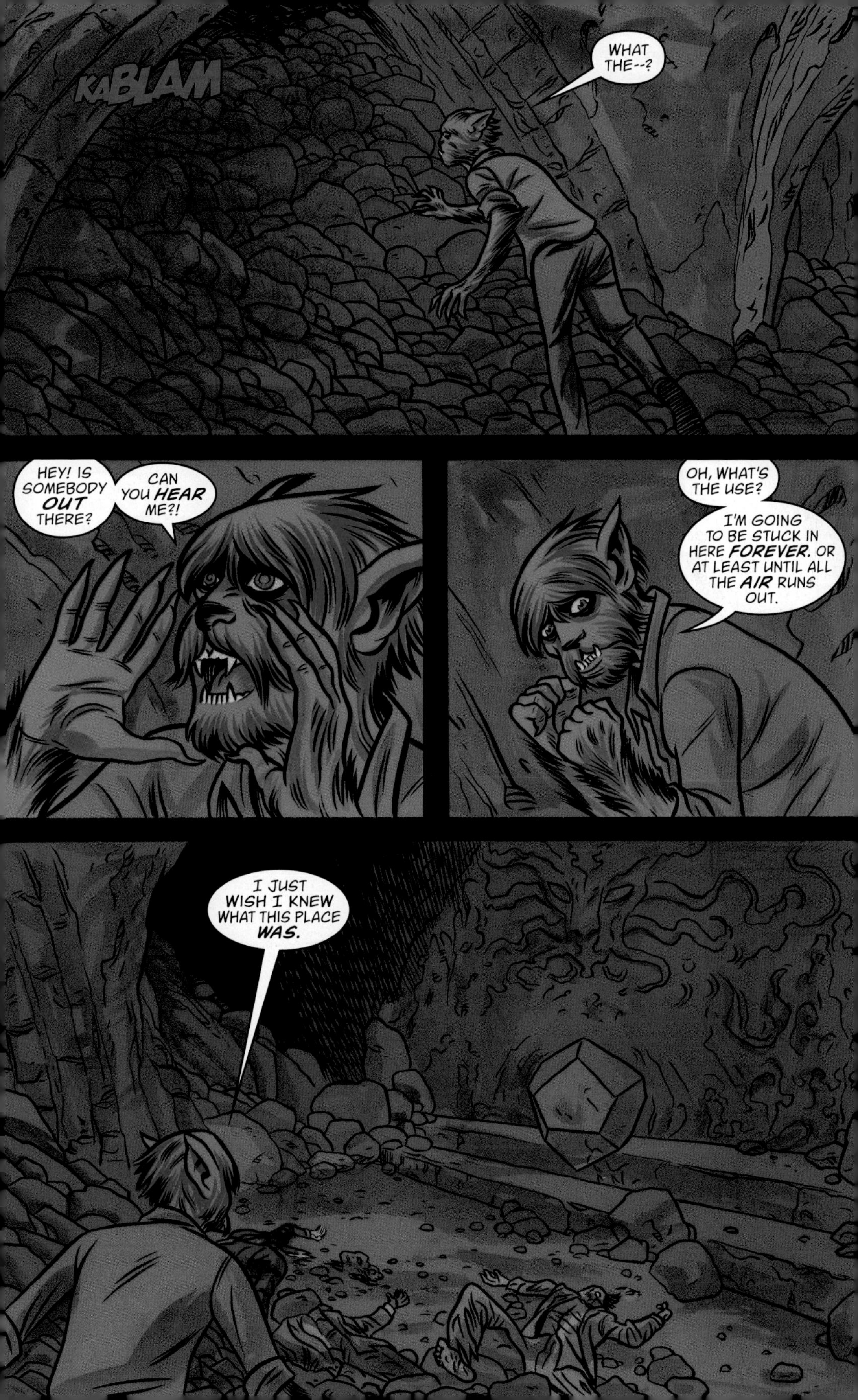
KABLAM
WHAT THE--?
HEY! IS SOMEBODY OUT THERE?
CAN YOU HEAR ME?!
OH, WHAT'S THE USE?
I'M GOING TO BE STUCK IN HERE FOREVER. OR AT LEAST UNTIL ALL THE AIR RUNS OUT.
I JUST WISH I KNEW WHAT THIS PLACE WAS.

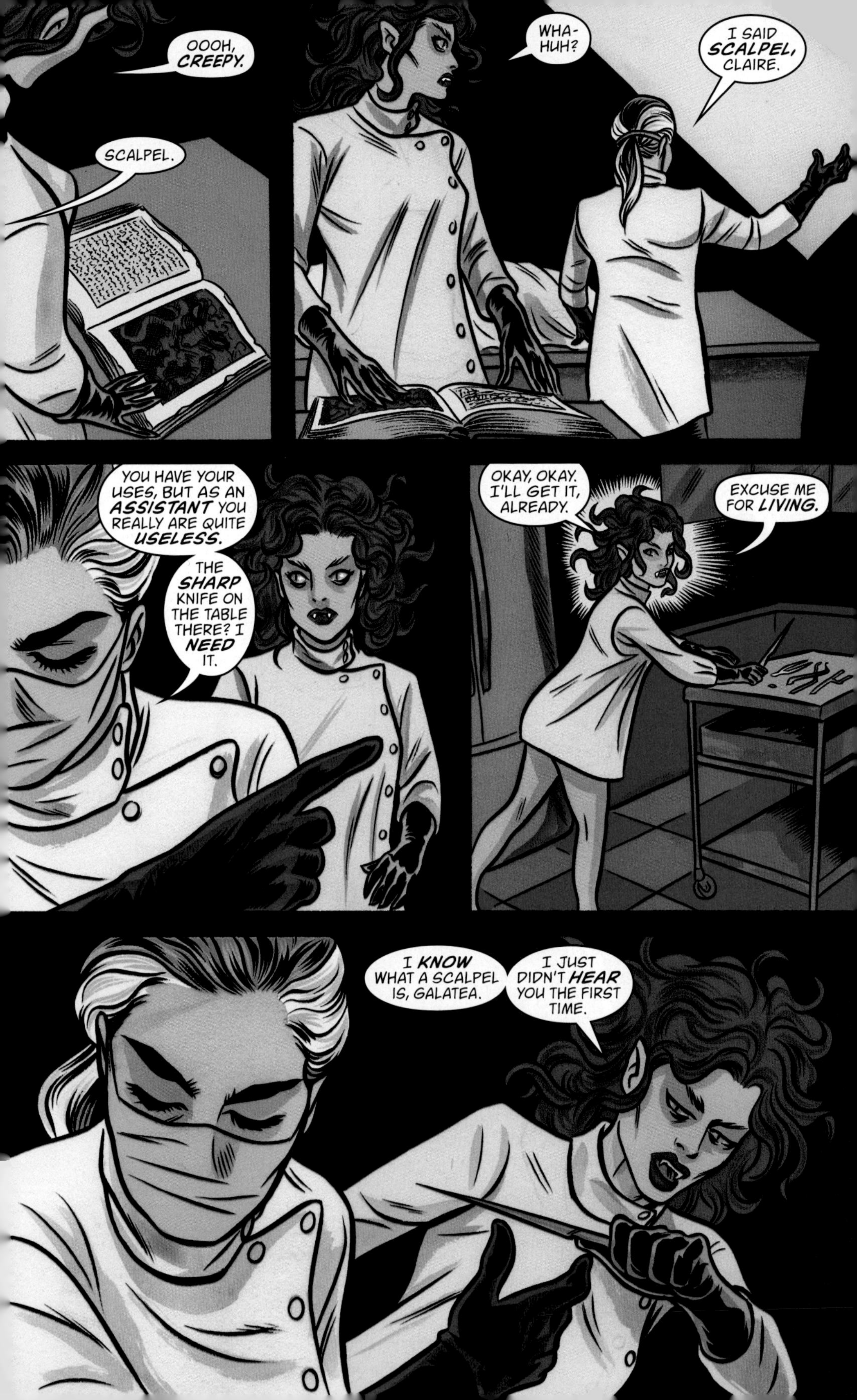
OOOH, CREEPY.
SCALPEL.
WHA-HUH?
I SAID SCALPEL, CLAIRE.
YOU HAVE YOUR USES, BUT AS AN ASSISTANT YOU REALLY ARE QUITE USELESS.
THE SHARP KNIFE ON THE TABLE THERE? I NEED IT.
OKAY, OKAY. I'LL GET IT, ALREADY.
EXCUSE ME FOR LIVING.
I KNOW WHAT A SCALPEL IS, GALATEA.
I JUST DIDN'T HEAR YOU THE FIRST TIME.

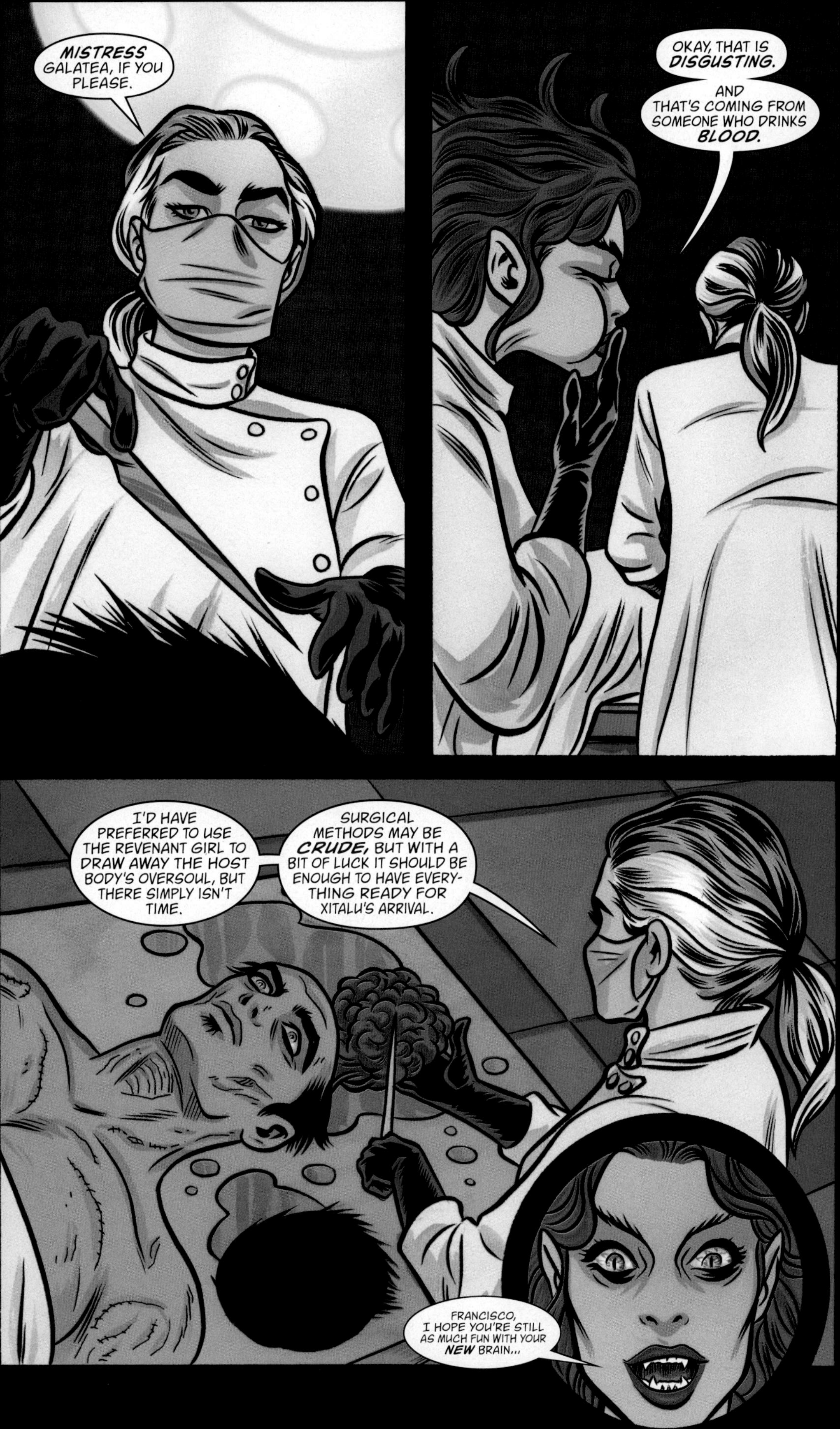
MISTRESS GALATEA, IF YOU PLEASE.
OKAY, THAT IS DISGUSTING.
AND THAT'S COMING FROM SOMEONE WHO DRINKS BLOOD.
I'D HAVE PREFERRED TO USE THE REVENANT GIRL TO DRAW AWAY THE HOST BODY'S OVERSOUL, BUT THERE SIMPLY ISN'T TIME.
SURGICAL METHODS MAY BE CRUDE, BUT WITH A BIT OF LUCK IT SHOULD BE ENOUGH TO HAVE EVERY-THING READY FOR XITALU'S ARRIVAL.
FRANCISCO, I HOPE YOU'RE STILL AS MUCH FUN WITH YOUR NEW BRAIN...

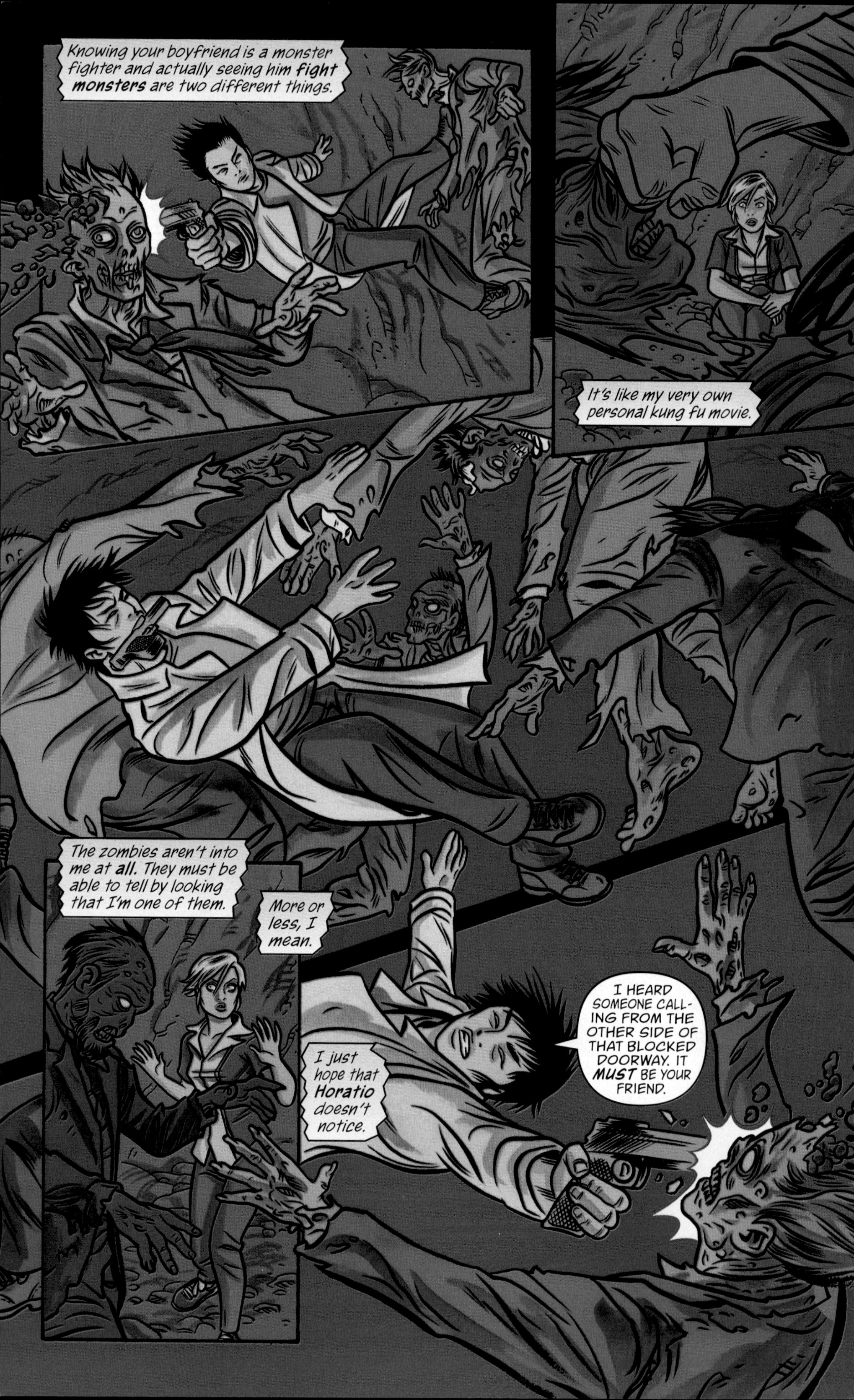

Knowing your boyfriend is a monster fighter and actually seeing him fight monsters are two different things.
It's like my very own personal kung fu movie.
The zombies aren't into me at all. They must be able to tell by looking that I'm one of them.
More or less, I mean.
I just hope that Horatio doesn't notice.
I HEARD SOMEONE CALLING FROM THE OTHER SIDE OF THAT BLOCKED DOORWAY. IT MUST BE YOUR FRIEND.

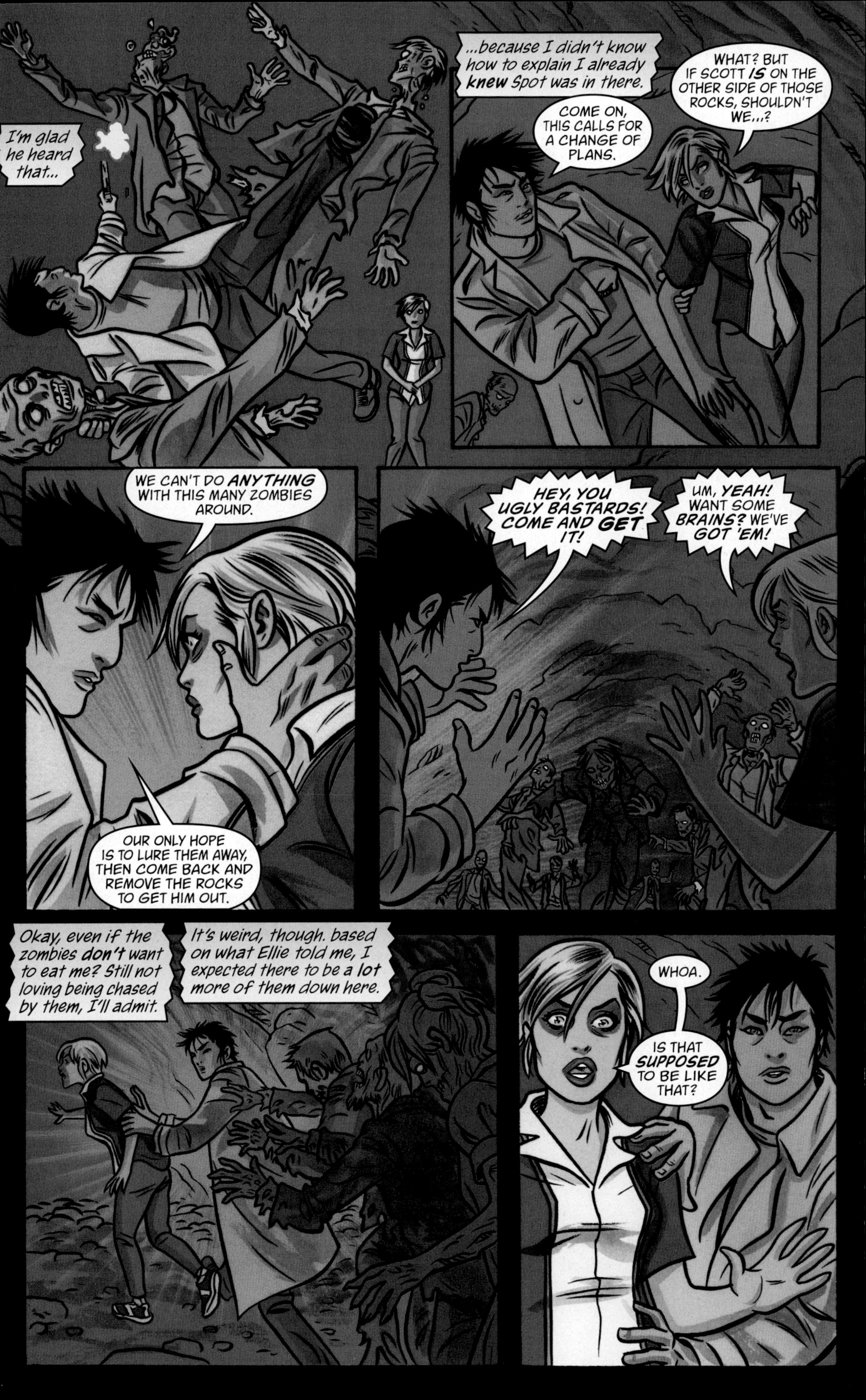

I'm glad he heard that...
...because I didn't know how to explain I already **knew** Spot was in there.
COME ON, THIS CALLS FOR A CHANGE OF PLANS.
WHAT? BUT IF SCOTT **IS** ON THE OTHER SIDE OF THOSE ROCKS, SHOULDN'T WE...?
WE CAN'T DO **ANYTHING** WITH THIS MANY ZOMBIES AROUND.
OUR ONLY HOPE IS TO LURE THEM AWAY, THEN COME BACK AND REMOVE THE ROCKS TO GET HIM OUT.
HEY, YOU UGLY BASTARDS! COME AND **GET** IT!
UM, **YEAH!** WANT SOME **BRAINS?** WE'VE GOT 'EM!
Okay, even if the zombies **don't** want to eat me? Still not loving being chased by them, I'll admit.
It's weird, though. based on what Ellie told me, I expected there to be a **lot** more of them down here.
WHOA.
IS THAT **SUPPOSED** TO BE LIKE THAT?

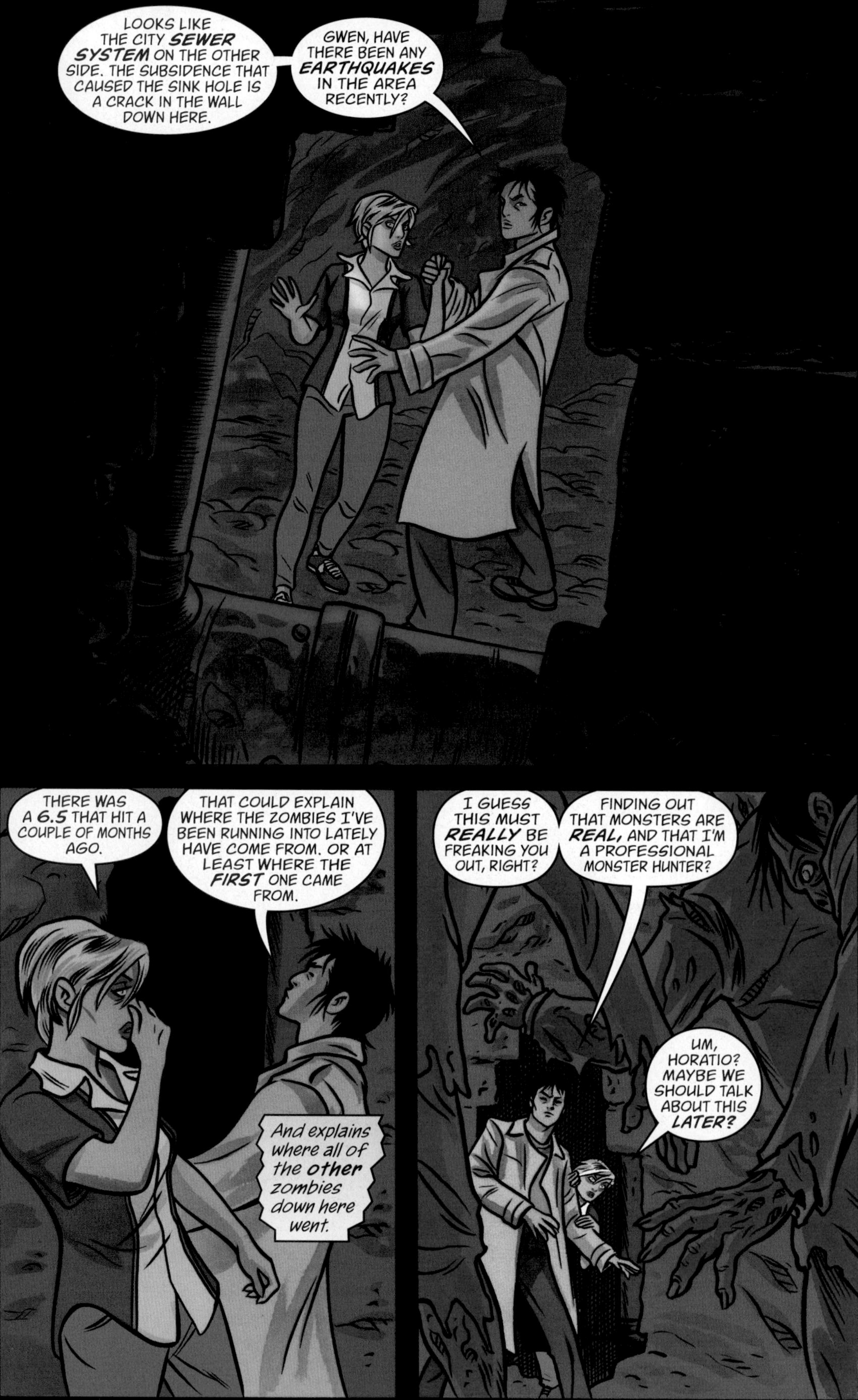
LOOKS LIKE THE CITY SEWER SYSTEM ON THE OTHER SIDE. THE SUBSIDENCE THAT CAUSED THE SINK HOLE IS A CRACK IN THE WALL DOWN HERE.
GWEN, HAVE THERE BEEN ANY EARTHQUAKES IN THE AREA RECENTLY?
THERE WAS A 6.5 THAT HIT A COUPLE OF MONTHS AGO.
THAT COULD EXPLAIN WHERE THE ZOMBIES I'VE BEEN RUNNING INTO LATELY HAVE COME FROM. OR AT LEAST WHERE THE FIRST ONE CAME FROM.
And explains where all of the other zombies down here went.
I GUESS THIS MUST REALLY BE FREAKING YOU OUT, RIGHT?
FINDING OUT THAT MONSTERS ARE REAL, AND THAT I'M A PROFESSIONAL MONSTER HUNTER?
UM, HORATIO? MAYBE WE SHOULD TALK ABOUT THIS LATER?

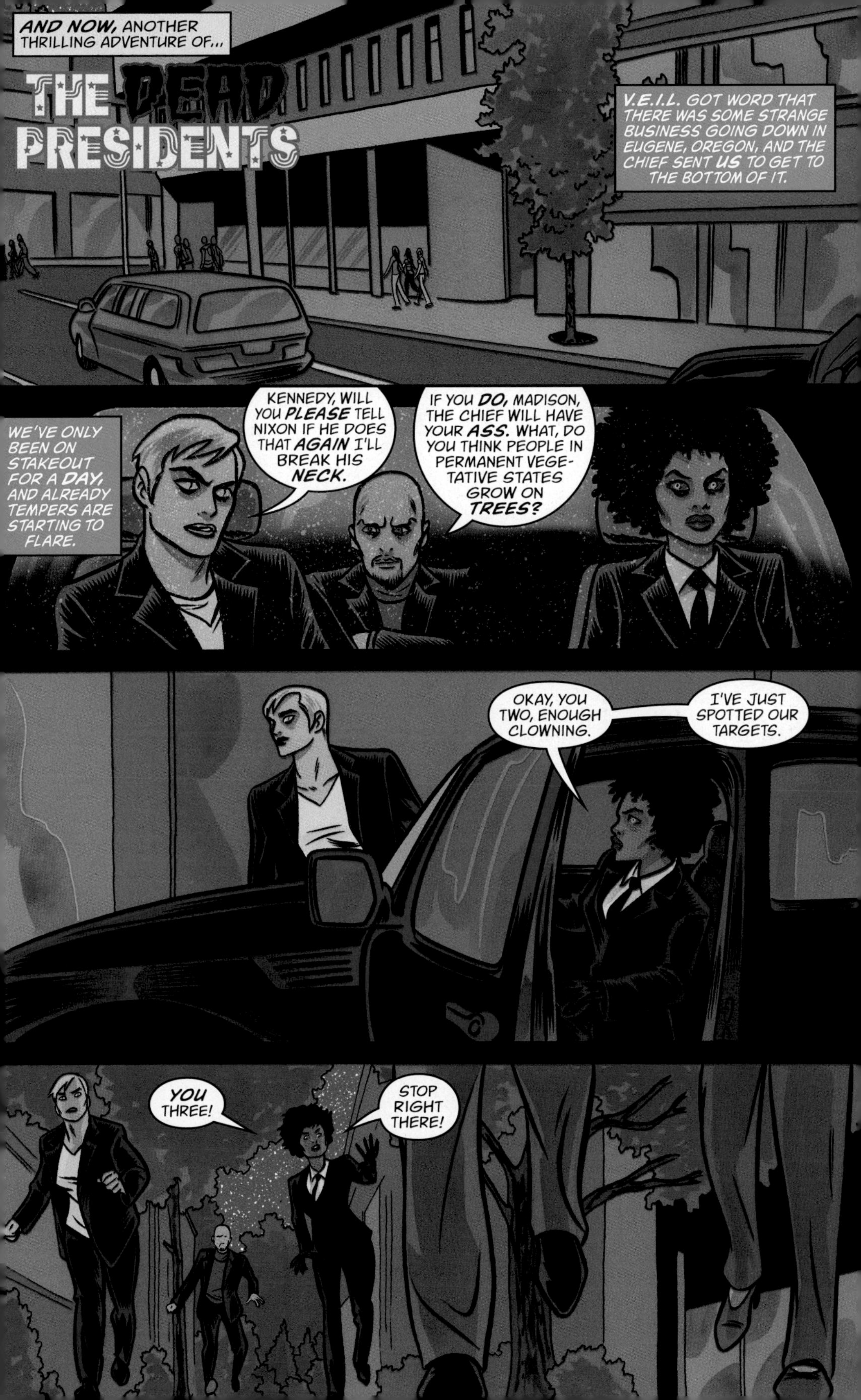
AND NOW, ANOTHER THRILLING ADVENTURE OF...
THE DEAD PRESIDENTS
V.E.I.L. GOT WORD THAT THERE WAS SOME STRANGE BUSINESS GOING DOWN IN EUGENE, OREGON, AND THE CHIEF SENT US TO GET TO THE BOTTOM OF IT.
WE'VE ONLY BEEN ON STAKEOUT FOR A DAY, AND ALREADY TEMPERS ARE STARTING TO FLARE.
KENNEDY, WILL YOU PLEASE TELL NIXON IF HE DOES THAT AGAIN I'LL BREAK HIS NECK.
IF YOU DO, MADISON, THE CHIEF WILL HAVE YOUR ASS. WHAT, DO YOU THINK PEOPLE IN PERMANENT VEGE-TATIVE STATES GROW ON TREES?
OKAY, YOU TWO, ENOUGH CLOWNING.
I'VE JUST SPOTTED OUR TARGETS.
YOU THREE!
STOP RIGHT THERE!

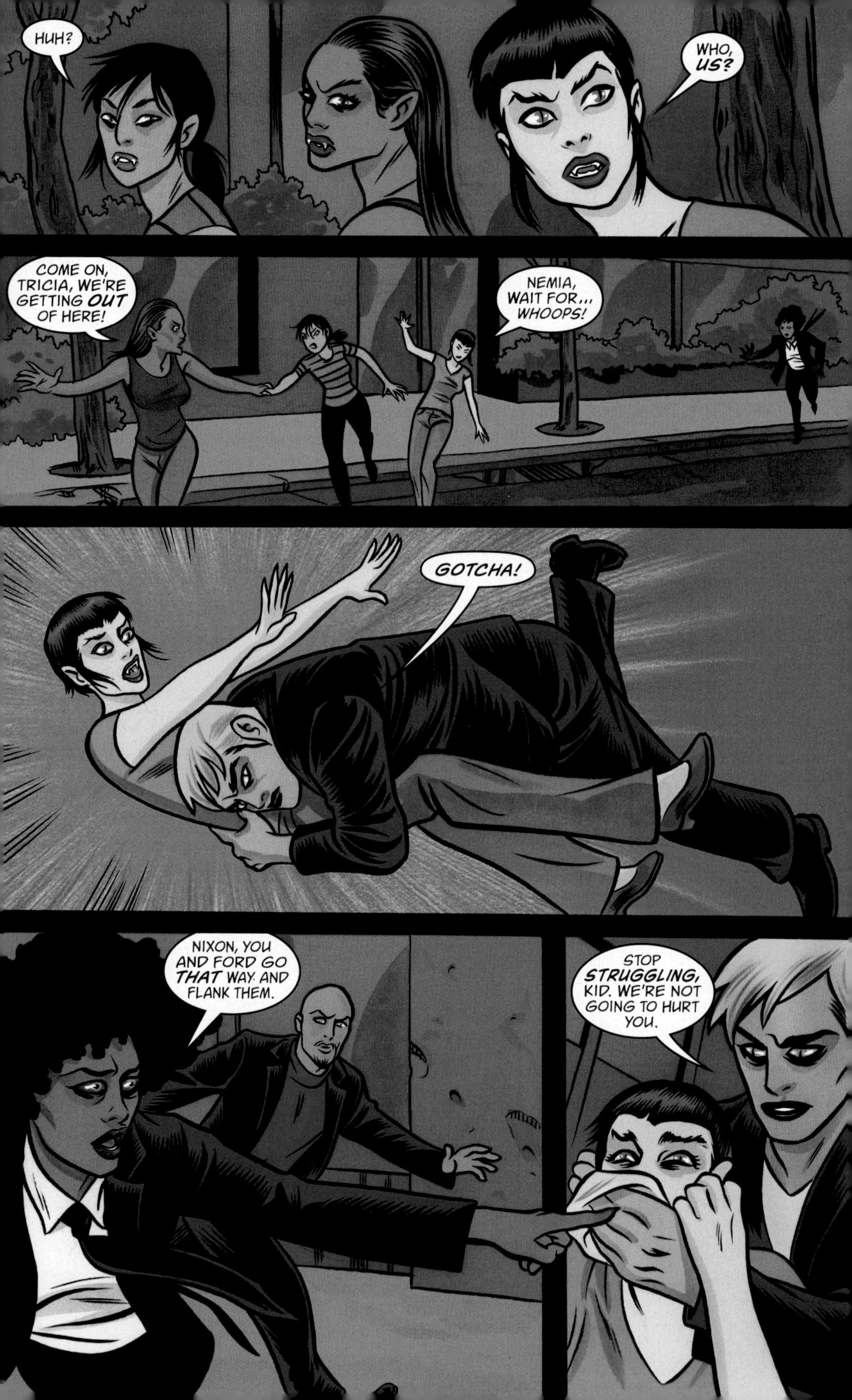
HUH?
WHO, US?
COME ON, TRICIA, WE'RE GETTING OUT OF HERE!
NEMIA, WAIT FOR... WHOOPS!
GOTCHA!
NIXON, YOU AND FORD GO THAT WAY AND FLANK THEM.
STOP STRUGGLING, KID. WE'RE NOT GOING TO HURT YOU.

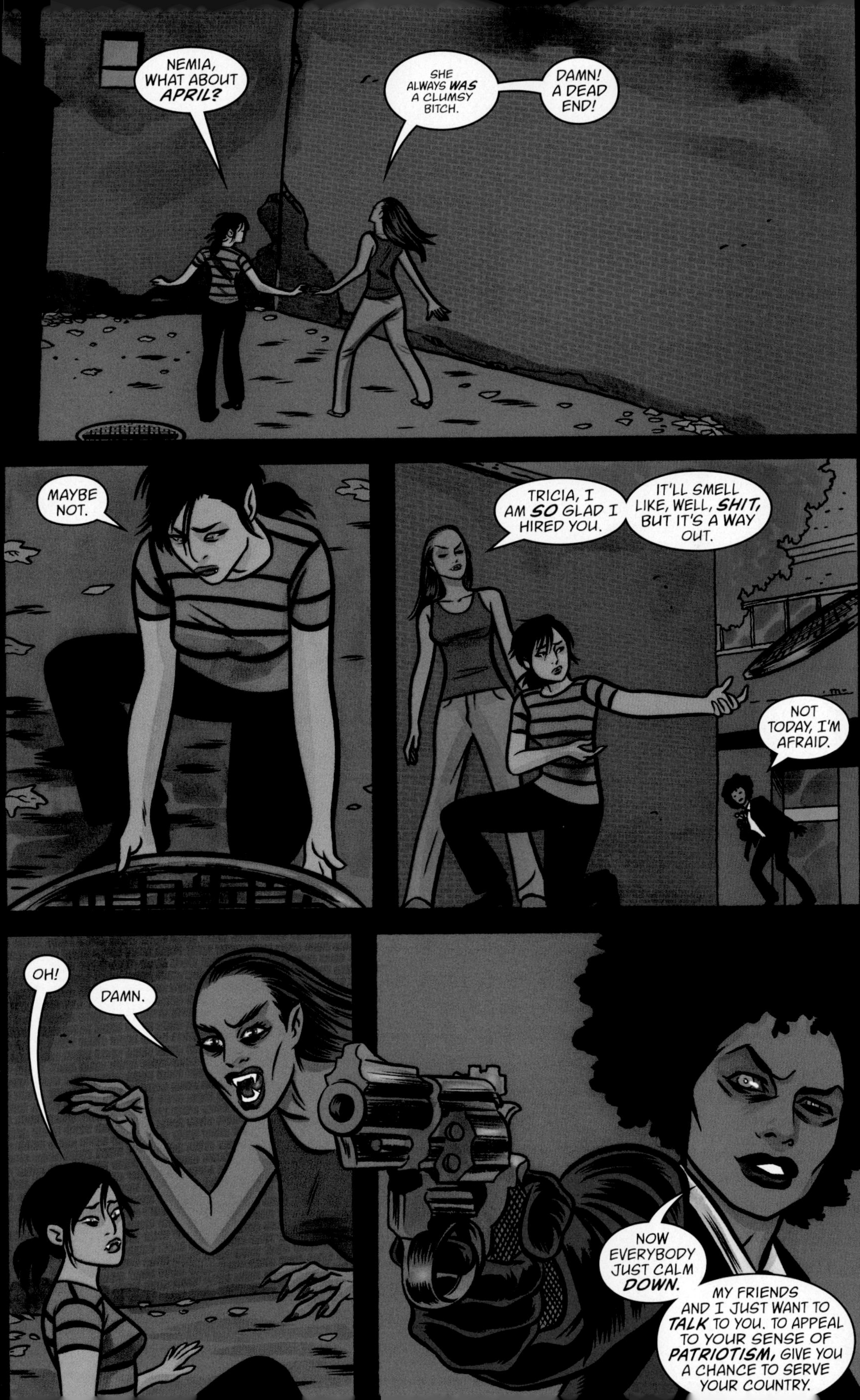
NEMIA, WHAT ABOUT APRIL?
SHE ALWAYS WAS A CLUMSY BITCH.
DAMN! A DEAD END!
MAYBE NOT.
TRICIA, I AM SO GLAD I HIRED YOU.
IT'LL SMELL LIKE, WELL, SHIT, BUT IT'S A WAY OUT.
NOT TODAY, I'M AFRAID.
OH!
DAMN.
NOW EVERYBODY JUST CALM DOWN.
MY FRIENDS AND I JUST WANT TO TALK TO YOU. TO APPEAL TO YOUR SENSE OF PATRIOTISM, GIVE YOU A CHANCE TO SERVE YOUR COUNTRY.

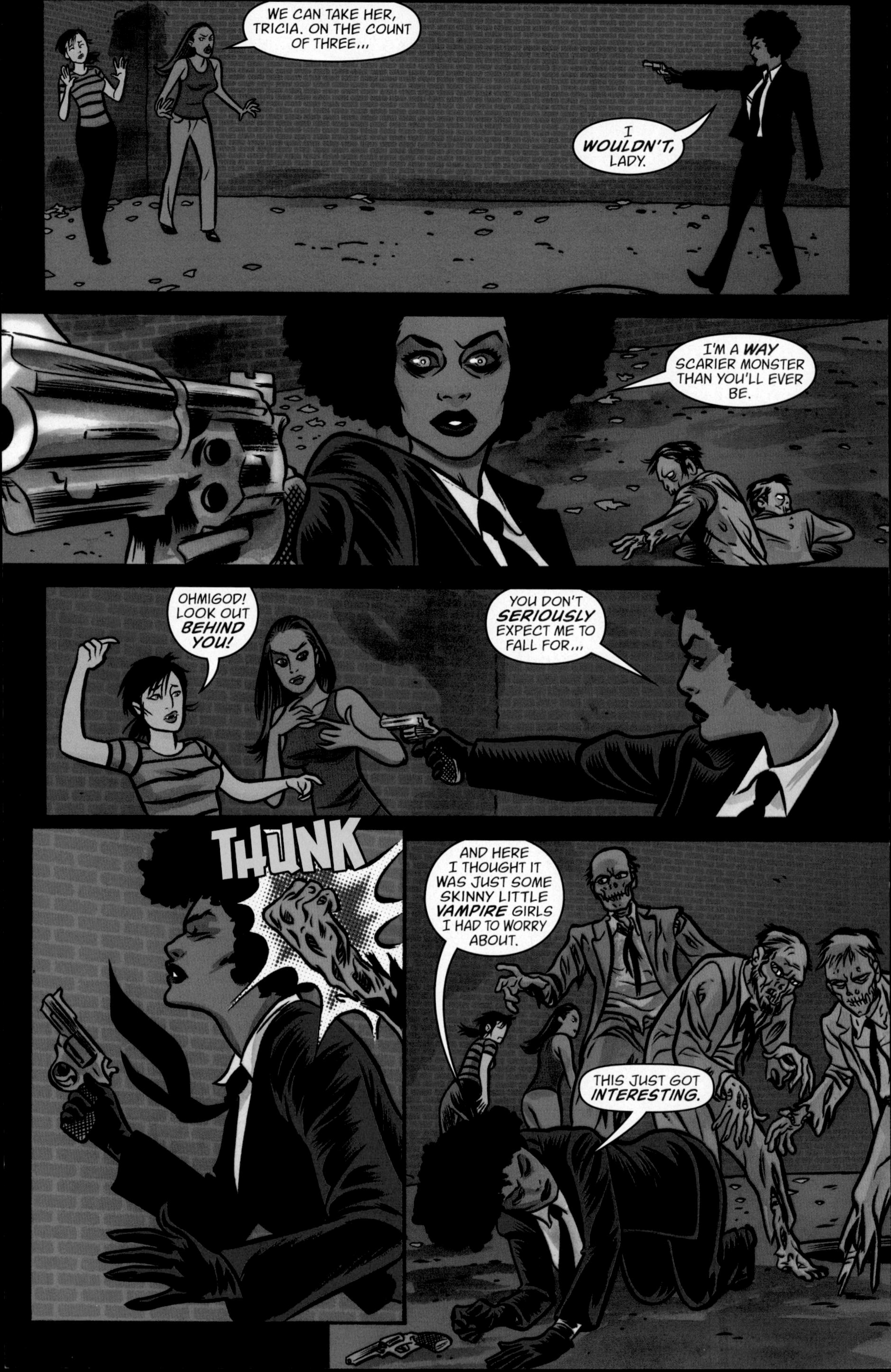

WE CAN TAKE HER, TRICIA. ON THE COUNT OF THREE...
I WOULDN'T, LADY.
I'M A WAY SCARIER MONSTER THAN YOU'LL EVER BE.
OHMIGOD! LOOK OUT BEHIND YOU!
YOU DON'T SERIOUSLY EXPECT ME TO FALL FOR...
THUNK
AND HERE I THOUGHT IT WAS JUST SOME SKINNY LITTLE VAMPIRE GIRLS I HAD TO WORRY ABOUT.
THIS JUST GOT INTERESTING.

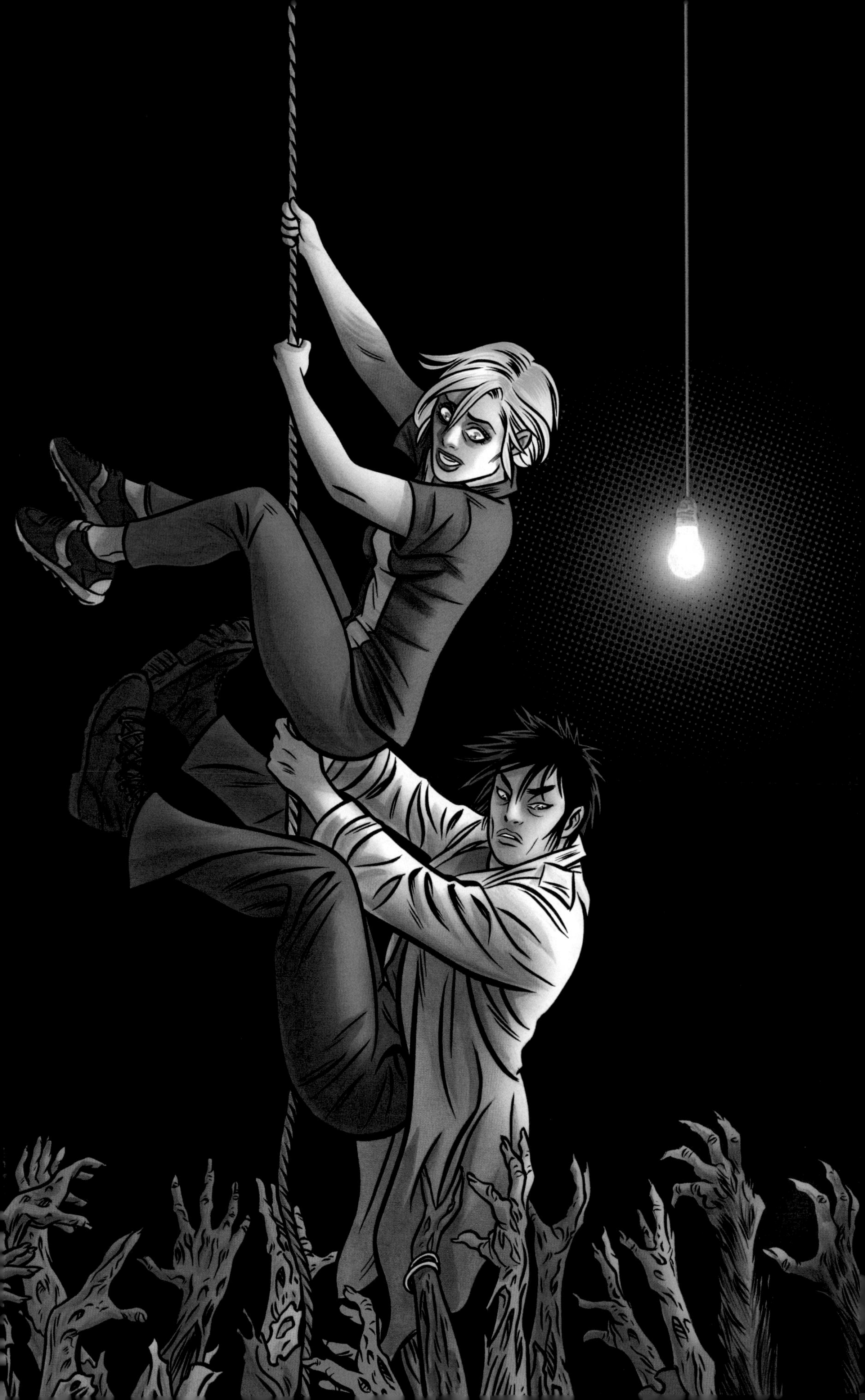

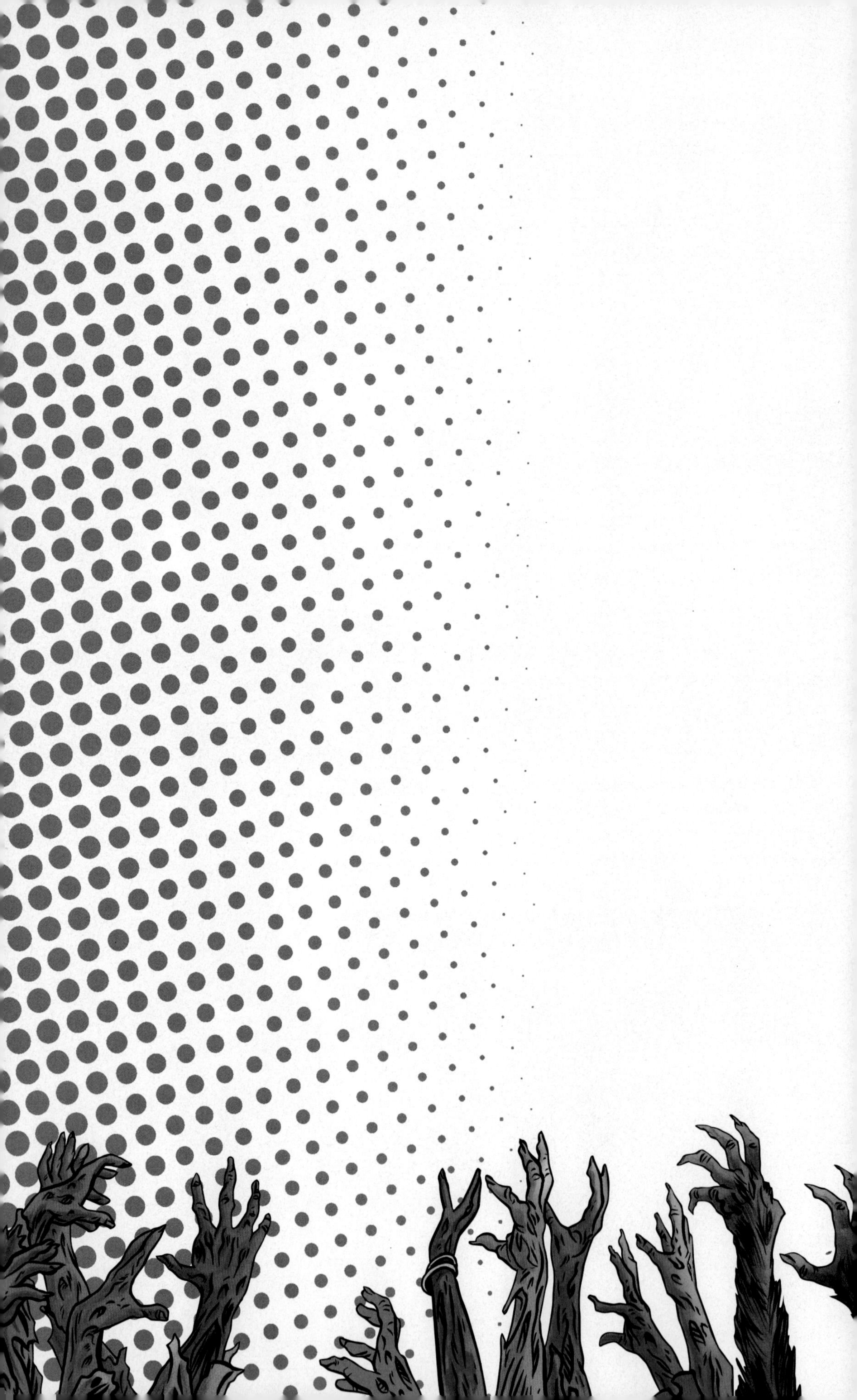

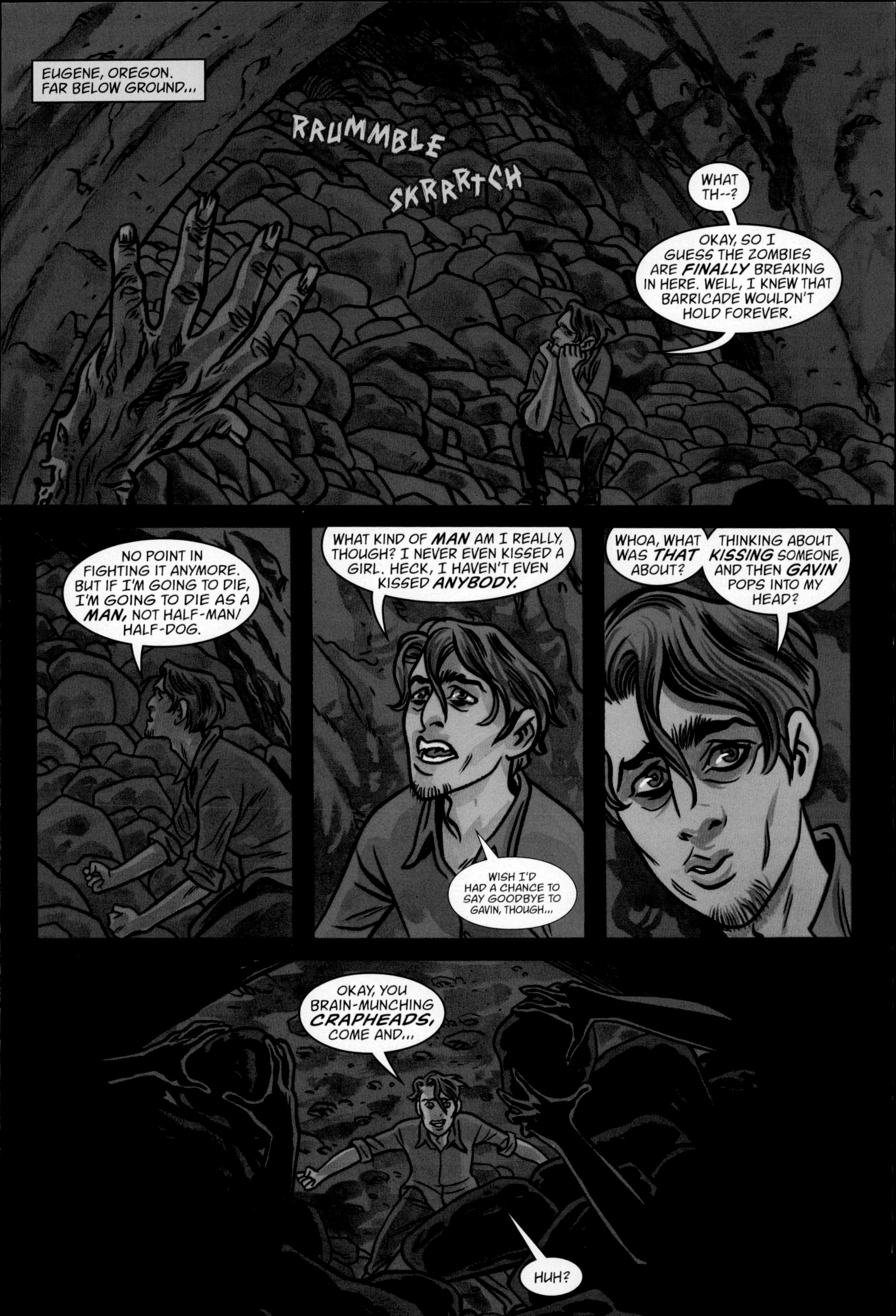
EUGENE, OREGON. FAR BELOW GROUND...
RRUMMBLE
SKRRRTCH
WHAT TH--?
OKAY, SO I GUESS THE ZOMBIES ARE FINALLY BREAKING IN HERE. WELL, I KNEW THAT BARRICADE WOULDN'T HOLD FOREVER.
NO POINT IN FIGHTING IT ANYMORE. BUT IF I'M GOING TO DIE, I'M GOING TO DIE AS A MAN, NOT HALF-MAN/ HALF-DOG.
WHAT KIND OF MAN AM I REALLY, THOUGH? I NEVER EVEN KISSED A GIRL. HECK, I HAVEN'T EVEN KISSED ANYBODY.
WISH I'D HAD A CHANCE TO SAY GOODBYE TO GAVIN, THOUGH...
WHOA, WHAT WAS THAT ABOUT?
THINKING ABOUT KISSING SOMEONE, AND THEN GAVIN POPS INTO MY HEAD?
OKAY, YOU BRAIN-MUNCHING CRAPHEADS, COME AND...
HUH?

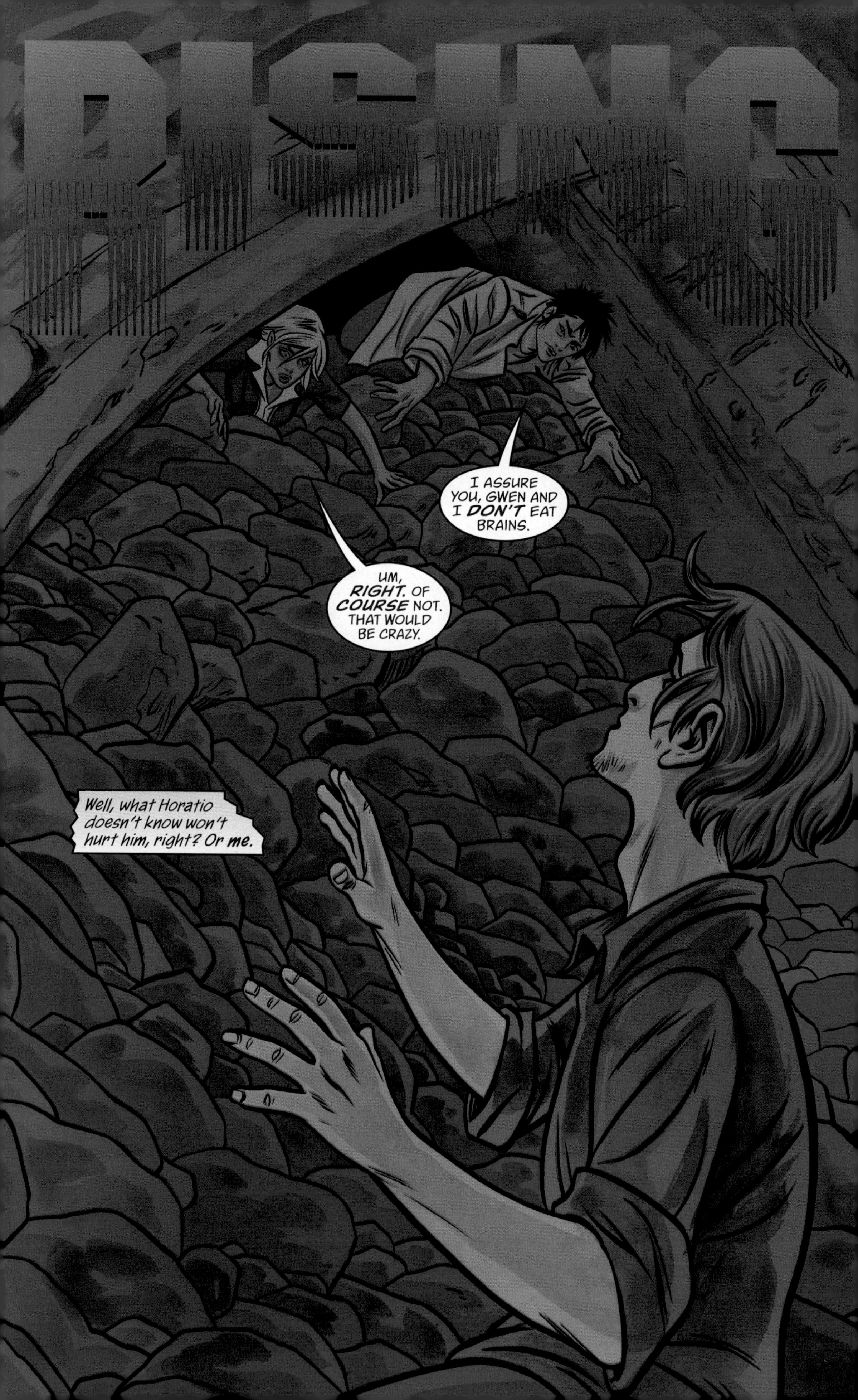
I ASSURE YOU, GWEN AND I **DON'T** EAT BRAINS.
UM, **RIGHT.** OF **COURSE** NOT. THAT WOULD BE CRAZY.
*Well, what Horatio doesn't know won't hurt him, right? Or **me**.*

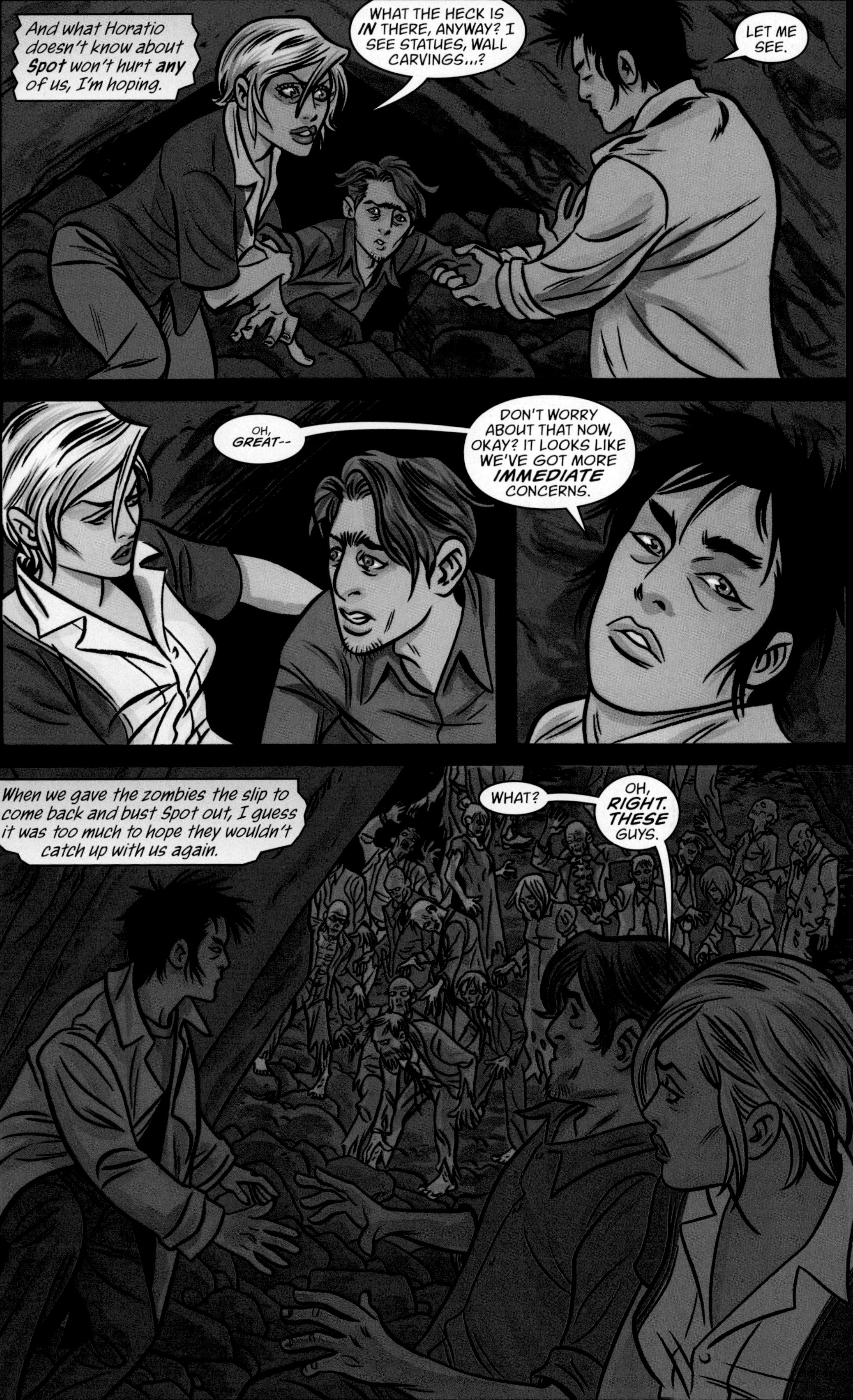
And what Horatio doesn't know about Spot won't hurt any of us, I'm hoping.
WHAT THE HECK IS IN THERE, ANYWAY? I SEE STATUES, WALL CARVINGS...?
LET ME SEE.
OH, GREAT--
DON'T WORRY ABOUT THAT NOW, OKAY? IT LOOKS LIKE WE'VE GOT MORE IMMEDIATE CONCERNS.
When we gave the zombies the slip to come back and bust Spot out, I guess it was too much to hope they wouldn't catch up with us again.
WHAT?
OH, RIGHT. THESE GUYS.

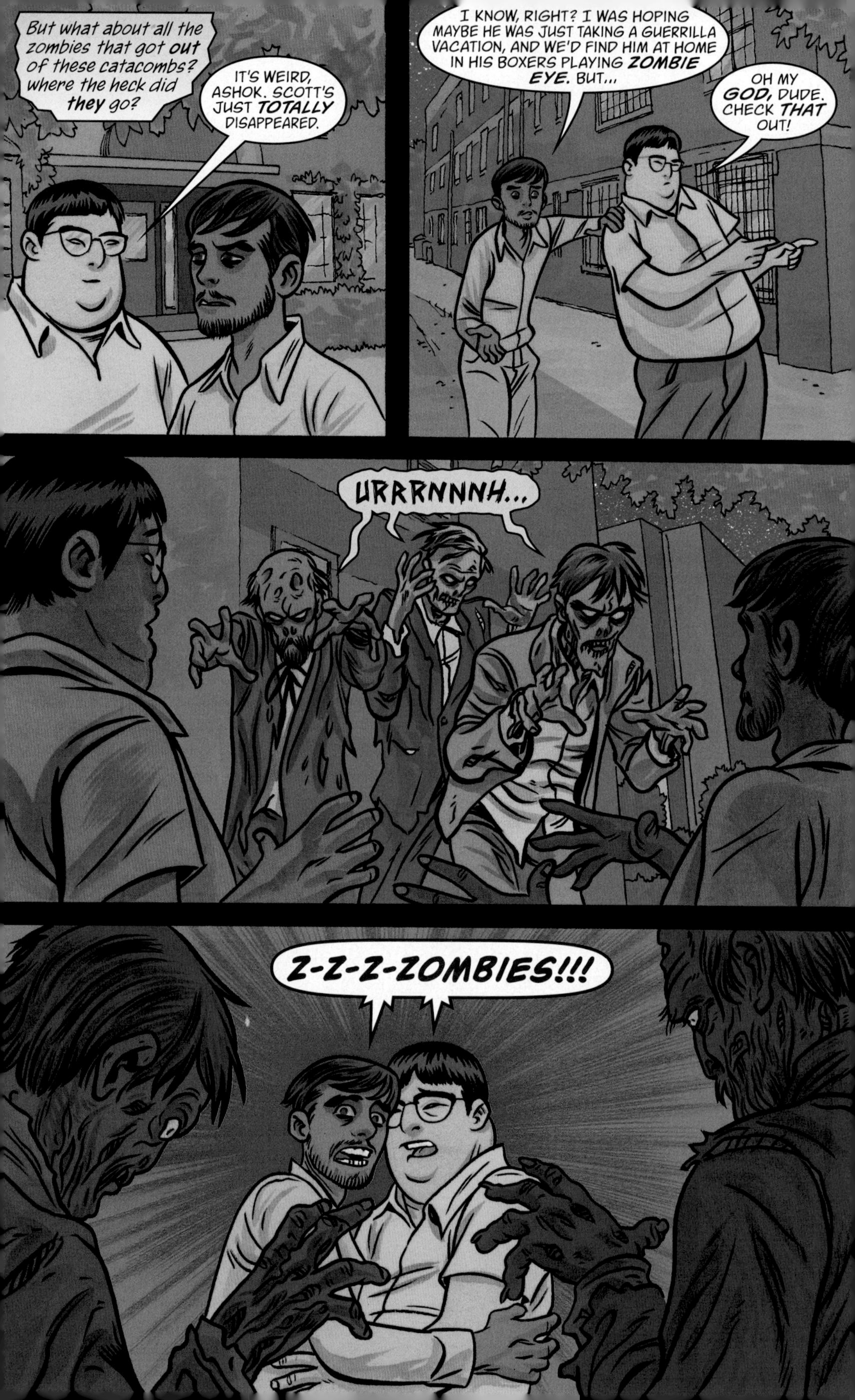
But what about all the zombies that got out of these catacombs? where the heck did they go?
IT'S WEIRD, ASHOK. SCOTT'S JUST TOTALLY DISAPPEARED.
I KNOW, RIGHT? I WAS HOPING MAYBE HE WAS JUST TAKING A GUERRILLA VACATION, AND WE'D FIND HIM AT HOME IN HIS BOXERS PLAYING ZOMBIE EYE. BUT...
OH MY GOD, DUDE. CHECK THAT OUT!
URRRNNNH...
Z-Z-Z-ZOMBIES!!!

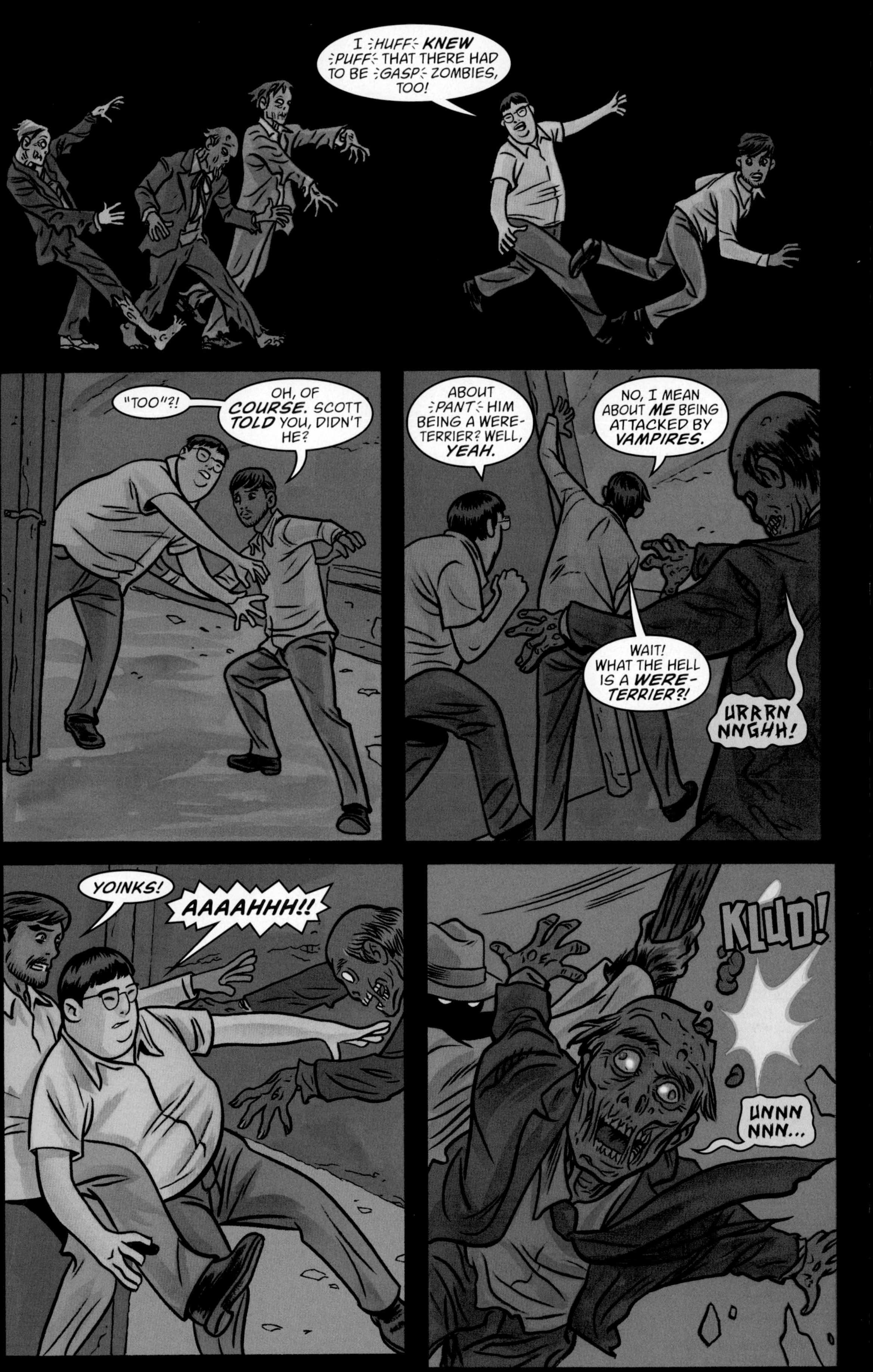

I ⁓HUFF⁓ KNEW ⁓PUFF⁓ THAT THERE HAD TO BE ⁓GASP⁓ ZOMBIES, TOO!
"TOO"?!
OH, OF COURSE. SCOTT TOLD YOU, DIDN'T HE?
ABOUT ⁓PANT⁓ HIM BEING A WERE-TERRIER? WELL, YEAH.
NO, I MEAN ABOUT ME BEING ATTACKED BY VAMPIRES.
WAIT! WHAT THE HELL IS A WERE-TERRIER?!
URRRN NNGHH!
YOINKS!
AAAAHHH!!
KLUD!
UNNN NNN...

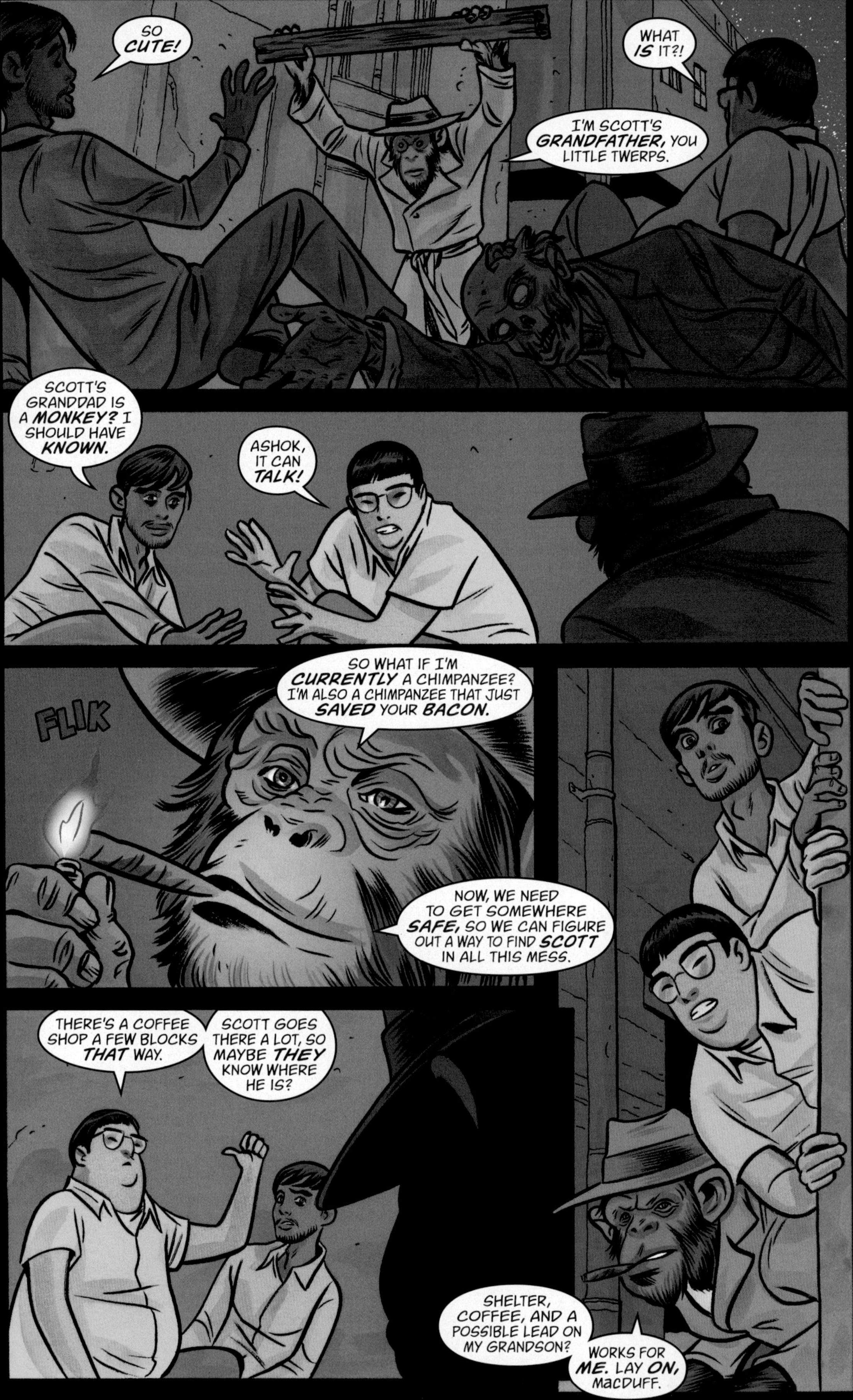
SO CUTE!
WHAT IS IT?!
I'M SCOTT'S GRANDFATHER, YOU LITTLE TWERPS.
SCOTT'S GRANDDAD IS A MONKEY? I SHOULD HAVE KNOWN.
ASHOK, IT CAN TALK!
FLIK
SO WHAT IF I'M CURRENTLY A CHIMPANZEE? I'M ALSO A CHIMPANZEE THAT JUST SAVED YOUR BACON.
NOW, WE NEED TO GET SOMEWHERE SAFE, SO WE CAN FIGURE OUT A WAY TO FIND SCOTT IN ALL THIS MESS.
THERE'S A COFFEE SHOP A FEW BLOCKS THAT WAY.
SCOTT GOES THERE A LOT, SO MAYBE THEY KNOW WHERE HE IS?
SHELTER, COFFEE, AND A POSSIBLE LEAD ON MY GRANDSON?
WORKS FOR ME. LAY ON, MacDUFF.

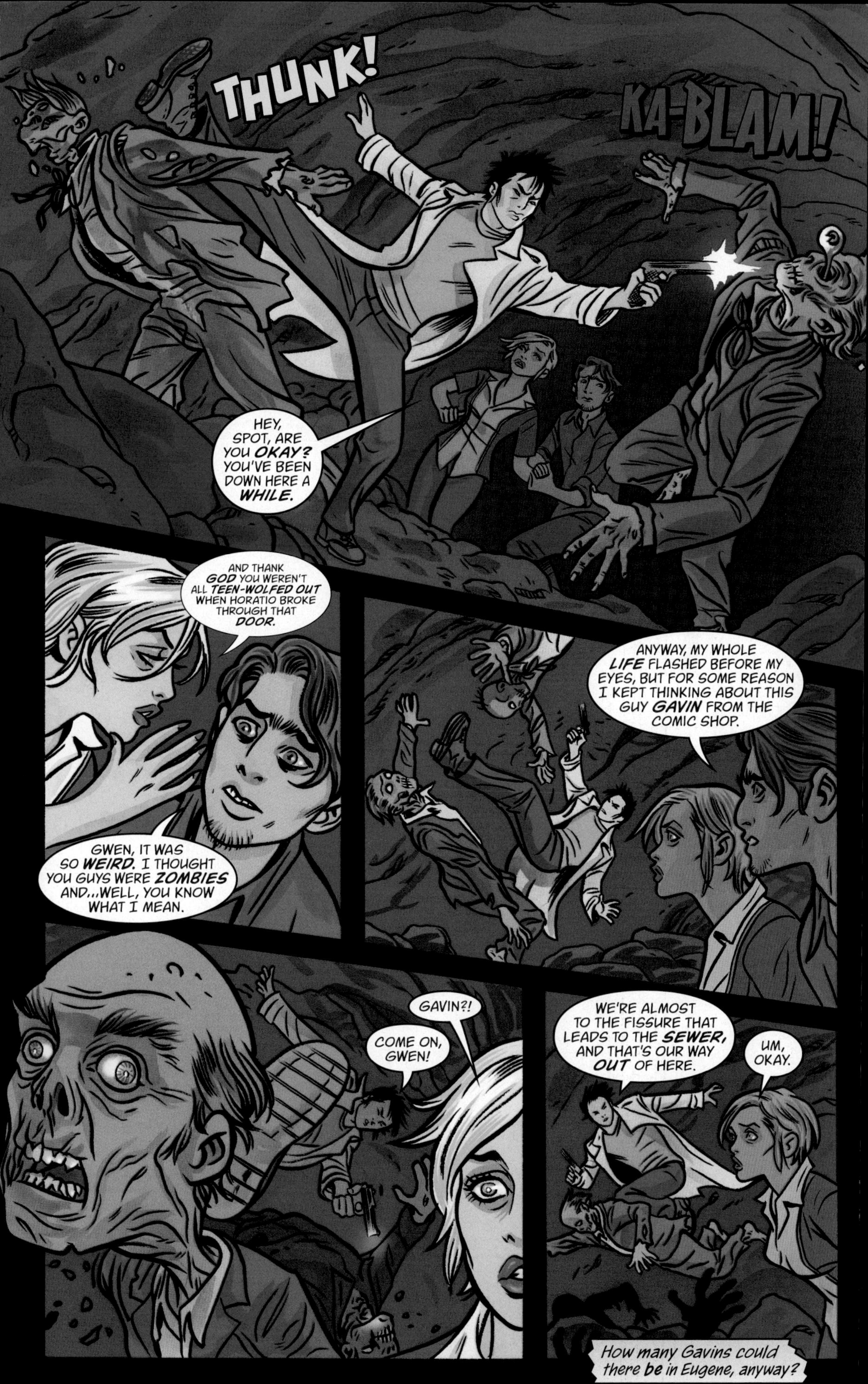
THUNK!
KA-BLAM!
HEY, SPOT, ARE YOU OKAY? YOU'VE BEEN DOWN HERE A WHILE.
AND THANK GOD YOU WEREN'T ALL TEEN-WOLFED OUT WHEN HORATIO BROKE THROUGH THAT DOOR.
GWEN, IT WAS SO WEIRD. I THOUGHT YOU GUYS WERE ZOMBIES AND...WELL, YOU KNOW WHAT I MEAN.
ANYWAY, MY WHOLE LIFE FLASHED BEFORE MY EYES, BUT FOR SOME REASON I KEPT THINKING ABOUT THIS GUY GAVIN FROM THE COMIC SHOP.
GAVIN?!
COME ON, GWEN!
WE'RE ALMOST TO THE FISSURE THAT LEADS TO THE SEWER, AND THAT'S OUR WAY OUT OF HERE.
UM, OKAY.
How many Gavins could there be in Eugene, anyway?

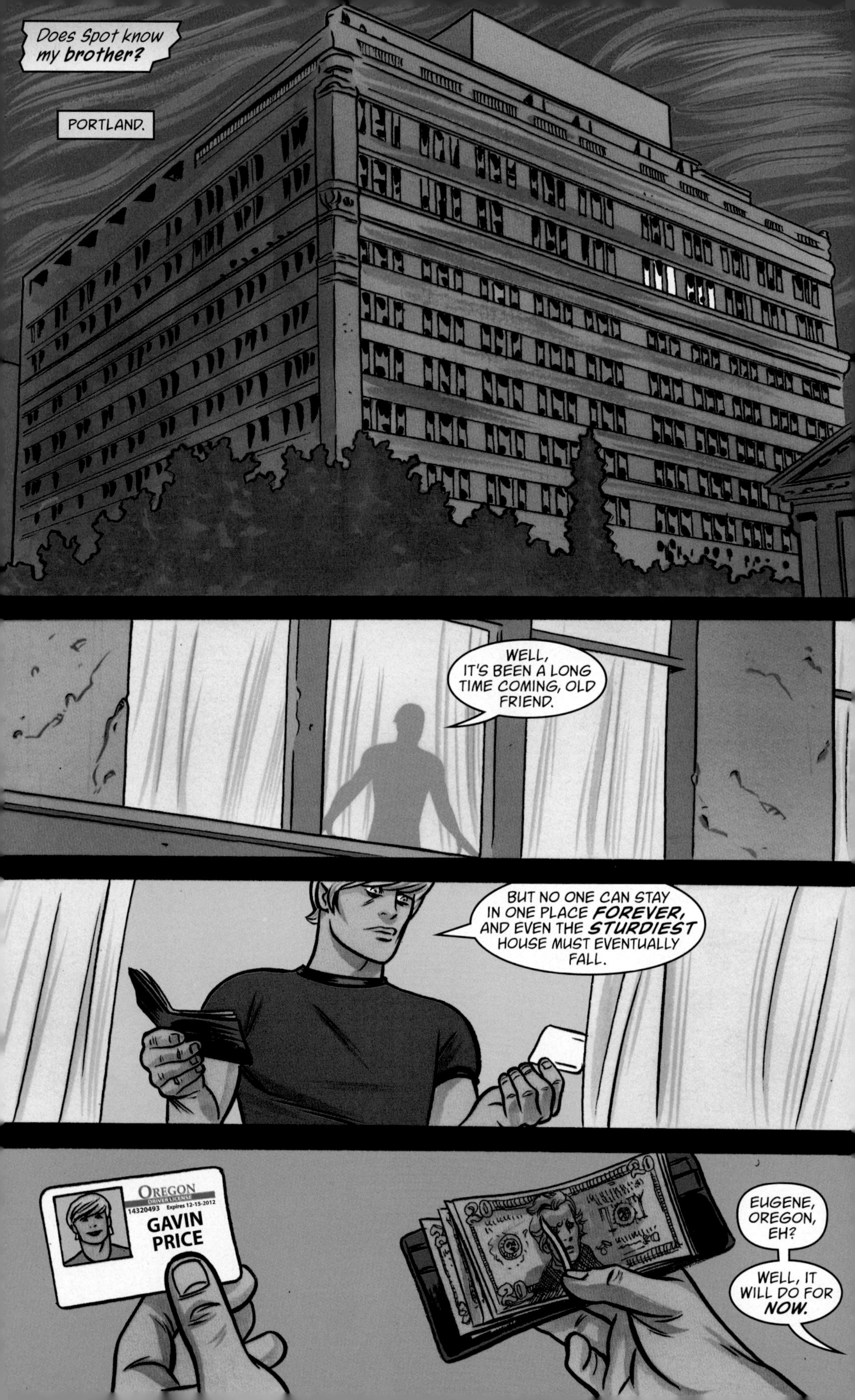
Does Spot know my brother?
PORTLAND.
WELL, IT'S BEEN A LONG TIME COMING, OLD FRIEND.
BUT NO ONE CAN STAY IN ONE PLACE FOREVER, AND EVEN THE STURDIEST HOUSE MUST EVENTUALLY FALL.
OREGON
DRIVER LICENSE
14320493 Expires 12-15-2012
GAVIN PRICE
EUGENE, OREGON, EH?
WELL, IT WILL DO FOR NOW.

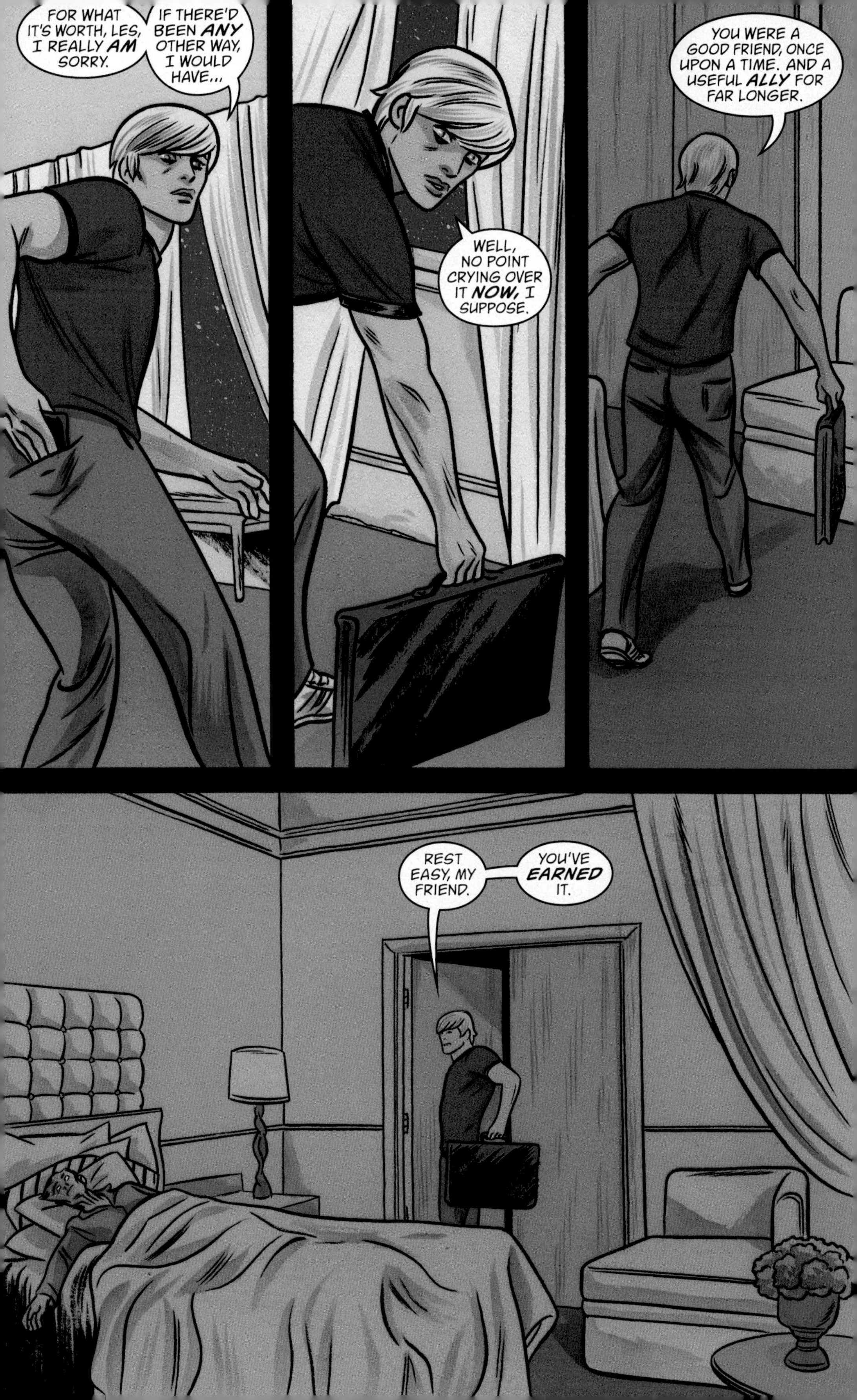
FOR WHAT IT'S WORTH, LES, I REALLY AM SORRY.
IF THERE'D BEEN ANY OTHER WAY, I WOULD HAVE...
WELL, NO POINT CRYING OVER IT NOW, I SUPPOSE.
YOU WERE A GOOD FRIEND, ONCE UPON A TIME. AND A USEFUL ALLY FOR FAR LONGER.
REST EASY, MY FRIEND.
YOU'VE EARNED IT.

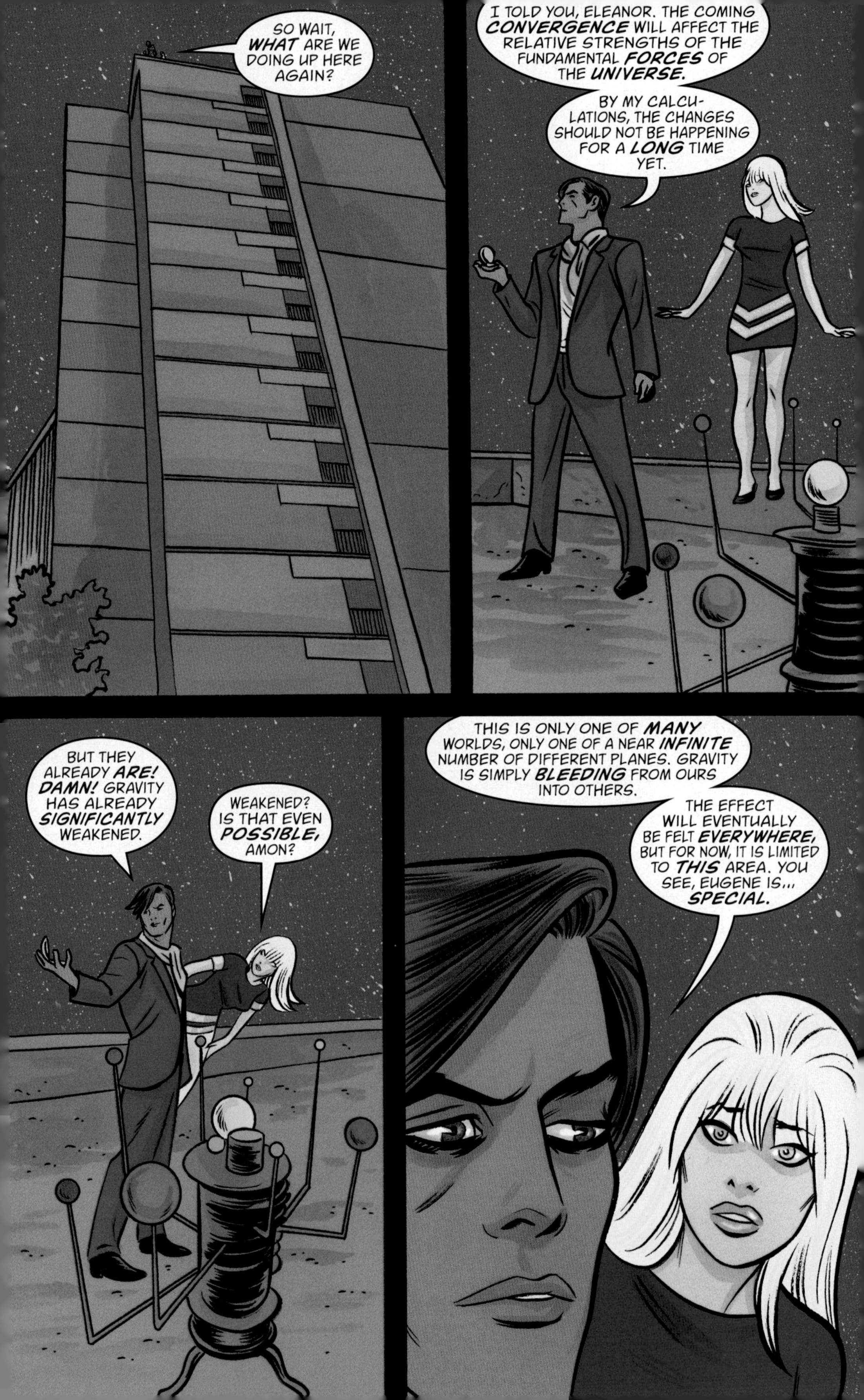
SO WAIT, WHAT ARE WE DOING UP HERE AGAIN?
I TOLD YOU, ELEANOR. THE COMING CONVERGENCE WILL AFFECT THE RELATIVE STRENGTHS OF THE FUNDAMENTAL FORCES OF THE UNIVERSE.
BY MY CALCU-LATIONS, THE CHANGES SHOULD NOT BE HAPPENING FOR A LONG TIME YET.
BUT THEY ALREADY ARE! DAMN! GRAVITY HAS ALREADY SIGNIFICANTLY WEAKENED.
WEAKENED? IS THAT EVEN POSSIBLE, AMON?
THIS IS ONLY ONE OF MANY WORLDS, ONLY ONE OF A NEAR INFINITE NUMBER OF DIFFERENT PLANES. GRAVITY IS SIMPLY BLEEDING FROM OURS INTO OTHERS.
THE EFFECT WILL EVENTUALLY BE FELT EVERYWHERE, BUT FOR NOW, IT IS LIMITED TO THIS AREA. YOU SEE, EUGENE IS... SPECIAL.

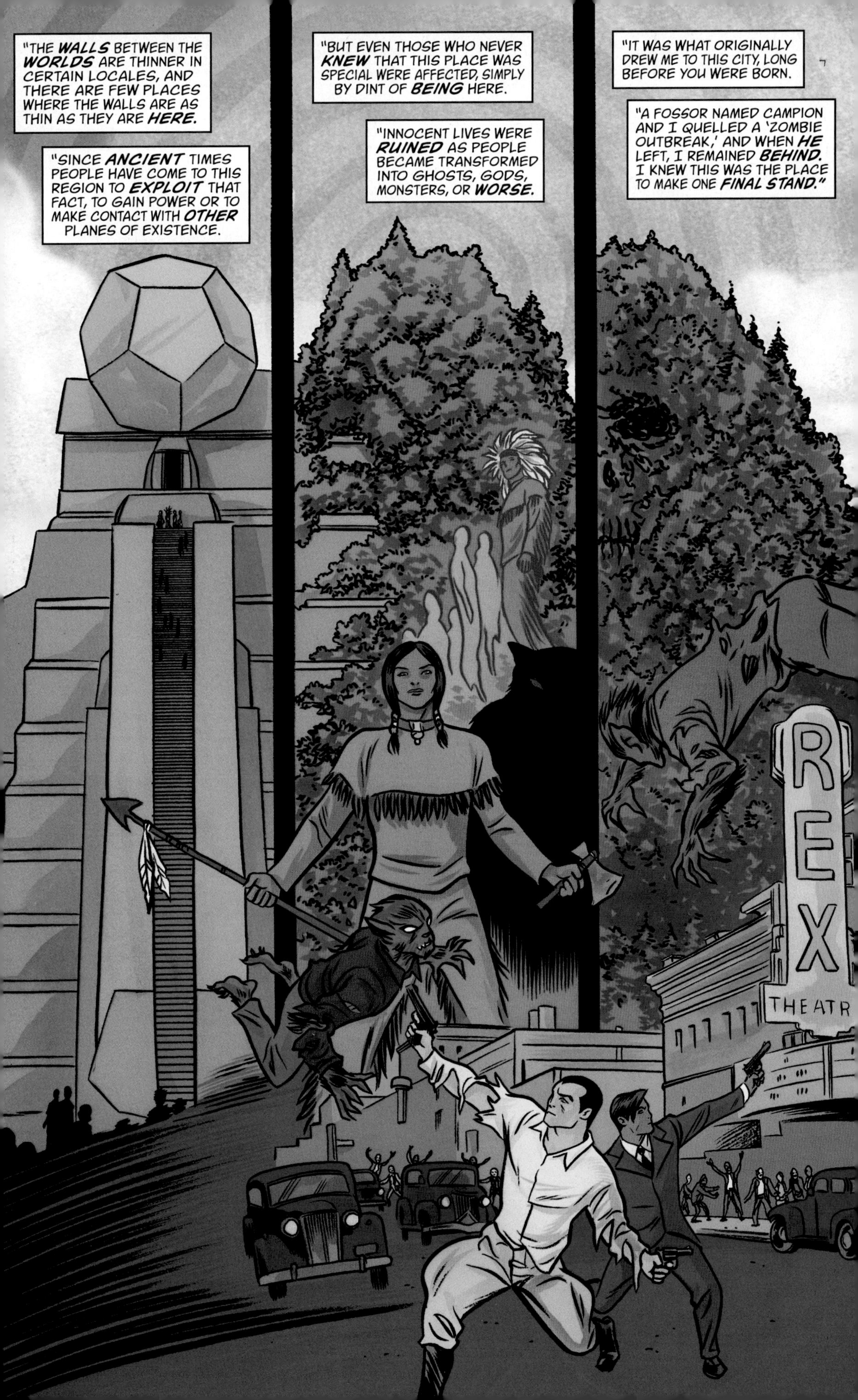
"THE WALLS BETWEEN THE WORLDS ARE THINNER IN CERTAIN LOCALES, AND THERE ARE FEW PLACES WHERE THE WALLS ARE AS THIN AS THEY ARE HERE.
"SINCE ANCIENT TIMES PEOPLE HAVE COME TO THIS REGION TO EXPLOIT THAT FACT, TO GAIN POWER OR TO MAKE CONTACT WITH OTHER PLANES OF EXISTENCE.
"BUT EVEN THOSE WHO NEVER KNEW THAT THIS PLACE WAS SPECIAL WERE AFFECTED, SIMPLY BY DINT OF BEING HERE.
"INNOCENT LIVES WERE RUINED AS PEOPLE BECAME TRANSFORMED INTO GHOSTS, GODS, MONSTERS, OR WORSE.
"IT WAS WHAT ORIGINALLY DREW ME TO THIS CITY, LONG BEFORE YOU WERE BORN.
"A FOSSOR NAMED CAMPION AND I QUELLED A 'ZOMBIE OUTBREAK,' AND WHEN HE LEFT, I REMAINED BEHIND. I KNEW THIS WAS THE PLACE TO MAKE ONE FINAL STAND."
REX
THEATR

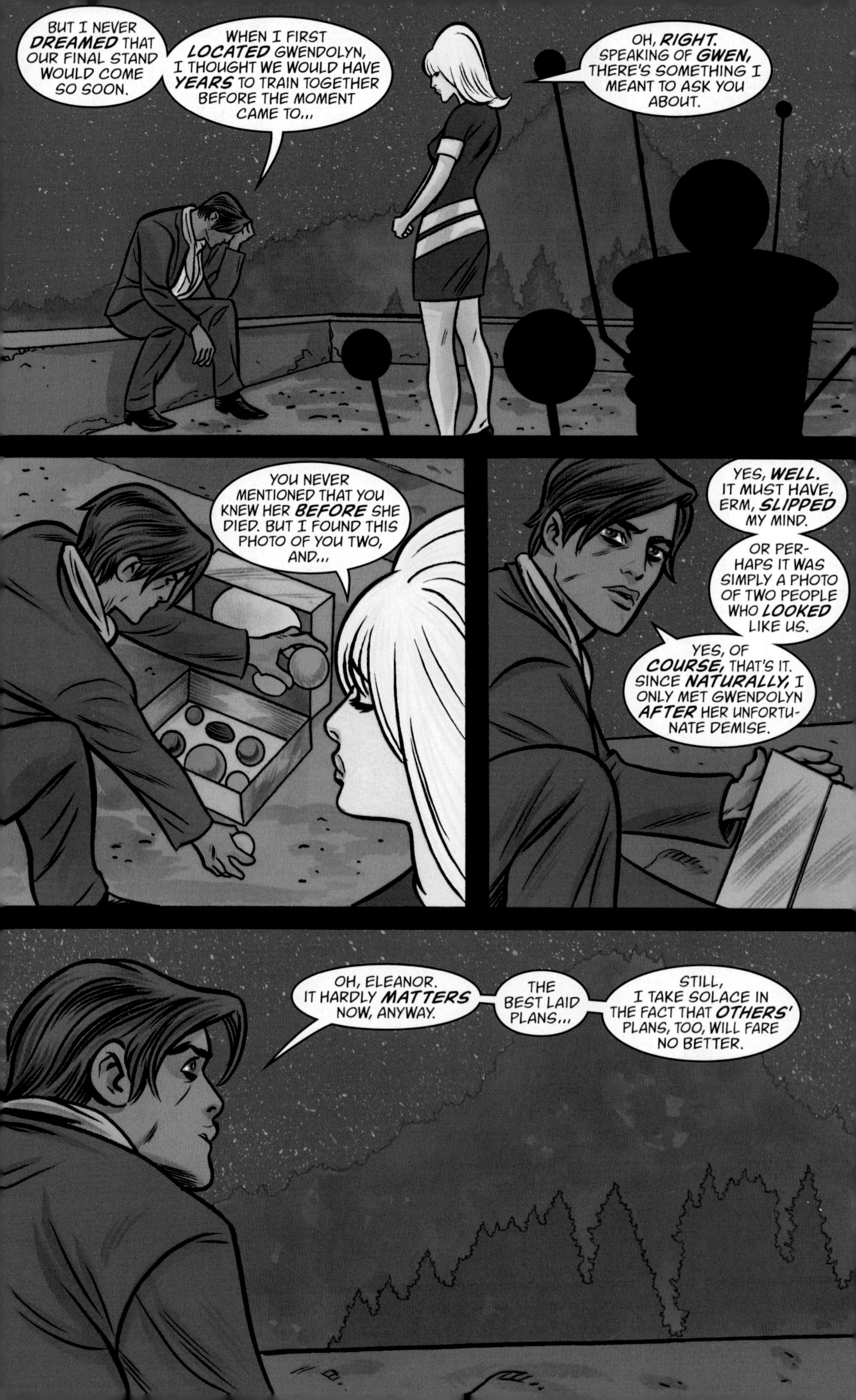
BUT I NEVER DREAMED THAT OUR FINAL STAND WOULD COME SO SOON.
WHEN I FIRST LOCATED GWENDOLYN, I THOUGHT WE WOULD HAVE YEARS TO TRAIN TOGETHER BEFORE THE MOMENT CAME TO...
OH, RIGHT. SPEAKING OF GWEN, THERE'S SOMETHING I MEANT TO ASK YOU ABOUT.
YOU NEVER MENTIONED THAT YOU KNEW HER BEFORE SHE DIED. BUT I FOUND THIS PHOTO OF YOU TWO, AND...
YES, WELL. IT MUST HAVE, ERM, SLIPPED MY MIND.
OR PERHAPS IT WAS SIMPLY A PHOTO OF TWO PEOPLE WHO LOOKED LIKE US.
YES, OF COURSE, THAT'S IT. SINCE NATURALLY, I ONLY MET GWENDOLYN AFTER HER UNFORTUNATE DEMISE.
OH, ELEANOR. IT HARDLY MATTERS NOW, ANYWAY.
THE BEST LAID PLANS...
STILL, I TAKE SOLACE IN THE FACT THAT OTHERS' PLANS, TOO, WILL FARE NO BETTER.

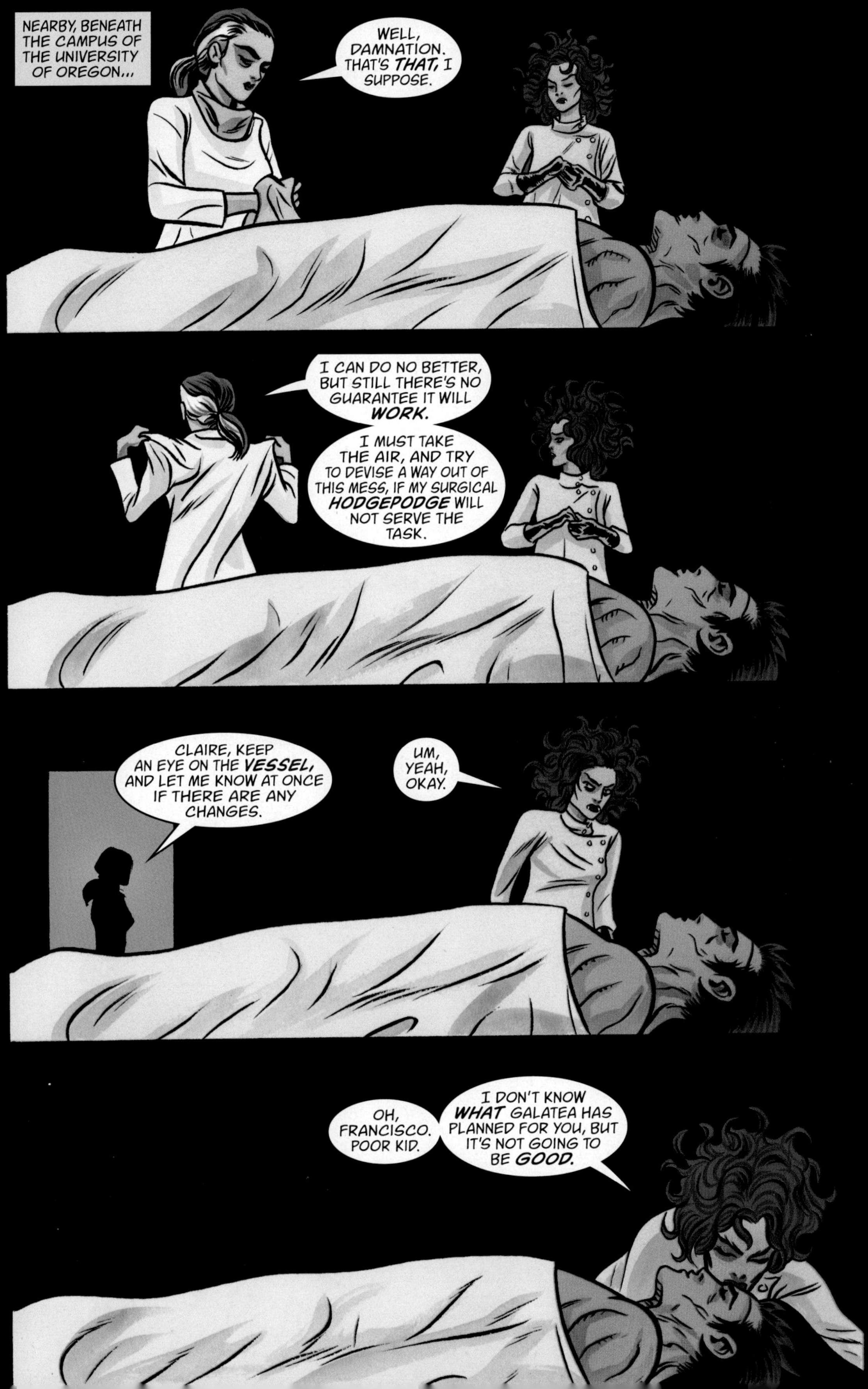
NEARBY, BENEATH THE CAMPUS OF THE UNIVERSITY OF OREGON...
WELL, DAMNATION. THAT'S *THAT*, I SUPPOSE.
I CAN DO NO BETTER, BUT STILL THERE'S NO GUARANTEE IT WILL *WORK.*
I MUST TAKE THE AIR, AND TRY TO DEVISE A WAY OUT OF THIS MESS, IF MY SURGICAL *HODGEPODGE* WILL NOT SERVE THE TASK.
CLAIRE, KEEP AN EYE ON THE *VESSEL,* AND LET ME KNOW AT ONCE IF THERE ARE ANY CHANGES.
UM, YEAH, OKAY.
OH, FRANCISCO. POOR KID.
I DON'T KNOW *WHAT* GALATEA HAS PLANNED FOR YOU, BUT IT'S NOT GOING TO BE *GOOD.*

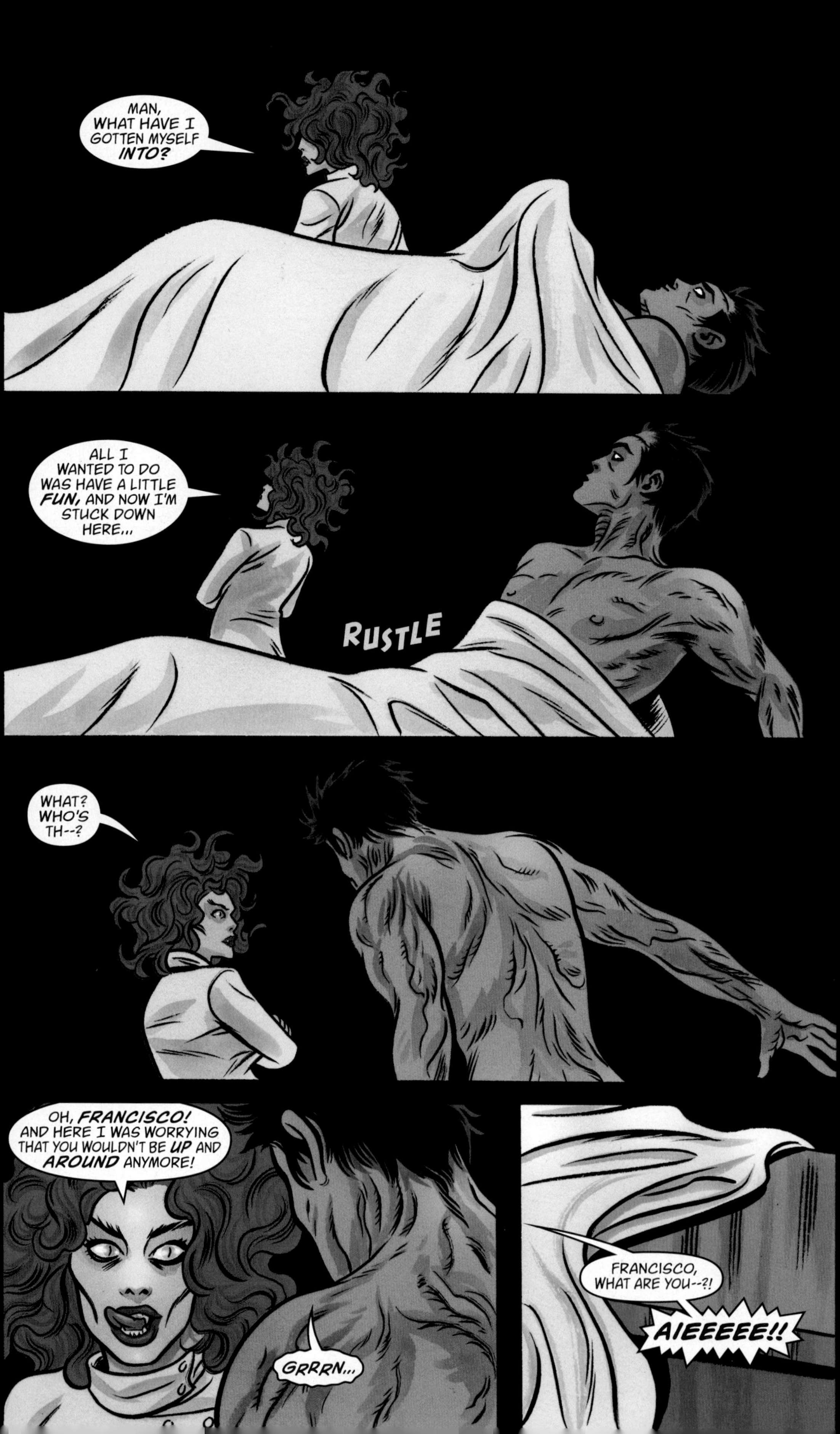
MAN, WHAT HAVE I GOTTEN MYSELF INTO?
ALL I WANTED TO DO WAS HAVE A LITTLE FUN, AND NOW I'M STUCK DOWN HERE...
RUSTLE
WHAT? WHO'S TH--?
OH, FRANCISCO! AND HERE I WAS WORRYING THAT YOU WOULDN'T BE UP AND AROUND ANYMORE!
GRRRN...
FRANCISCO, WHAT ARE YOU--?!
AIEEEEEE!!

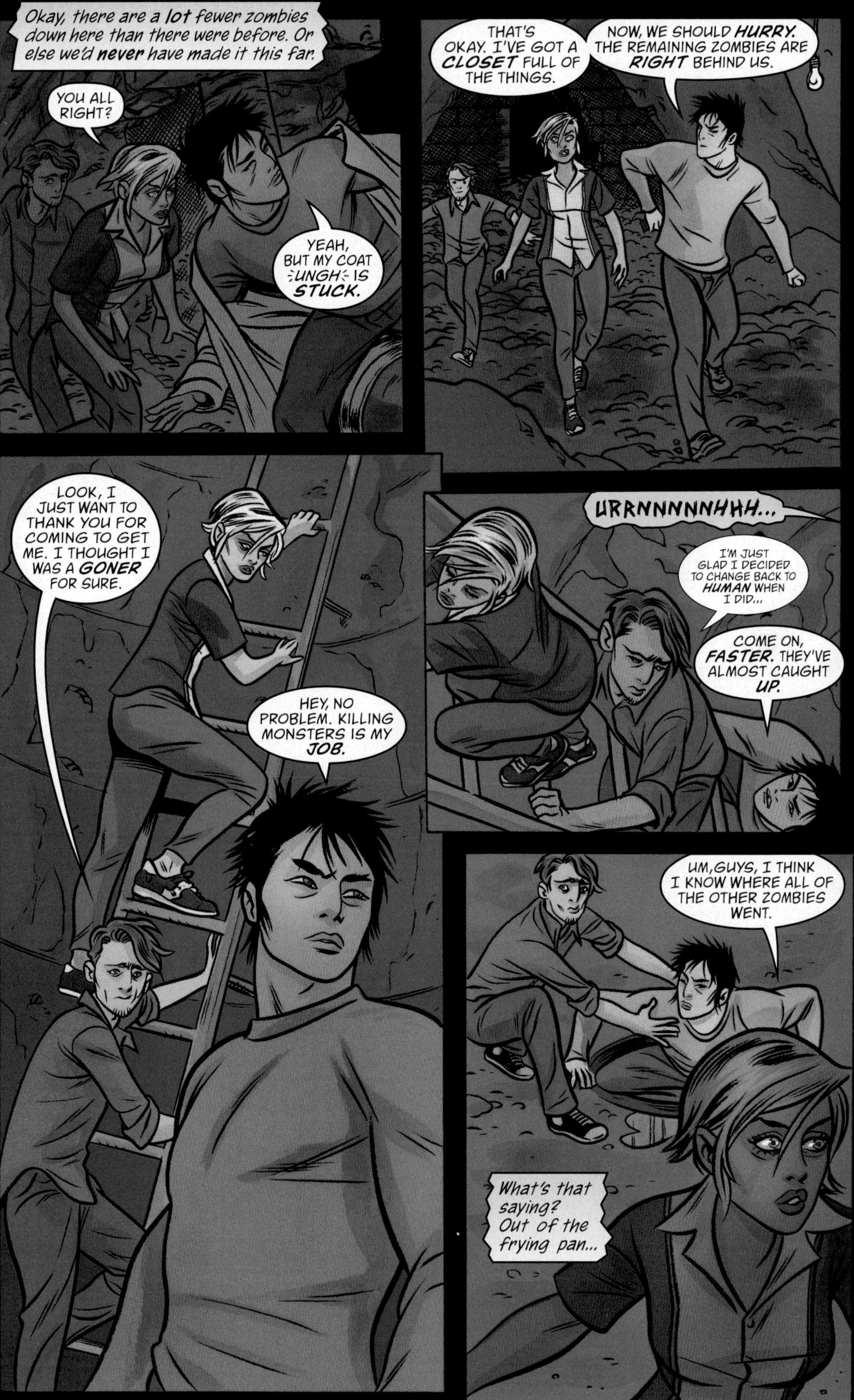
Okay, there are a **lot** fewer zombies down here than there were before. Or else we'd **never** have made it this far.
YOU ALL RIGHT?
YEAH, BUT MY COAT -UNGH- IS **STUCK.**
THAT'S OKAY. I'VE GOT A **CLOSET** FULL OF THE THINGS.
NOW, WE SHOULD **HURRY.** THE REMAINING ZOMBIES ARE **RIGHT** BEHIND US.
LOOK, I JUST WANT TO THANK YOU FOR COMING TO GET ME. I THOUGHT I WAS A **GONER** FOR SURE.
HEY, NO PROBLEM. KILLING MONSTERS IS MY **JOB.**
URRNNNNNHHH...
I'M JUST GLAD I DECIDED TO CHANGE BACK TO **HUMAN** WHEN I DID...
COME ON, **FASTER.** THEY'VE ALMOST CAUGHT **UP.**
UM, GUYS, I THINK I KNOW WHERE ALL OF THE OTHER ZOMBIES WENT.
What's that saying? Out of the frying pan...

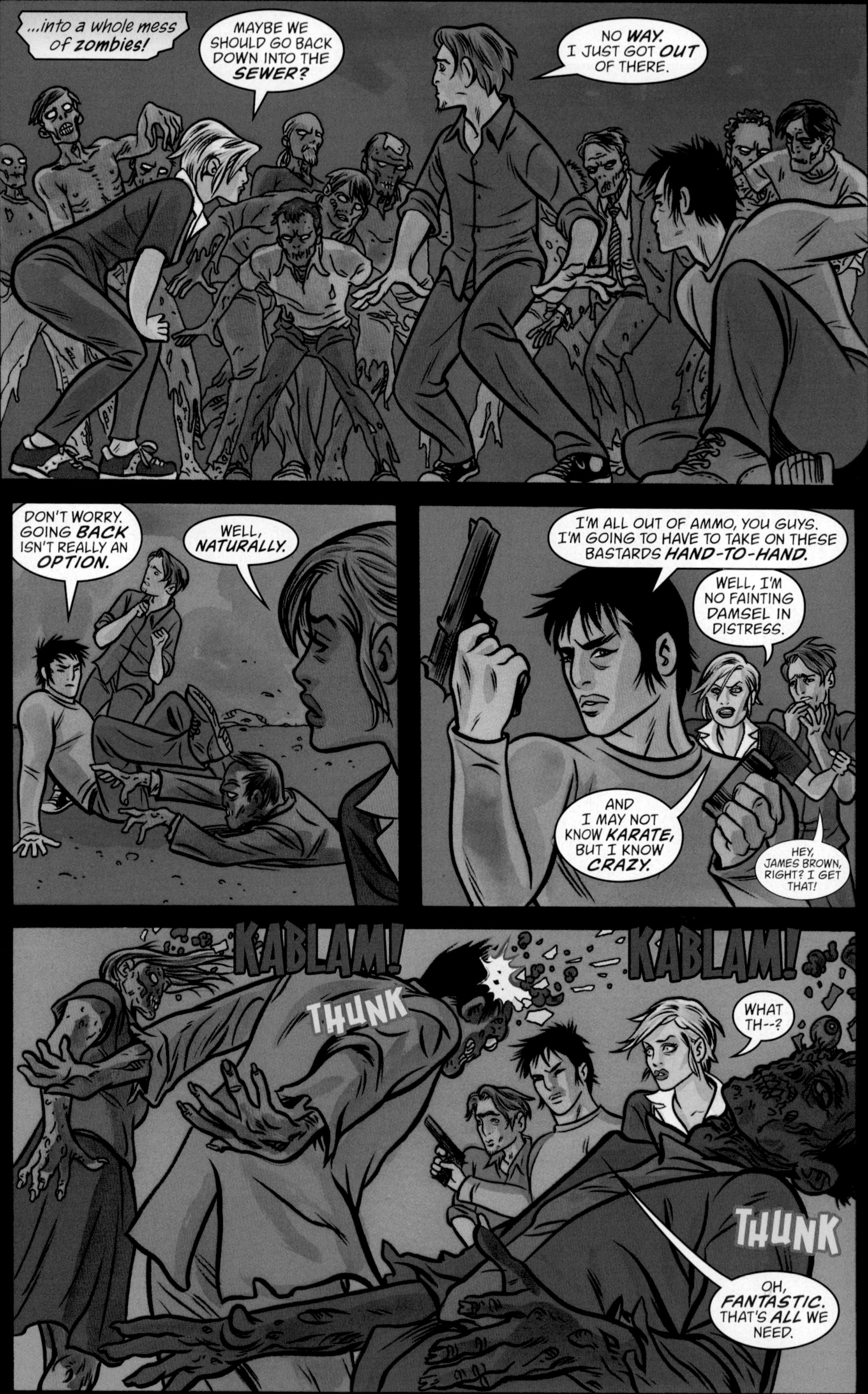
...into a whole mess of zombies!
MAYBE WE SHOULD GO BACK DOWN INTO THE SEWER?
NO WAY. I JUST GOT OUT OF THERE.
DON'T WORRY. GOING BACK ISN'T REALLY AN OPTION.
WELL, NATURALLY.
I'M ALL OUT OF AMMO, YOU GUYS. I'M GOING TO HAVE TO TAKE ON THESE BASTARDS HAND-TO-HAND.
WELL, I'M NO FAINTING DAMSEL IN DISTRESS.
AND I MAY NOT KNOW KARATE, BUT I KNOW CRAZY.
HEY, JAMES BROWN, RIGHT? I GET THAT!
KABLAM!
KABLAM!
THUNK
WHAT TH--?
THUNK
OH, FANTASTIC. THAT'S ALL WE NEED.

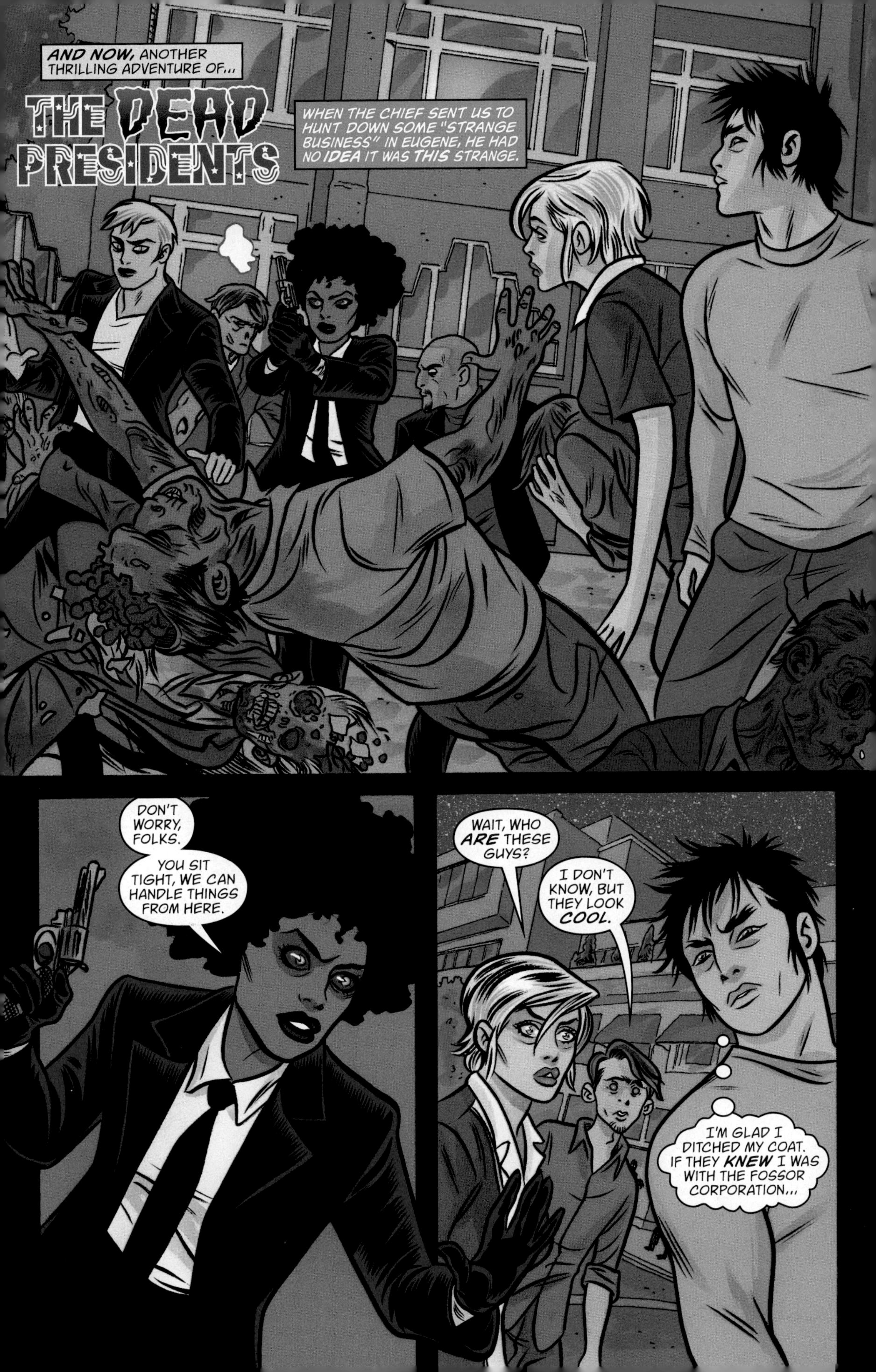
AND NOW, ANOTHER THRILLING ADVENTURE OF...
THE DEAD PRESIDENTS
WHEN THE CHIEF SENT US TO HUNT DOWN SOME "STRANGE BUSINESS" IN EUGENE, HE HAD NO IDEA IT WAS THIS STRANGE.
DON'T WORRY, FOLKS.
YOU SIT TIGHT, WE CAN HANDLE THINGS FROM HERE.
WAIT, WHO ARE THESE GUYS?
I DON'T KNOW, BUT THEY LOOK COOL.
I'M GLAD I DITCHED MY COAT. IF THEY KNEW I WAS WITH THE FOSSOR CORPORATION...

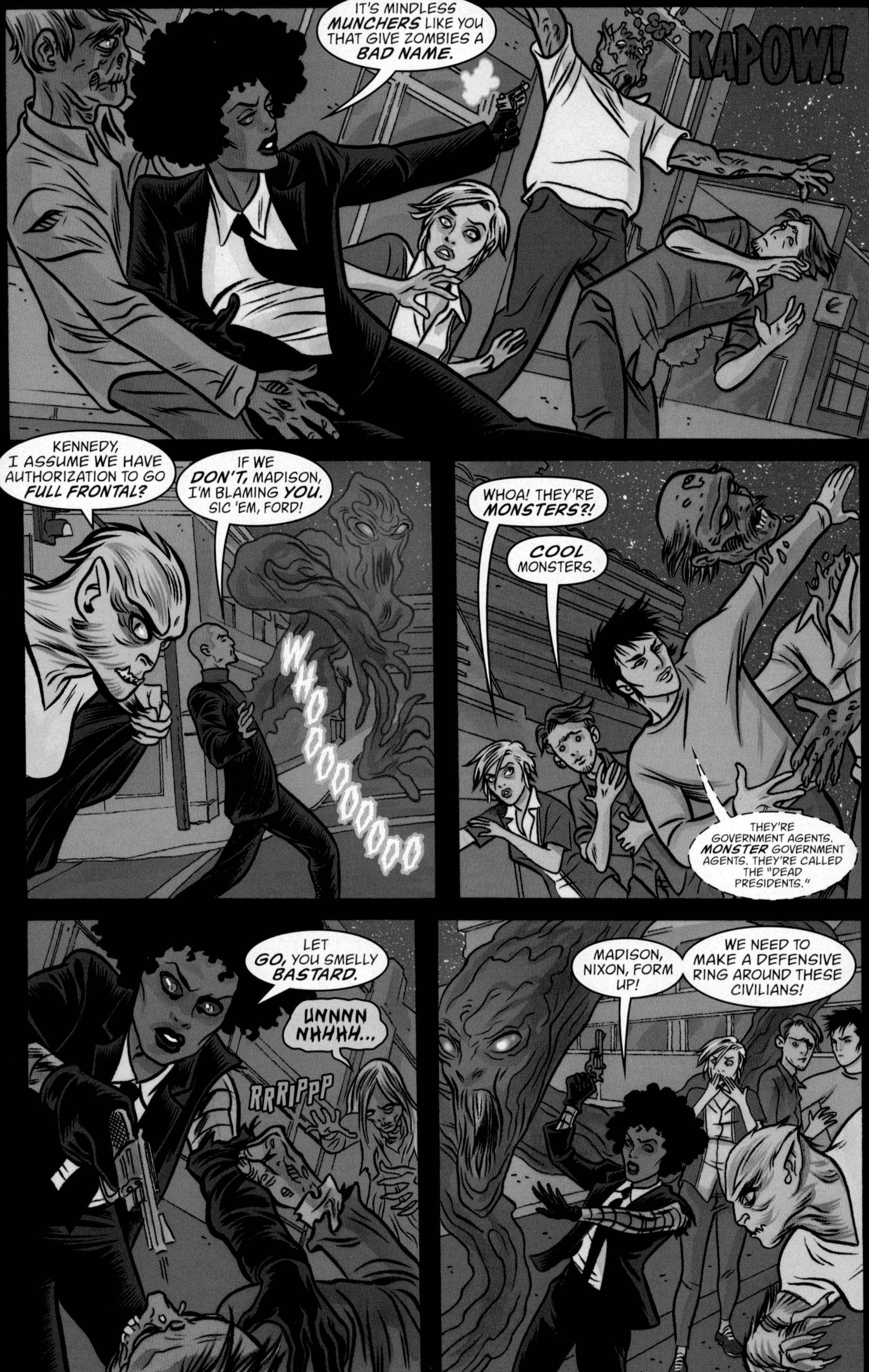

IT'S MINDLESS MUNCHERS LIKE YOU THAT GIVE ZOMBIES A BAD NAME.
KAPOW!
KENNEDY, I ASSUME WE HAVE AUTHORIZATION TO GO FULL FRONTAL?
IF WE DON'T, MADISON, I'M BLAMING YOU. SIC 'EM, FORD!
WHOOOOOOOOOO
WHOA! THEY'RE MONSTERS?!
COOL MONSTERS.
THEY'RE GOVERNMENT AGENTS. MONSTER GOVERNMENT AGENTS. THEY'RE CALLED THE "DEAD PRESIDENTS."
LET GO, YOU SMELLY BASTARD.
UNNNN NHHHH...
RRRIPPP
MADISON, NIXON, FORM UP!
WE NEED TO MAKE A DEFENSIVE RING AROUND THESE CIVILIANS!

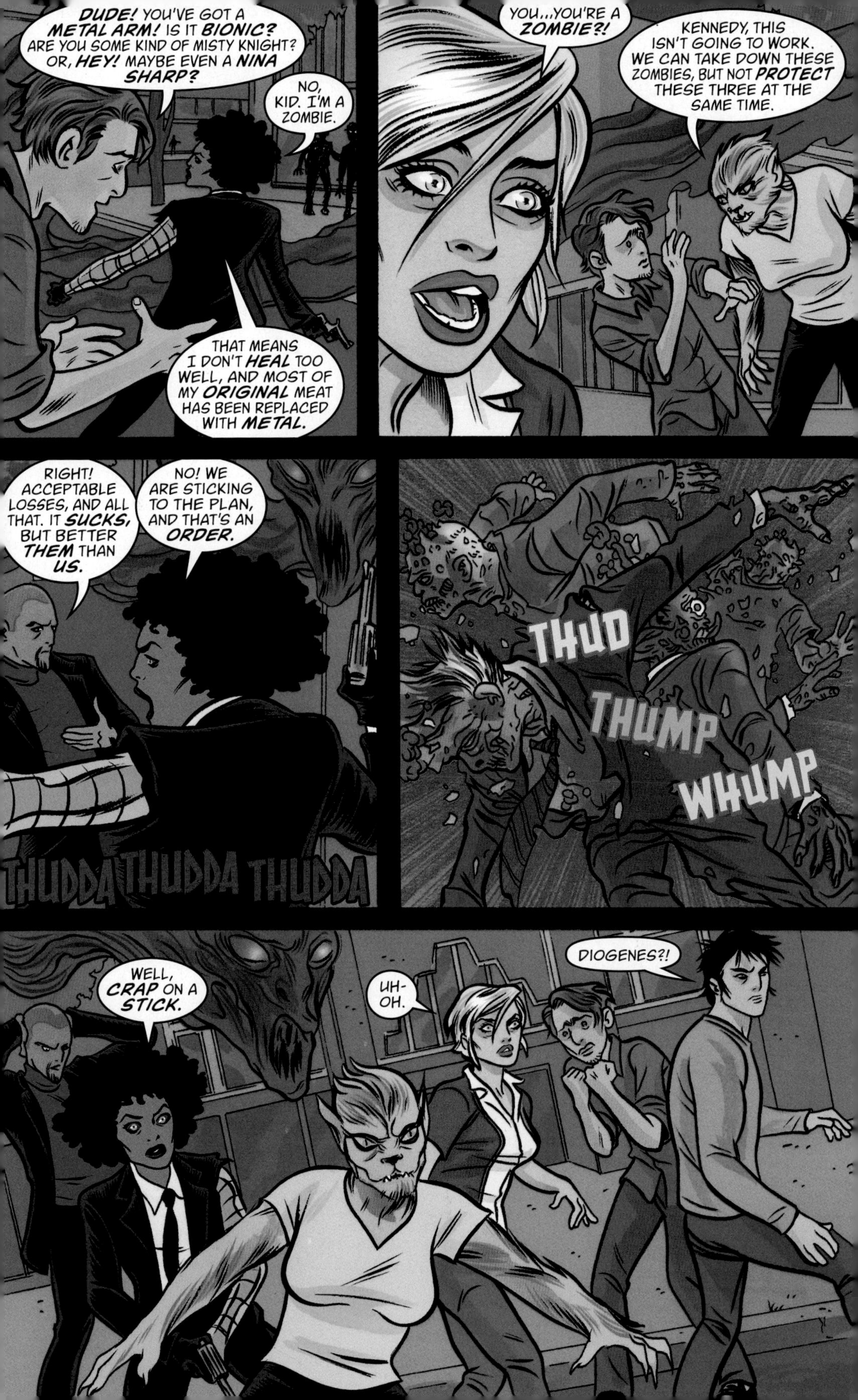
DUDE! YOU'VE GOT A METAL ARM! IS IT BIONIC? ARE YOU SOME KIND OF MISTY KNIGHT? OR, HEY! MAYBE EVEN A NINA SHARP?
NO, KID. I'M A ZOMBIE.
THAT MEANS I DON'T HEAL TOO WELL, AND MOST OF MY ORIGINAL MEAT HAS BEEN REPLACED WITH METAL.
YOU...YOU'RE A ZOMBIE?!
KENNEDY, THIS ISN'T GOING TO WORK. WE CAN TAKE DOWN THESE ZOMBIES, BUT NOT PROTECT THESE THREE AT THE SAME TIME.
RIGHT! ACCEPTABLE LOSSES, AND ALL THAT. IT SUCKS, BUT BETTER THEM THAN US.
NO! WE ARE STICKING TO THE PLAN, AND THAT'S AN ORDER.
THUDDA THUDDA THUDDA
THUD
THUMP
WHUMP
WELL, CRAP ON A STICK.
UH-OH.
DIOGENES?!

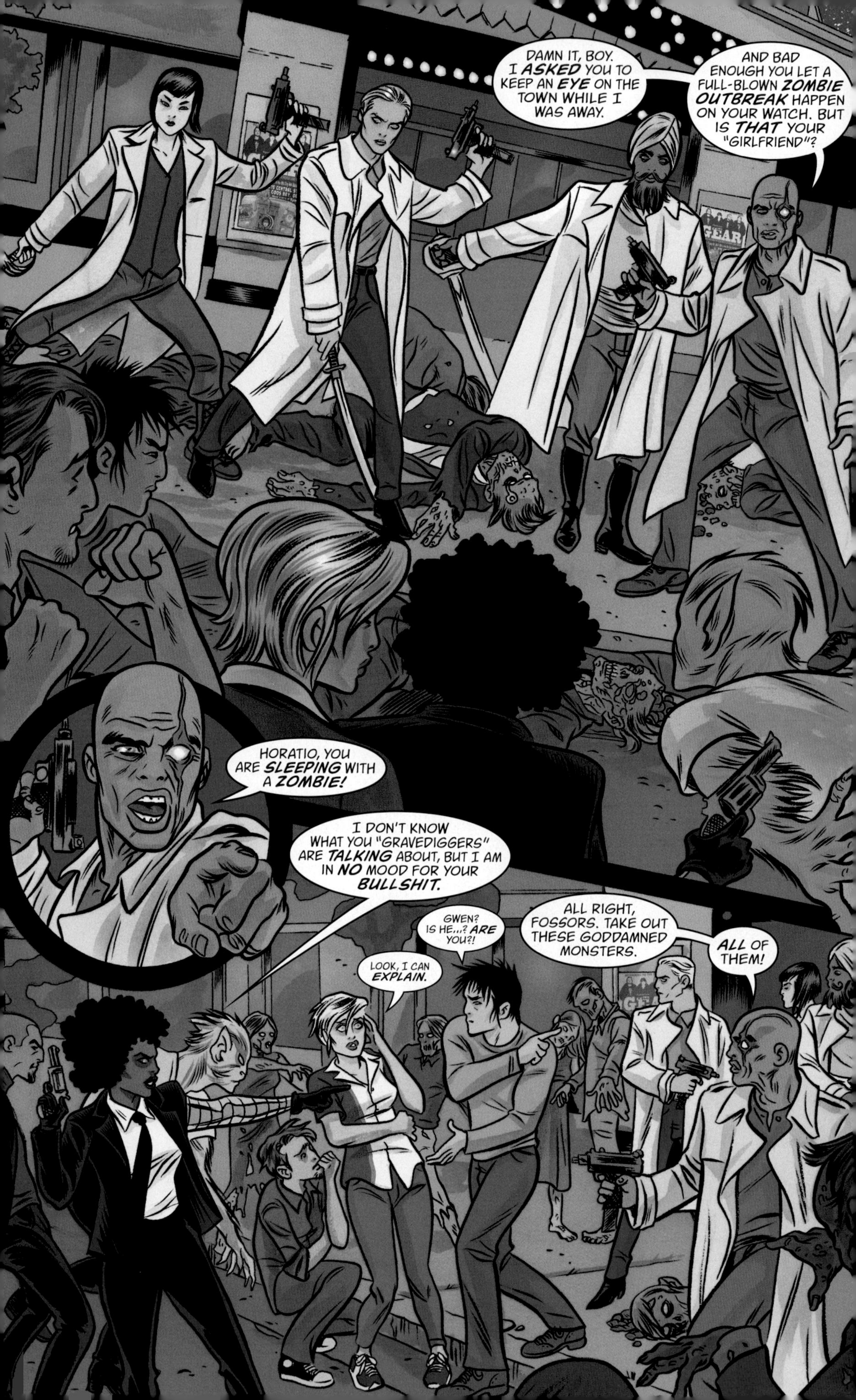
DAMN IT, BOY. I ASKED YOU TO KEEP AN EYE ON THE TOWN WHILE I WAS AWAY.
AND BAD ENOUGH YOU LET A FULL-BLOWN ZOMBIE OUTBREAK HAPPEN ON YOUR WATCH. BUT IS THAT YOUR "GIRLFRIEND"?
HORATIO, YOU ARE SLEEPING WITH A ZOMBIE!
I DON'T KNOW WHAT YOU "GRAVEDIGGERS" ARE TALKING ABOUT, BUT I AM IN NO MOOD FOR YOUR BULLSHIT.
LOOK, I CAN EXPLAIN.
GWEN? IS HE...? ARE YOU?!
ALL RIGHT, FOSSORS. TAKE OUT THESE GODDAMNED MONSTERS.
ALL OF THEM!

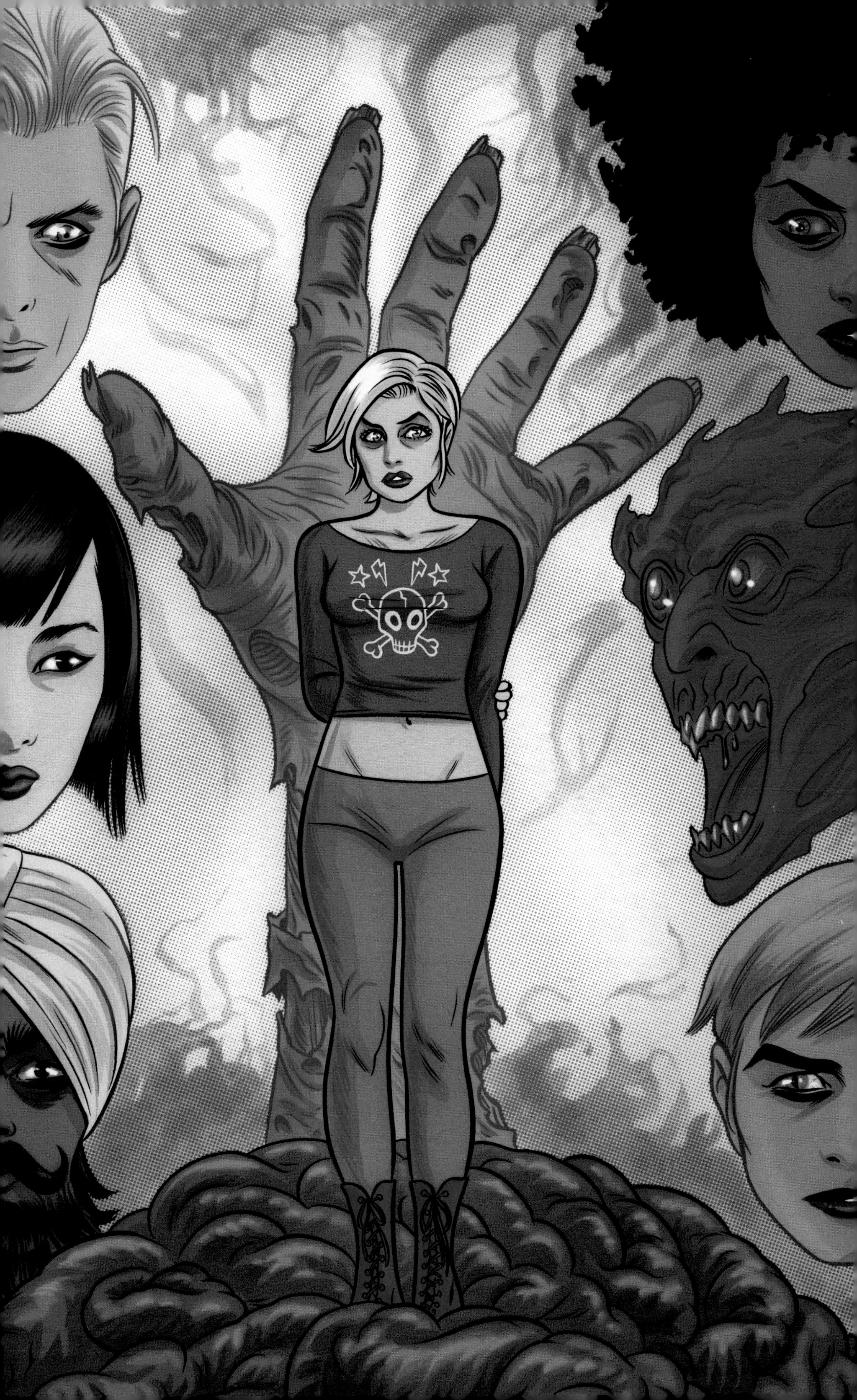

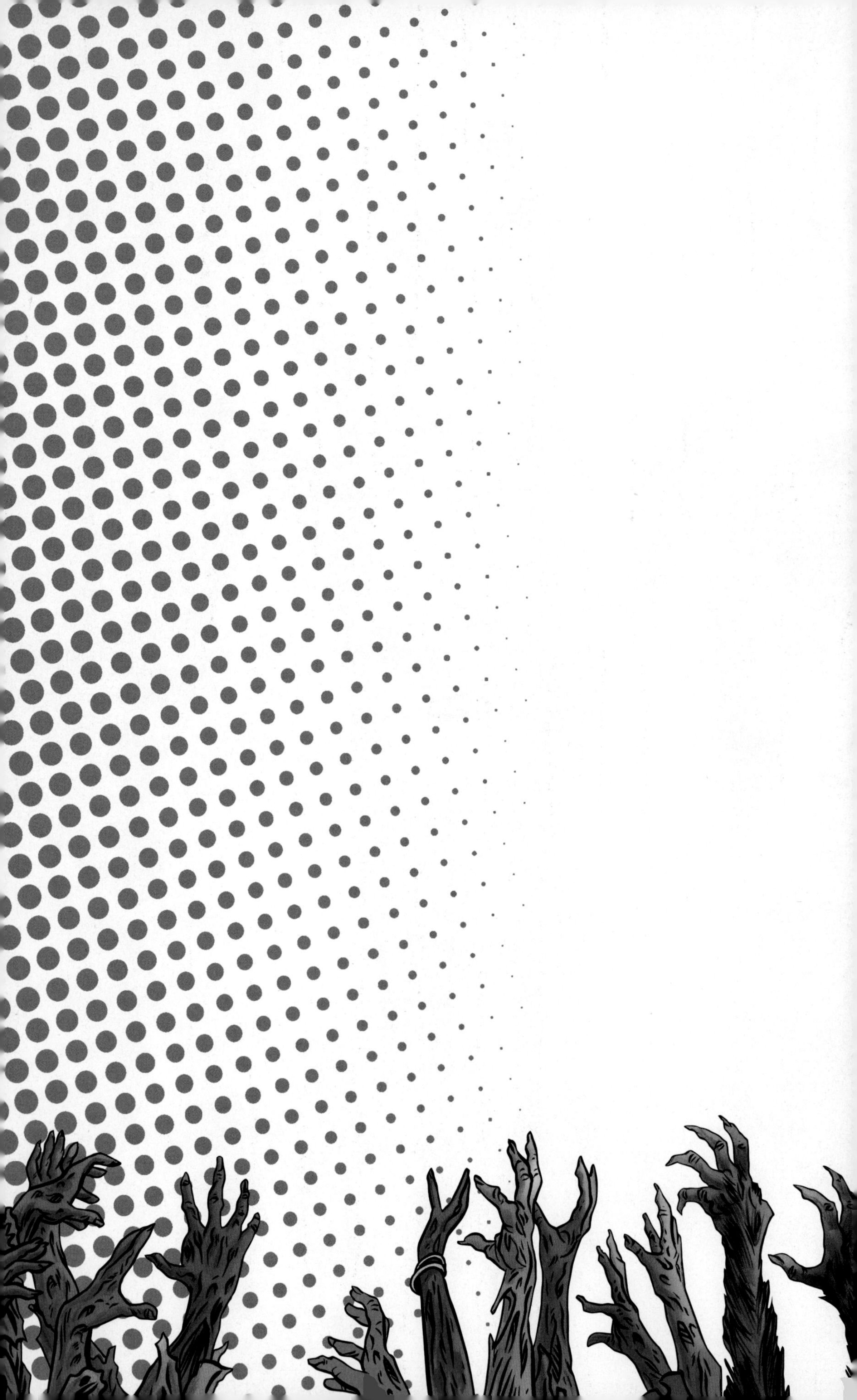

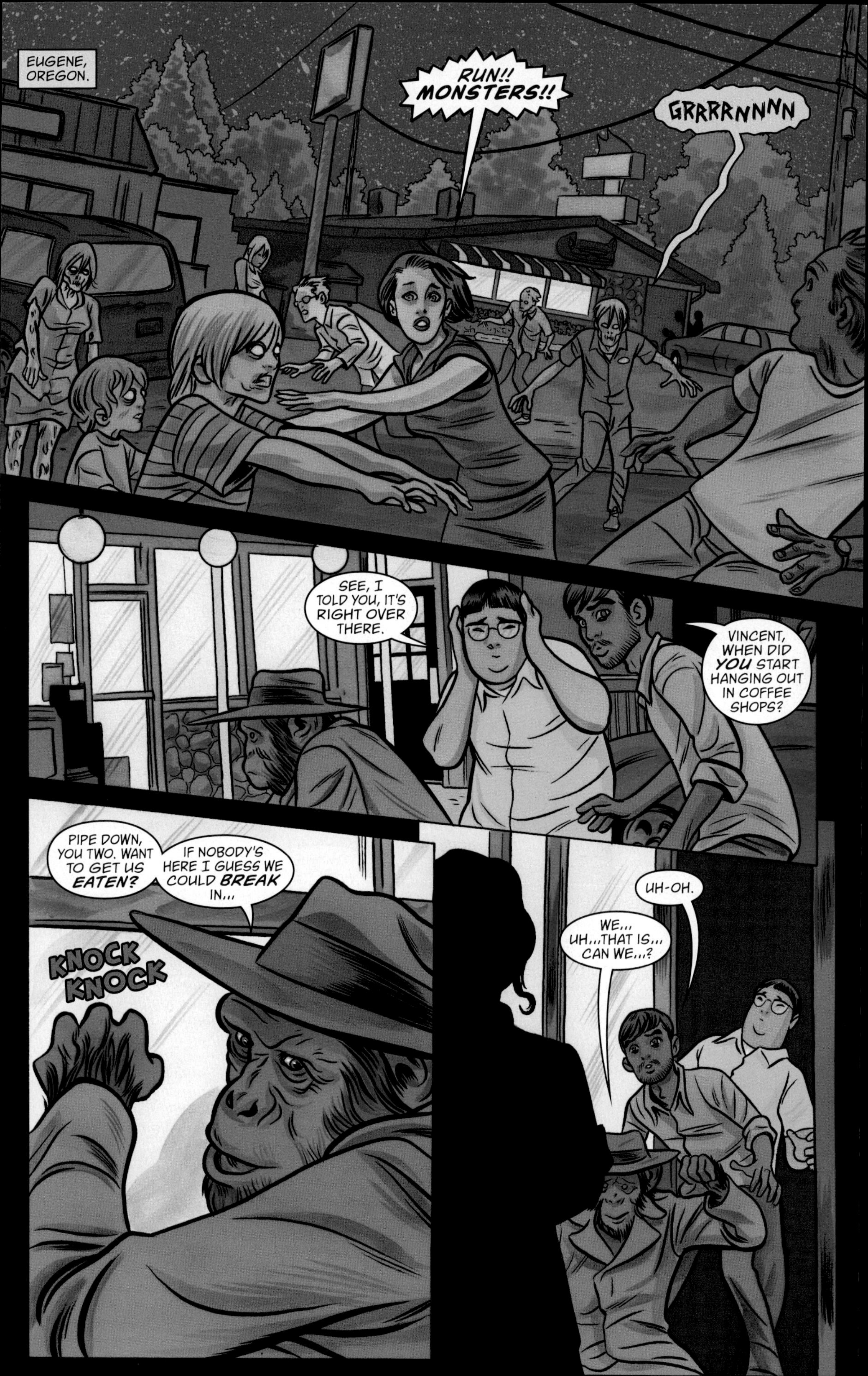
EUGENE, OREGON.
RUN!! MONSTERS!!
GRRRRNNNN
SEE, I TOLD YOU, IT'S RIGHT OVER THERE.
VINCENT, WHEN DID YOU START HANGING OUT IN COFFEE SHOPS?
PIPE DOWN, YOU TWO. WANT TO GET US EATEN?
IF NOBODY'S HERE I GUESS WE COULD BREAK IN...
KNOCK KNOCK
UH-OH.
WE... UH...THAT IS... CAN WE...?

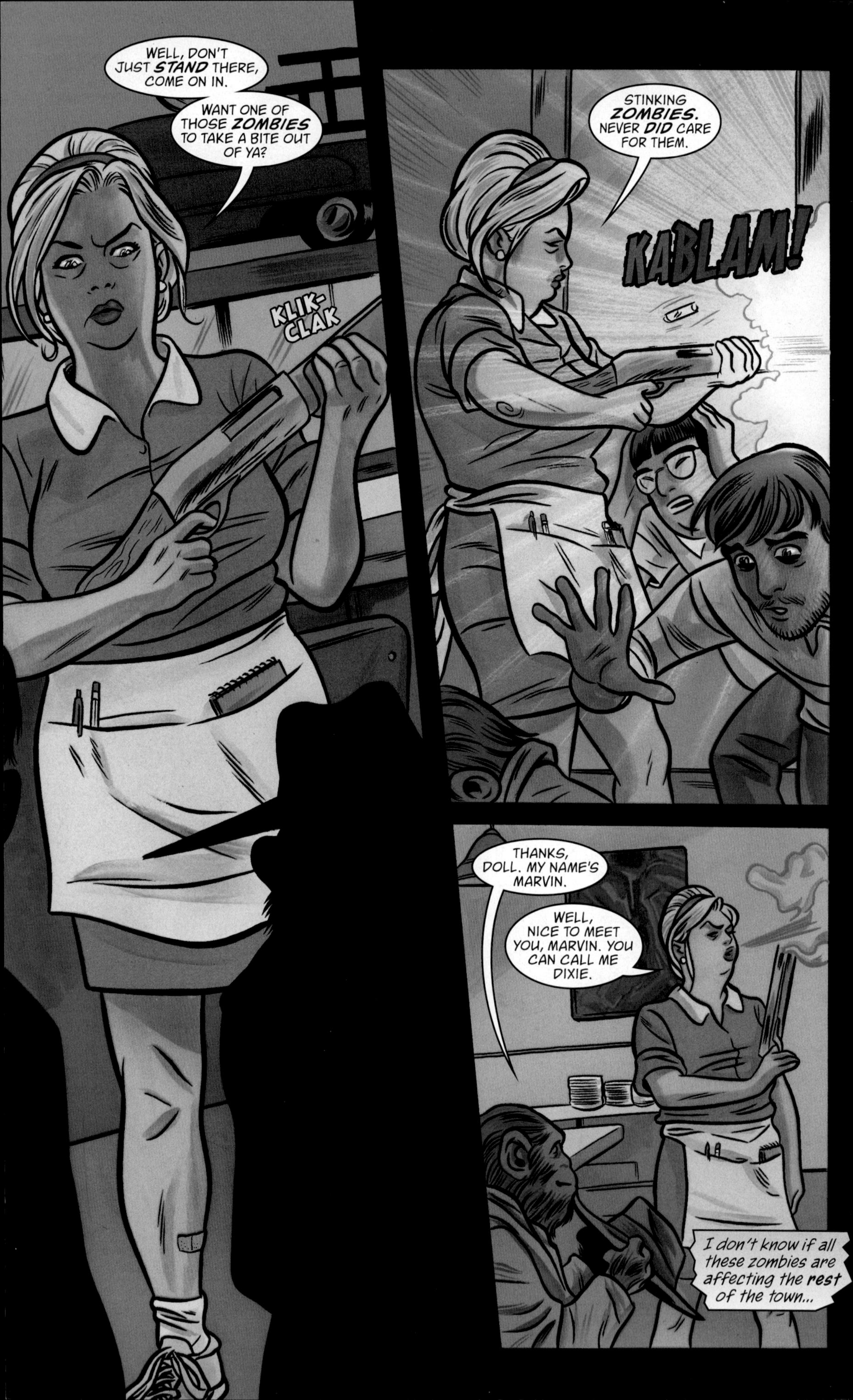
WELL, DON'T JUST STAND THERE, COME ON IN.
WANT ONE OF THOSE ZOMBIES TO TAKE A BITE OUT OF YA?
KLIK-CLAK
STINKING ZOMBIES. NEVER DID CARE FOR THEM.
KABLAM!
THANKS, DOLL. MY NAME'S MARVIN.
WELL, NICE TO MEET YOU, MARVIN. YOU CAN CALL ME DIXIE.
I don't know if all these zombies are affecting the rest of the town...

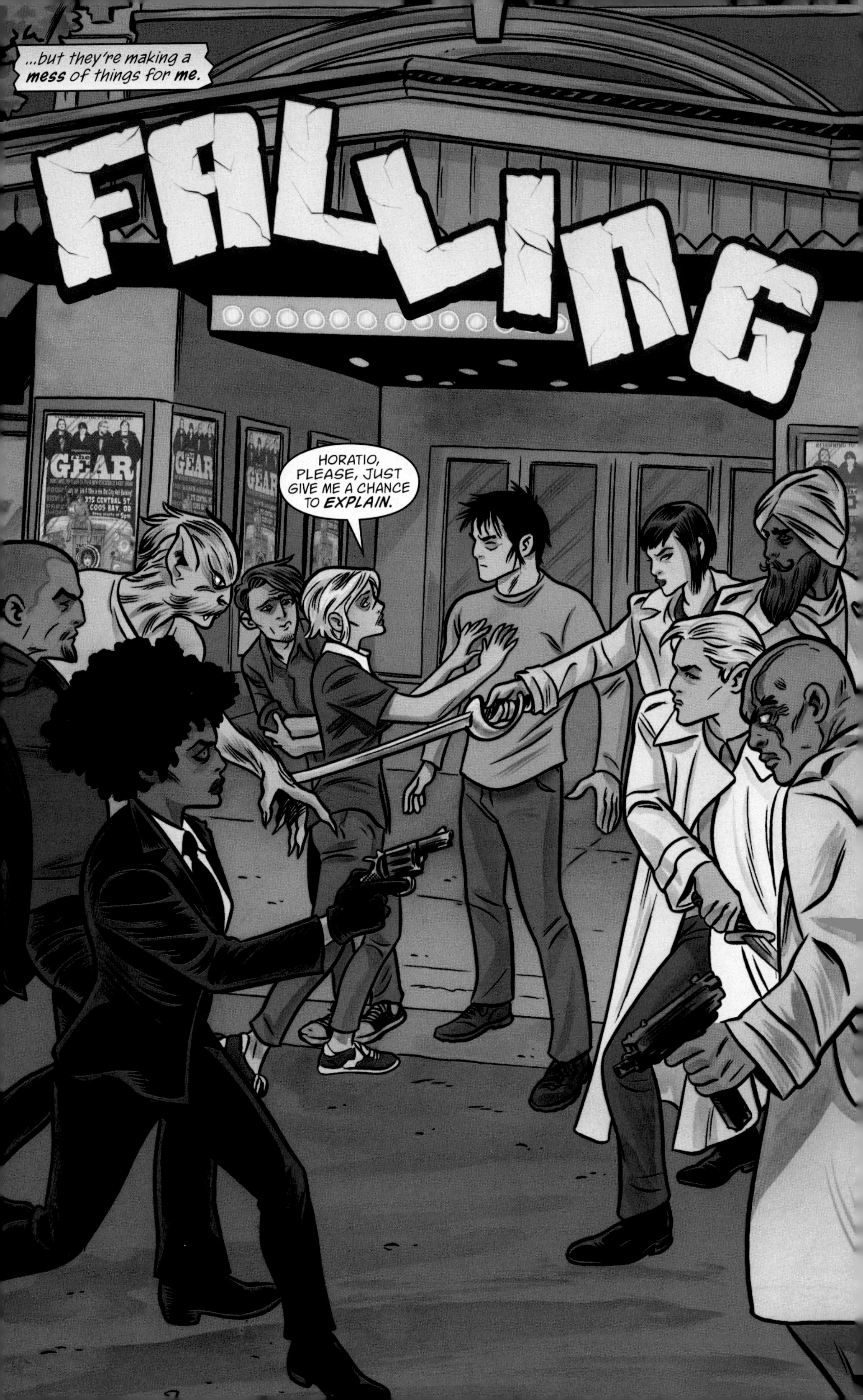
...but they're making a mess of things for me.
FALLING
HORATIO, PLEASE, JUST GIVE ME A CHANCE TO EXPLAIN.

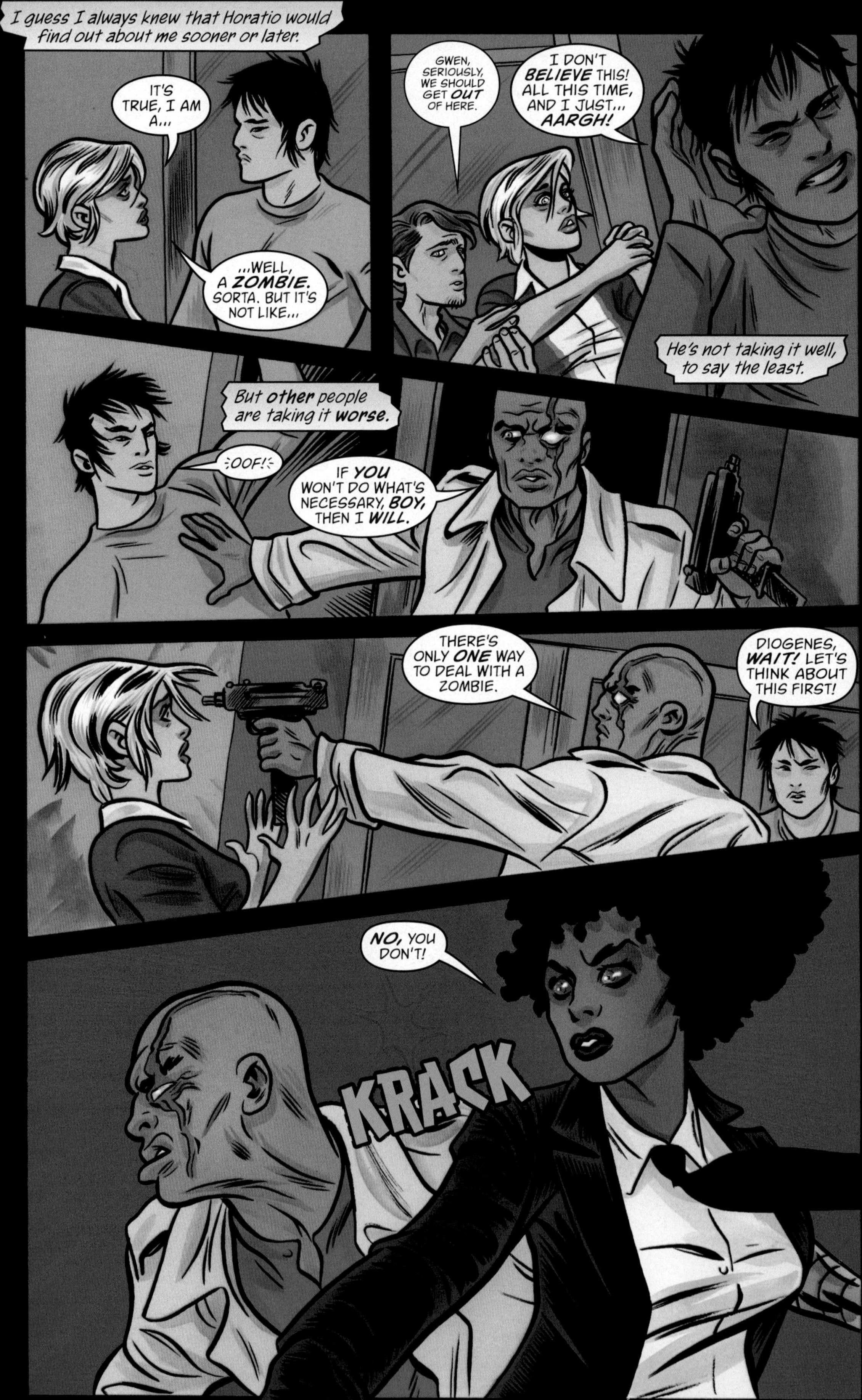
I guess I always knew that Horatio would find out about me sooner or later.
IT'S TRUE, I AM A...
...WELL, A ZOMBIE. SORTA. BUT IT'S NOT LIKE...
GWEN, SERIOUSLY, WE SHOULD GET OUT OF HERE.
I DON'T BELIEVE THIS! ALL THIS TIME, AND I JUST... AARGH!
He's not taking it well, to say the least.
But other people are taking it worse.
OOF!
IF YOU WON'T DO WHAT'S NECESSARY, BOY, THEN I WILL.
THERE'S ONLY ONE WAY TO DEAL WITH A ZOMBIE.
DIOGENES, WAIT! LET'S THINK ABOUT THIS FIRST!
NO, YOU DON'T!
KRACK

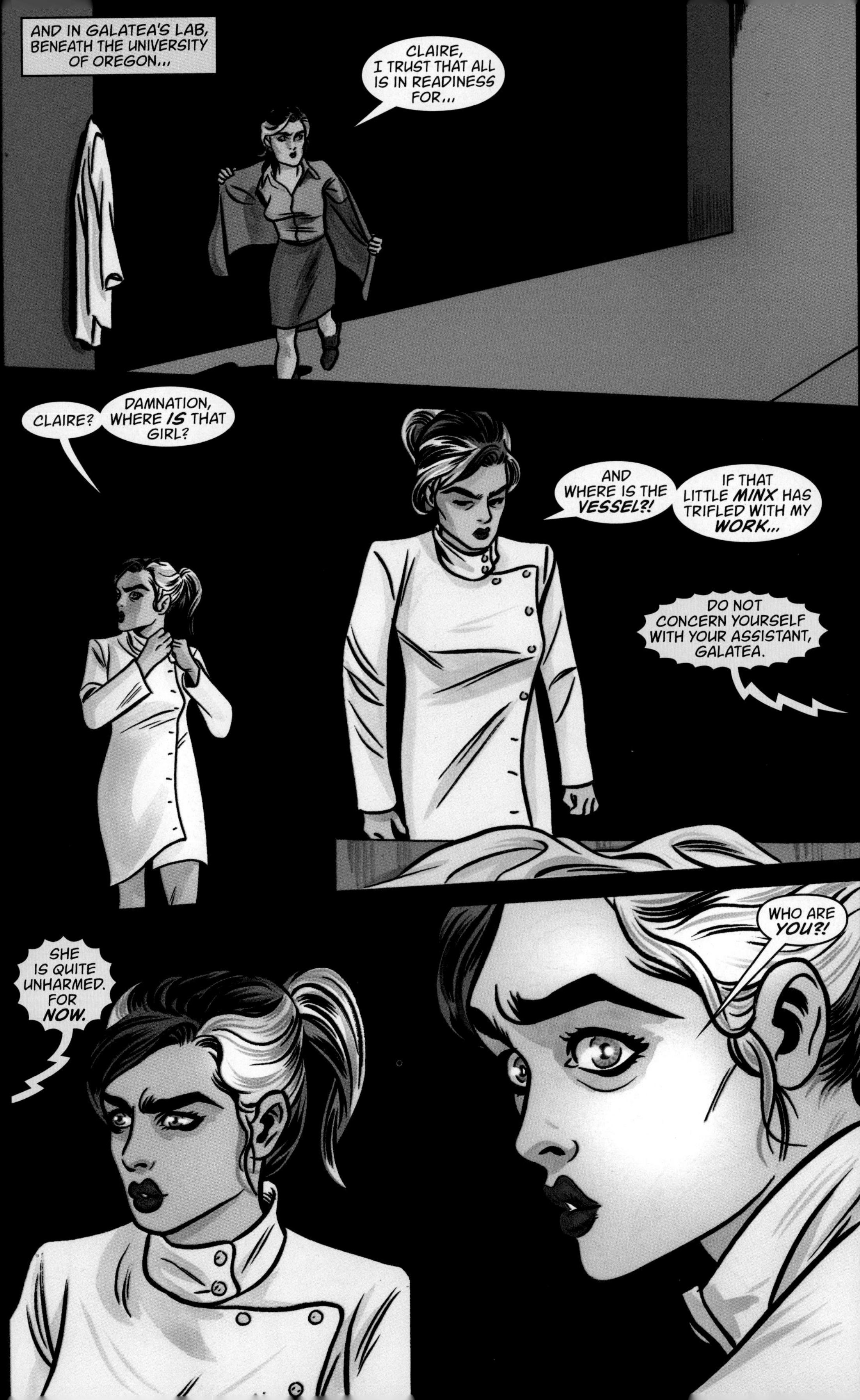
AND IN GALATEA'S LAB, BENEATH THE UNIVERSITY OF OREGON...
CLAIRE, I TRUST THAT ALL IS IN READINESS FOR...
CLAIRE?
DAMNATION, WHERE IS THAT GIRL?
AND WHERE IS THE VESSEL?!
IF THAT LITTLE MINX HAS TRIFLED WITH MY WORK...
DO NOT CONCERN YOURSELF WITH YOUR ASSISTANT, GALATEA.
SHE IS QUITE UNHARMED. FOR NOW.
WHO ARE YOU?!

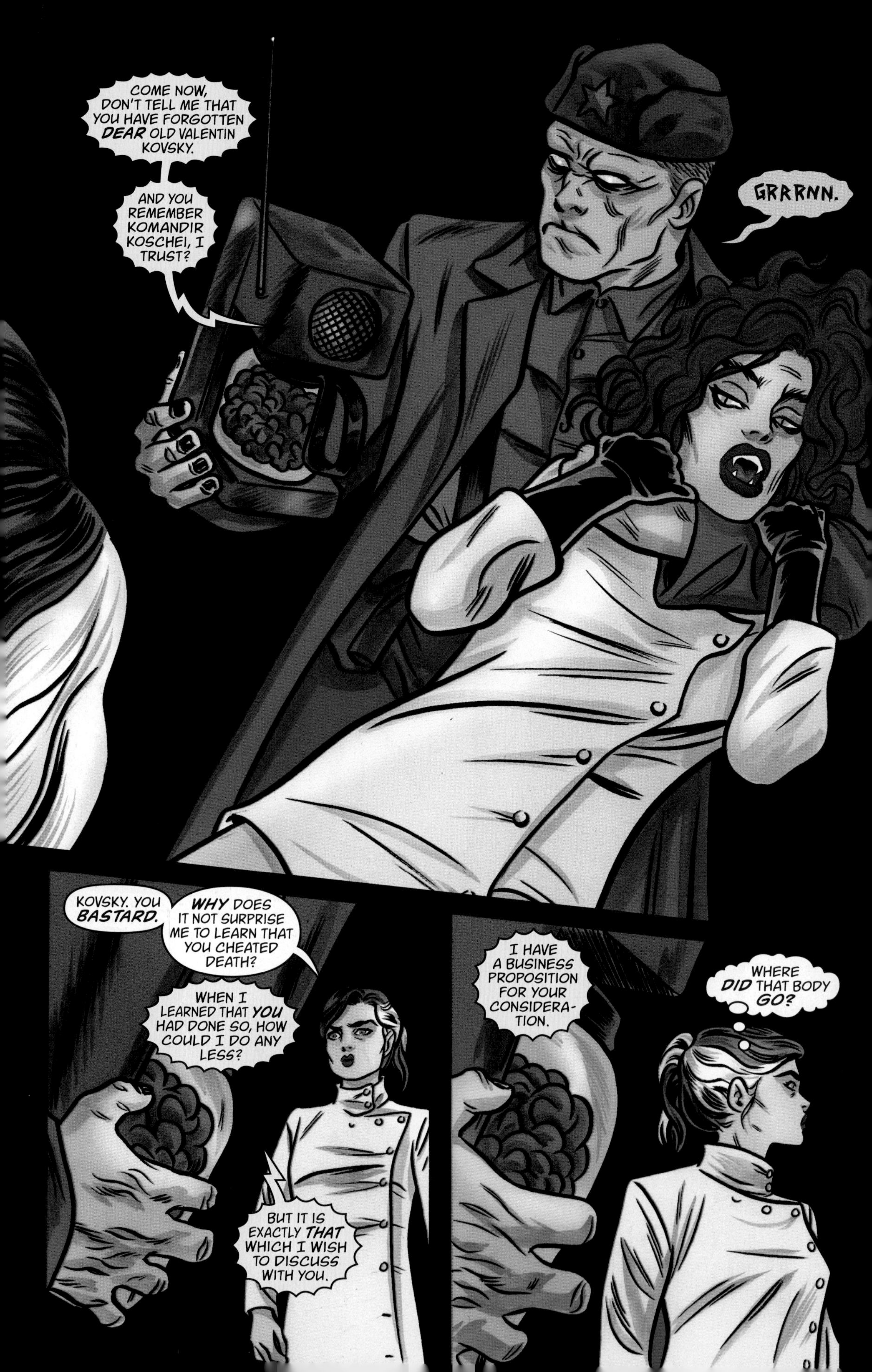
COME NOW, DON'T TELL ME THAT YOU HAVE FORGOTTEN **DEAR** OLD VALENTIN KOVSKY.
AND YOU REMEMBER KOMANDIR KOSCHEI, I TRUST?
GRRRNN.
KOVSKY. YOU **BASTARD.**
WHY DOES IT NOT SURPRISE ME TO LEARN THAT YOU CHEATED DEATH?
WHEN I LEARNED THAT **YOU** HAD DONE SO, HOW COULD I DO ANY LESS?
BUT IT IS EXACTLY **THAT** WHICH I WISH TO DISCUSS WITH YOU.
I HAVE A BUSINESS PROPOSITION FOR YOUR CONSIDERA-TION.
WHERE **DID** THAT BODY **GO?**

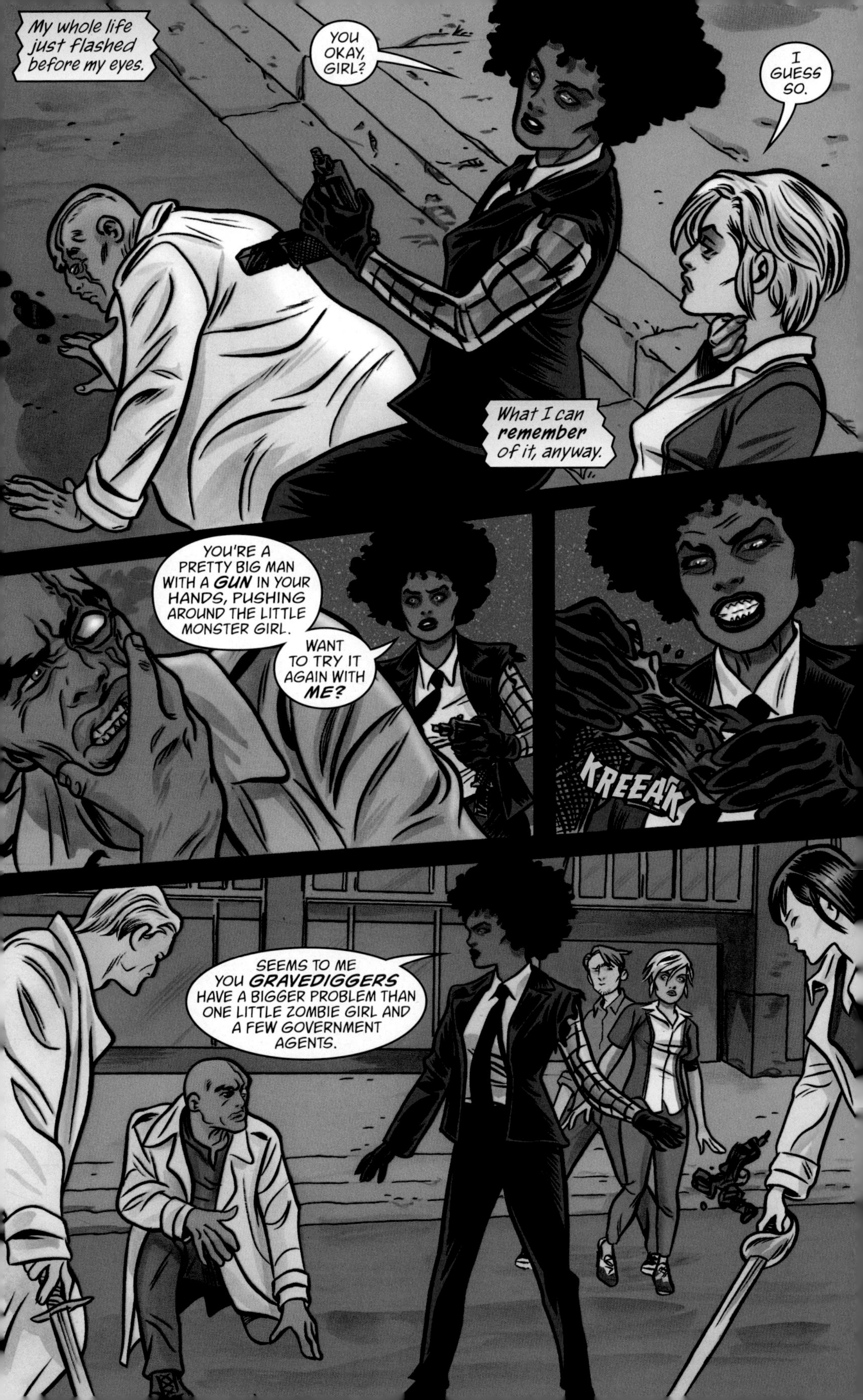
My whole life just flashed before my eyes.
YOU OKAY, GIRL?
I GUESS SO.
What I can **remember** of it, anyway.
YOU'RE A PRETTY BIG MAN WITH A ***GUN*** IN YOUR HANDS, PUSHING AROUND THE LITTLE MONSTER GIRL.
WANT TO TRY IT AGAIN WITH ***ME?***
KREEAK
SEEMS TO ME YOU ***GRAVEDIGGERS*** HAVE A BIGGER PROBLEM THAN ONE LITTLE ZOMBIE GIRL AND A FEW GOVERNMENT AGENTS.

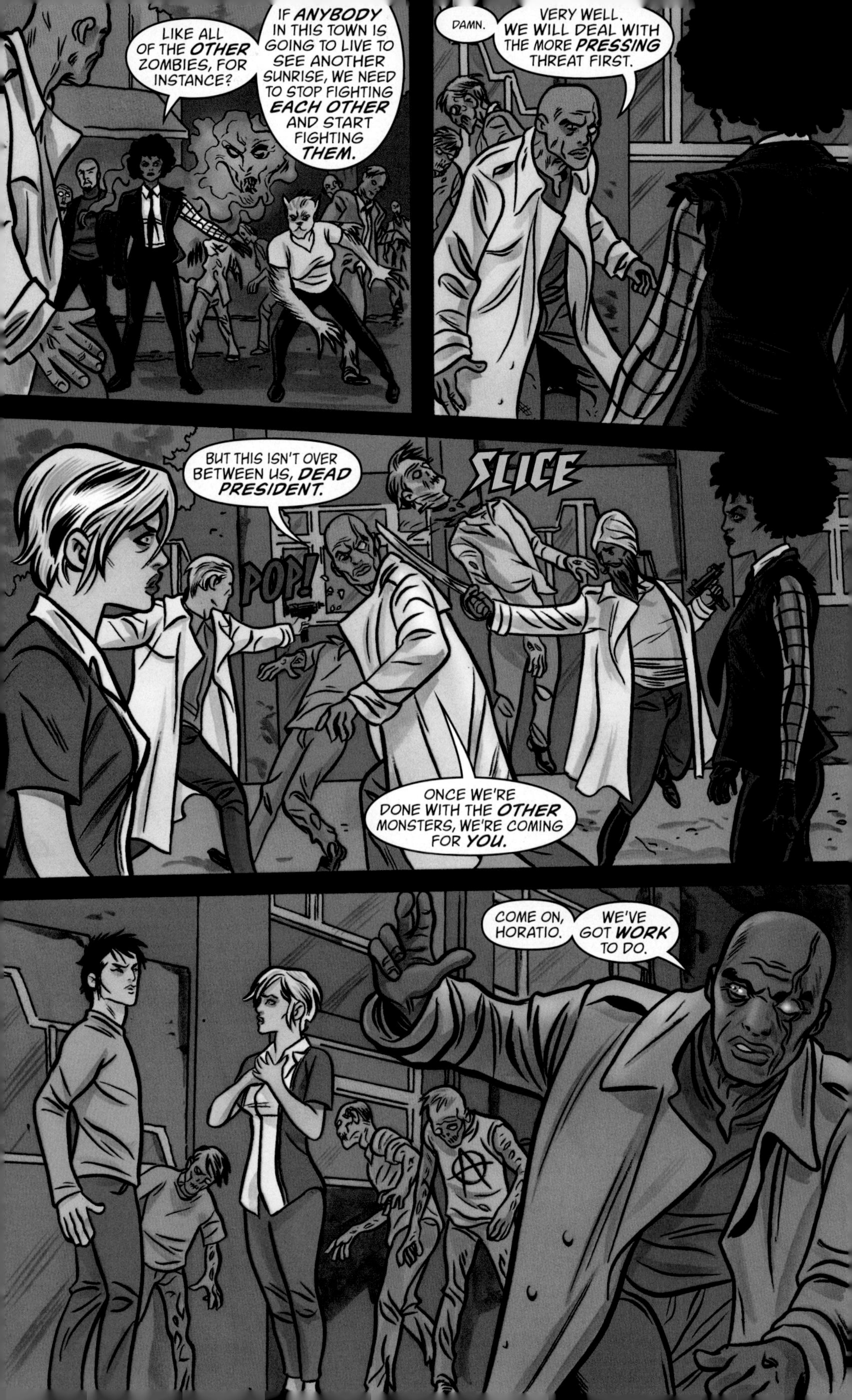
LIKE ALL OF THE OTHER ZOMBIES, FOR INSTANCE?
IF ANYBODY IN THIS TOWN IS GOING TO LIVE TO SEE ANOTHER SUNRISE, WE NEED TO STOP FIGHTING EACH OTHER AND START FIGHTING THEM.
DAMN.
VERY WELL. WE WILL DEAL WITH THE MORE PRESSING THREAT FIRST.
BUT THIS ISN'T OVER BETWEEN US, DEAD PRESIDENT.
SLICE
POP!
ONCE WE'RE DONE WITH THE OTHER MONSTERS, WE'RE COMING FOR YOU.
COME ON, HORATIO.
WE'VE GOT WORK TO DO.

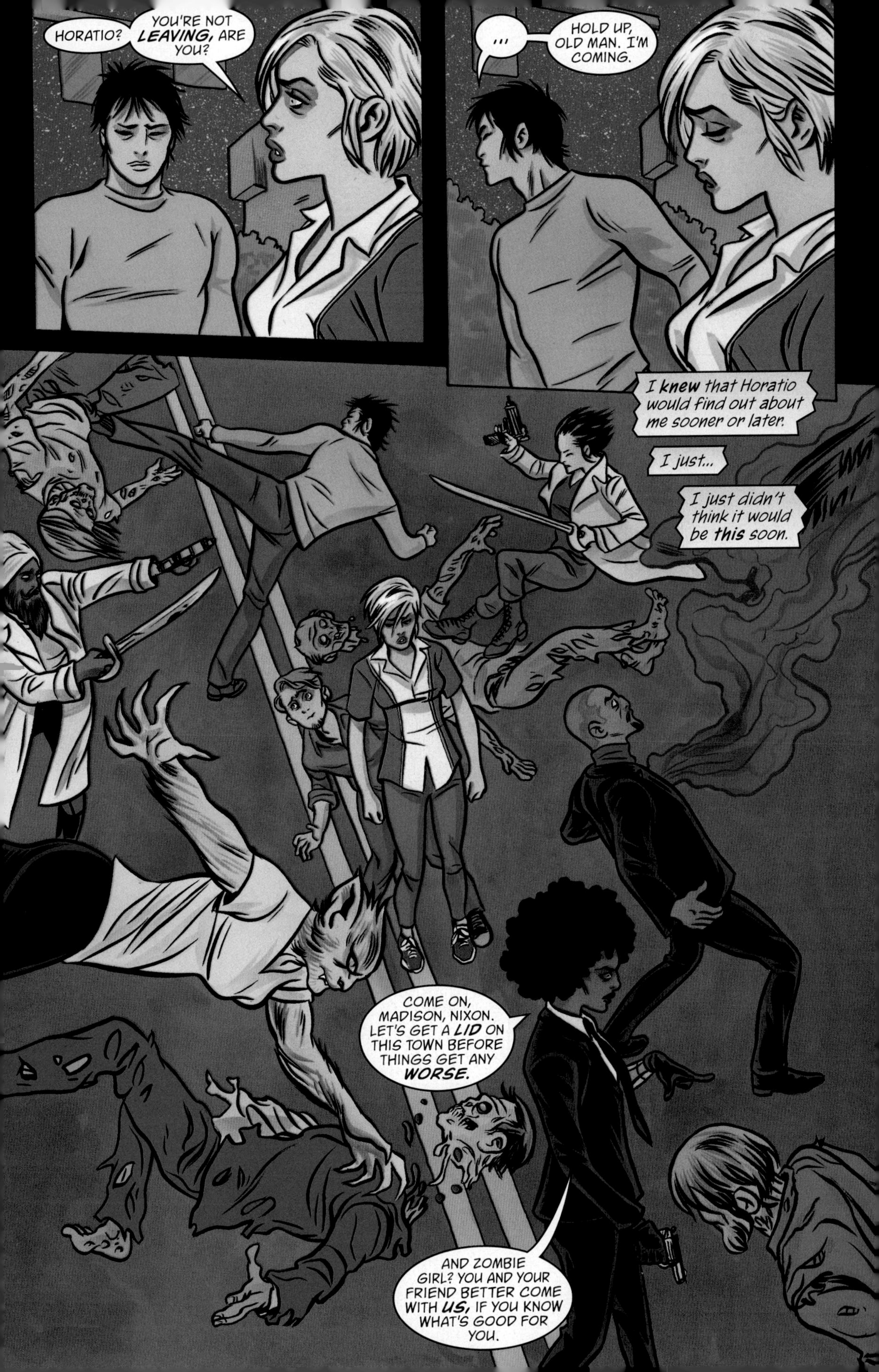
HORATIO?
YOU'RE NOT LEAVING, ARE YOU?
...
HOLD UP, OLD MAN. I'M COMING.
I knew that Horatio would find out about me sooner or later.
I just...
I just didn't think it would be this soon.
COME ON, MADISON, NIXON. LET'S GET A LID ON THIS TOWN BEFORE THINGS GET ANY WORSE.
AND ZOMBIE GIRL? YOU AND YOUR FRIEND BETTER COME WITH US, IF YOU KNOW WHAT'S GOOD FOR YOU.

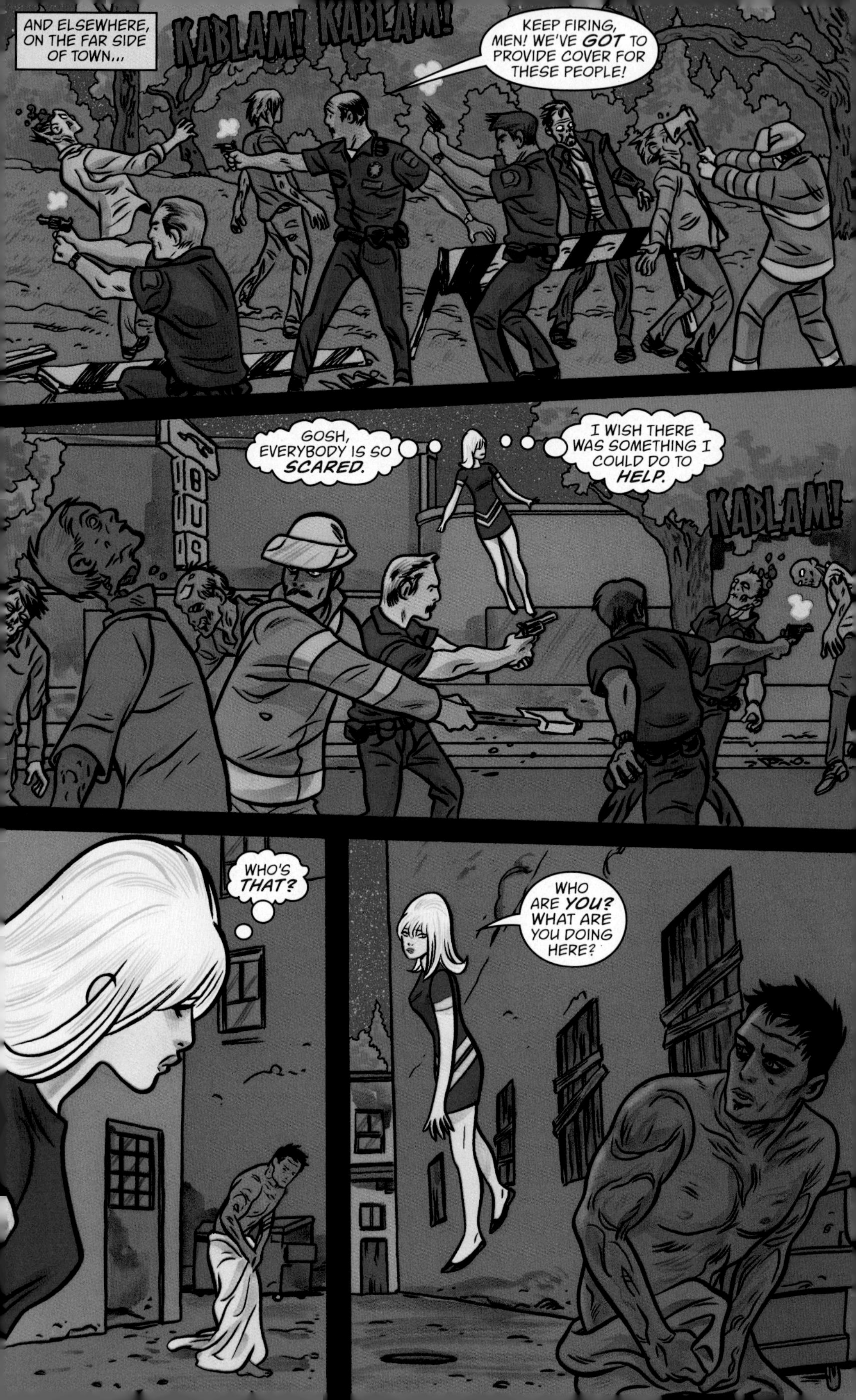
AND ELSEWHERE, ON THE FAR SIDE OF TOWN...
KABLAM! KABLAM!
KEEP FIRING, MEN! WE'VE GOT TO PROVIDE COVER FOR THESE PEOPLE!
GOSH, EVERYBODY IS SO SCARED.
I WISH THERE WAS SOMETHING I COULD DO TO HELP.
KABLAM!
WHO'S THAT?
WHO ARE YOU? WHAT ARE YOU DOING HERE?

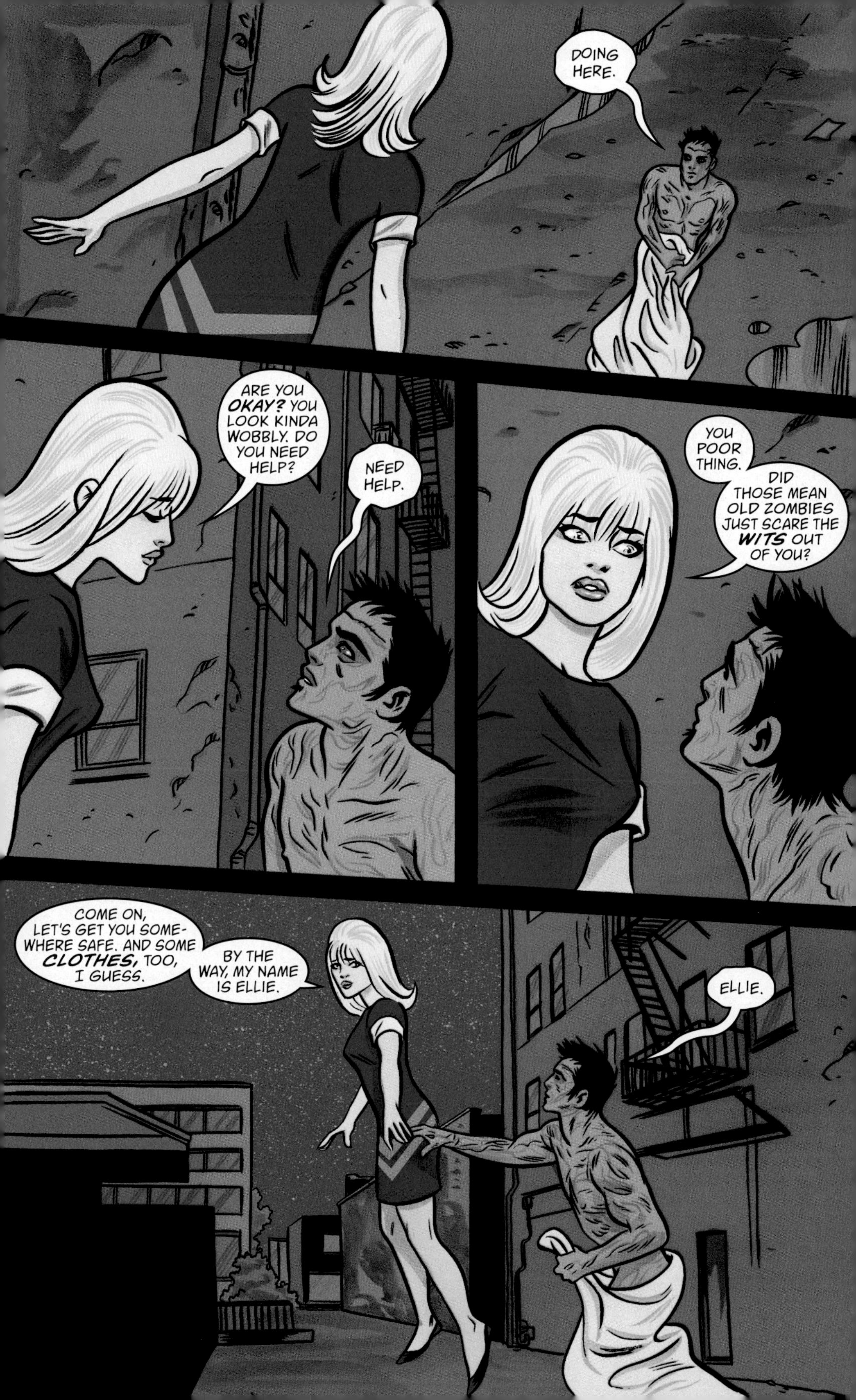
DOING HERE.
ARE YOU OKAY? YOU LOOK KINDA WOBBLY. DO YOU NEED HELP?
NEED HELP.
YOU POOR THING.
DID THOSE MEAN OLD ZOMBIES JUST SCARE THE WITS OUT OF YOU?
COME ON, LET'S GET YOU SOME-WHERE SAFE. AND SOME CLOTHES, TOO, I GUESS.
BY THE WAY, MY NAME IS ELLIE.
ELLIE.

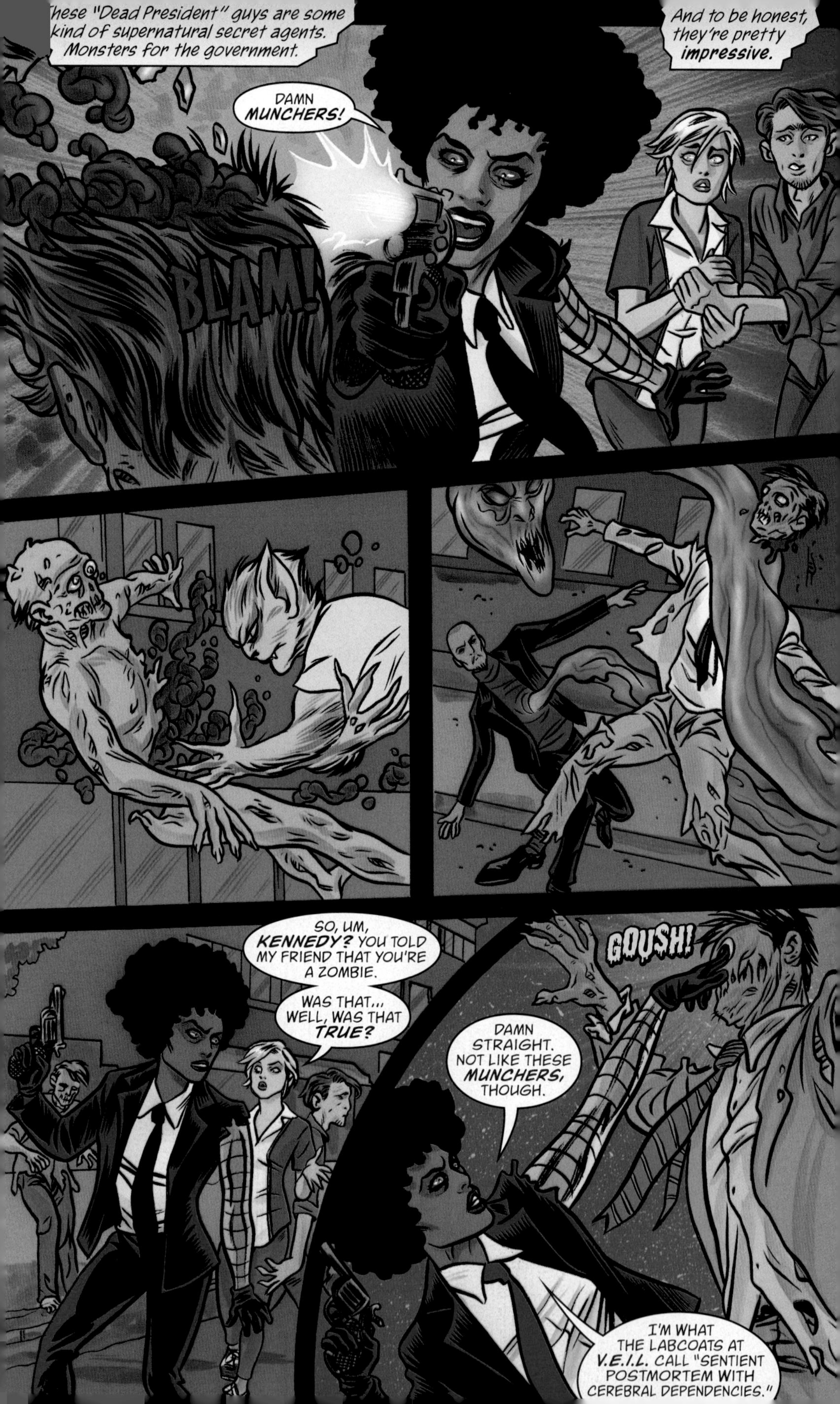
These "Dead President" guys are some kind of supernatural secret agents. Monsters for the government.
And to be honest, they're pretty impressive.
DAMN MUNCHERS!
BLAM!
SO, UM, KENNEDY? YOU TOLD MY FRIEND THAT YOU'RE A ZOMBIE.
WAS THAT... WELL, WAS THAT TRUE?
GOUSH!
DAMN STRAIGHT. NOT LIKE THESE MUNCHERS, THOUGH.
I'M WHAT THE LABCOATS AT V.E.I.L. CALL "SENTIENT POSTMORTEM WITH CEREBRAL DEPENDENCIES."

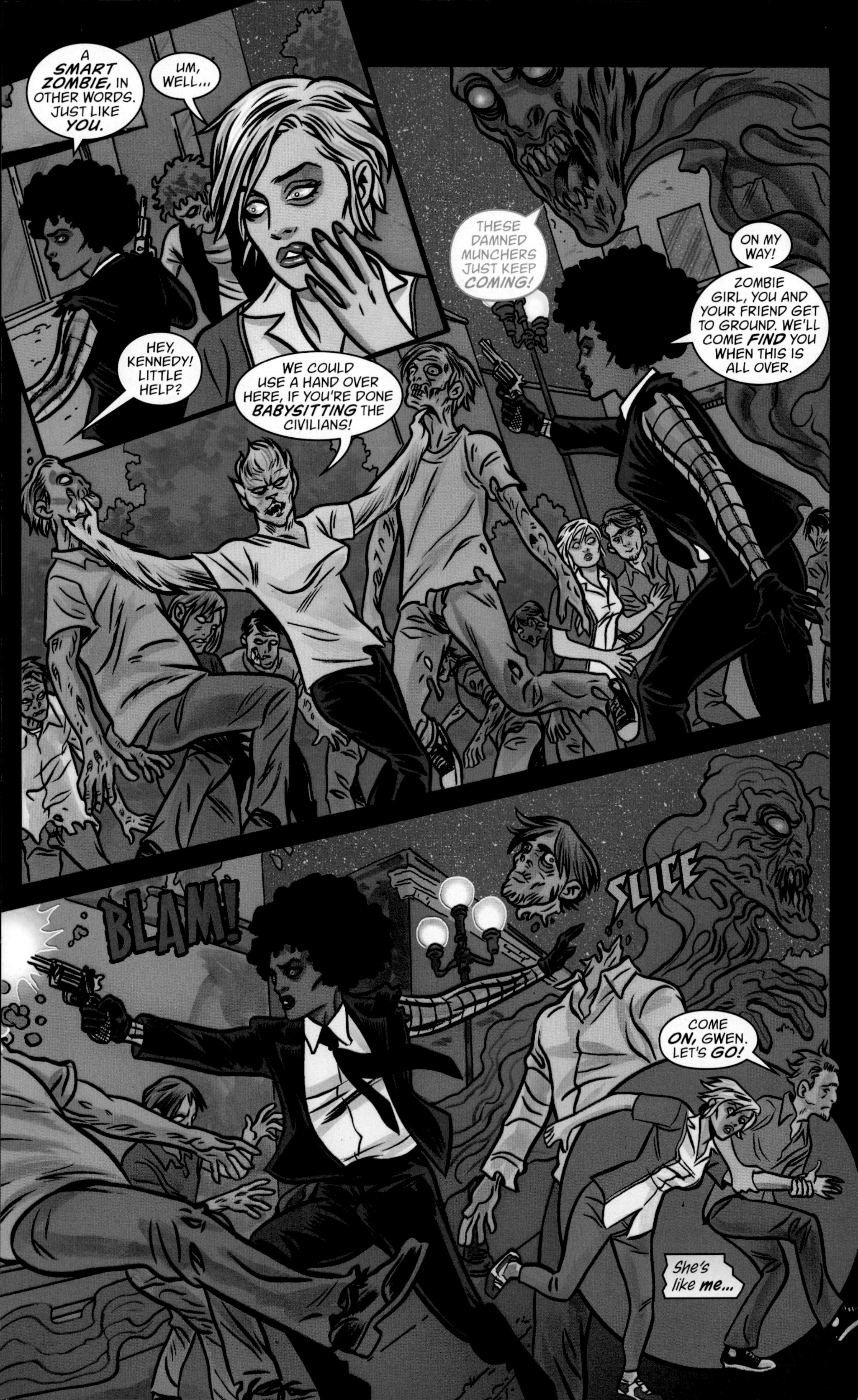
A SMART ZOMBIE, IN OTHER WORDS. JUST LIKE YOU.
UM, WELL...
HEY, KENNEDY! LITTLE HELP?
WE COULD USE A HAND OVER HERE, IF YOU'RE DONE BABYSITTING THE CIVILIANS!
THESE DAMNED MUNCHERS JUST KEEP COMING!
ON MY WAY!
ZOMBIE GIRL, YOU AND YOUR FRIEND GET TO GROUND. WE'LL COME FIND YOU WHEN THIS IS ALL OVER.
BLAM!
SLICE
COME ON, GWEN. LET'S GO!
She's like me...

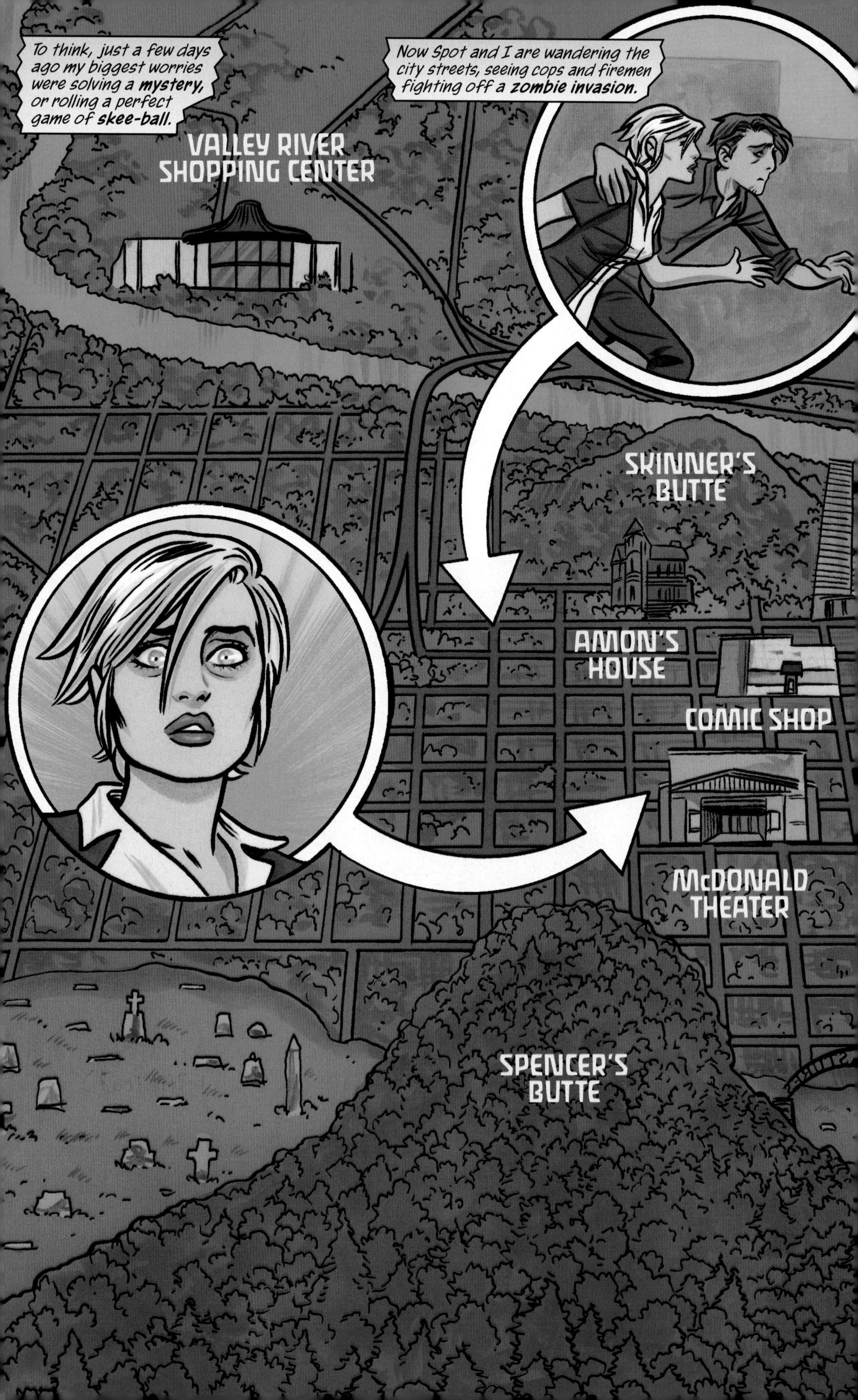
To think, just a few days ago my biggest worries were solving a **mystery**, or rolling a perfect game of **skee-ball**.
Now Spot and I are wandering the city streets, seeing cops and firemen fighting off a **zombie invasion**.
VALLEY RIVER SHOPPING CENTER
SKINNER'S BUTTE
AMON'S HOUSE
COMIC SHOP
McDONALD THEATER
SPENCER'S BUTTE

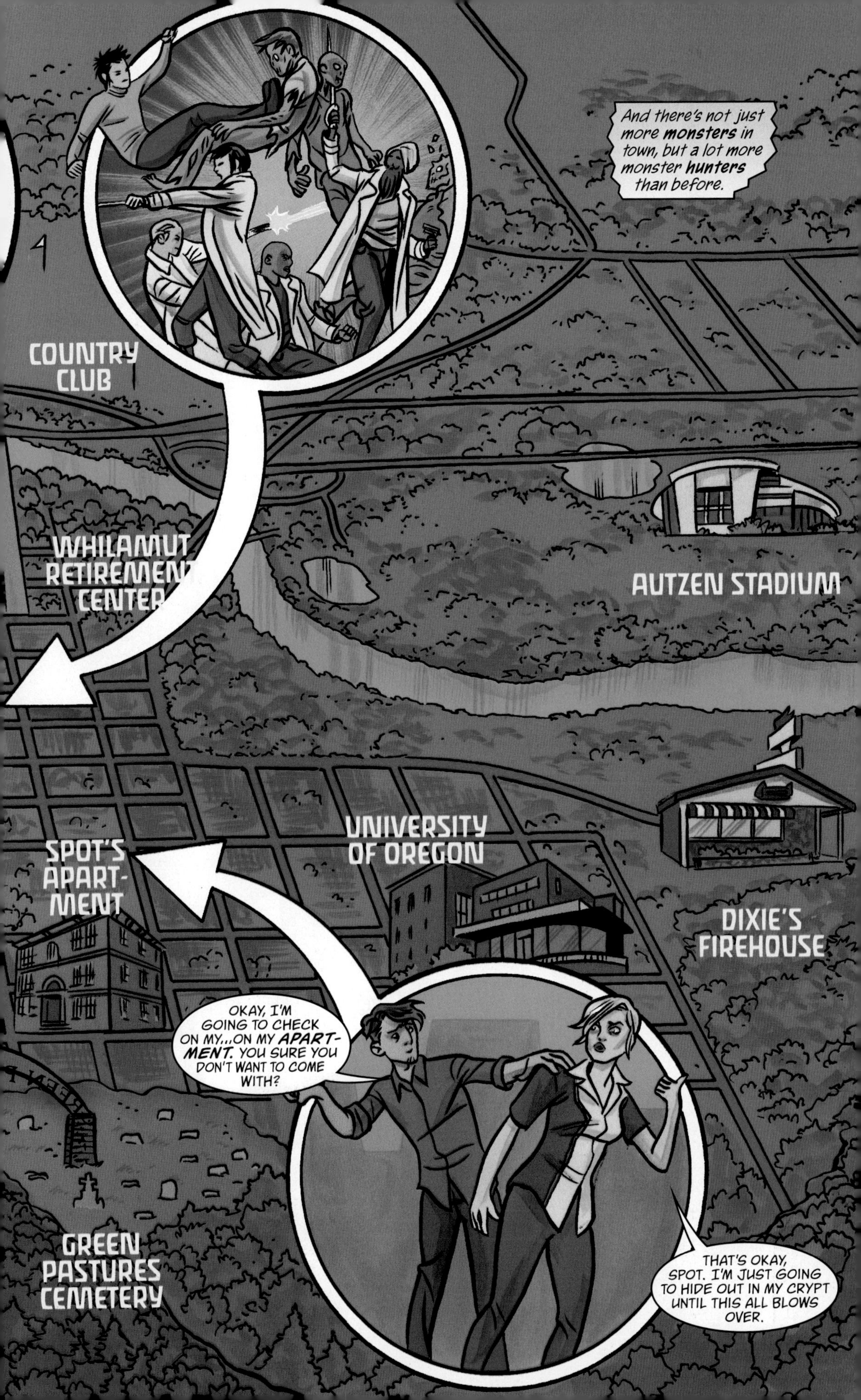
And there's not just more monsters in town, but a lot more monster hunters than before.
COUNTRY CLUB
WHILAMUT RETIREMENT CENTER
AUTZEN STADIUM
UNIVERSITY OF OREGON
SPOT'S APARTMENT
DIXIE'S FIREHOUSE
OKAY, I'M GOING TO CHECK ON MY...ON MY APARTMENT. YOU SURE YOU DON'T WANT TO COME WITH?
GREEN PASTURES CEMETERY
THAT'S OKAY, SPOT. I'M JUST GOING TO HIDE OUT IN MY CRYPT UNTIL THIS ALL BLOWS OVER.

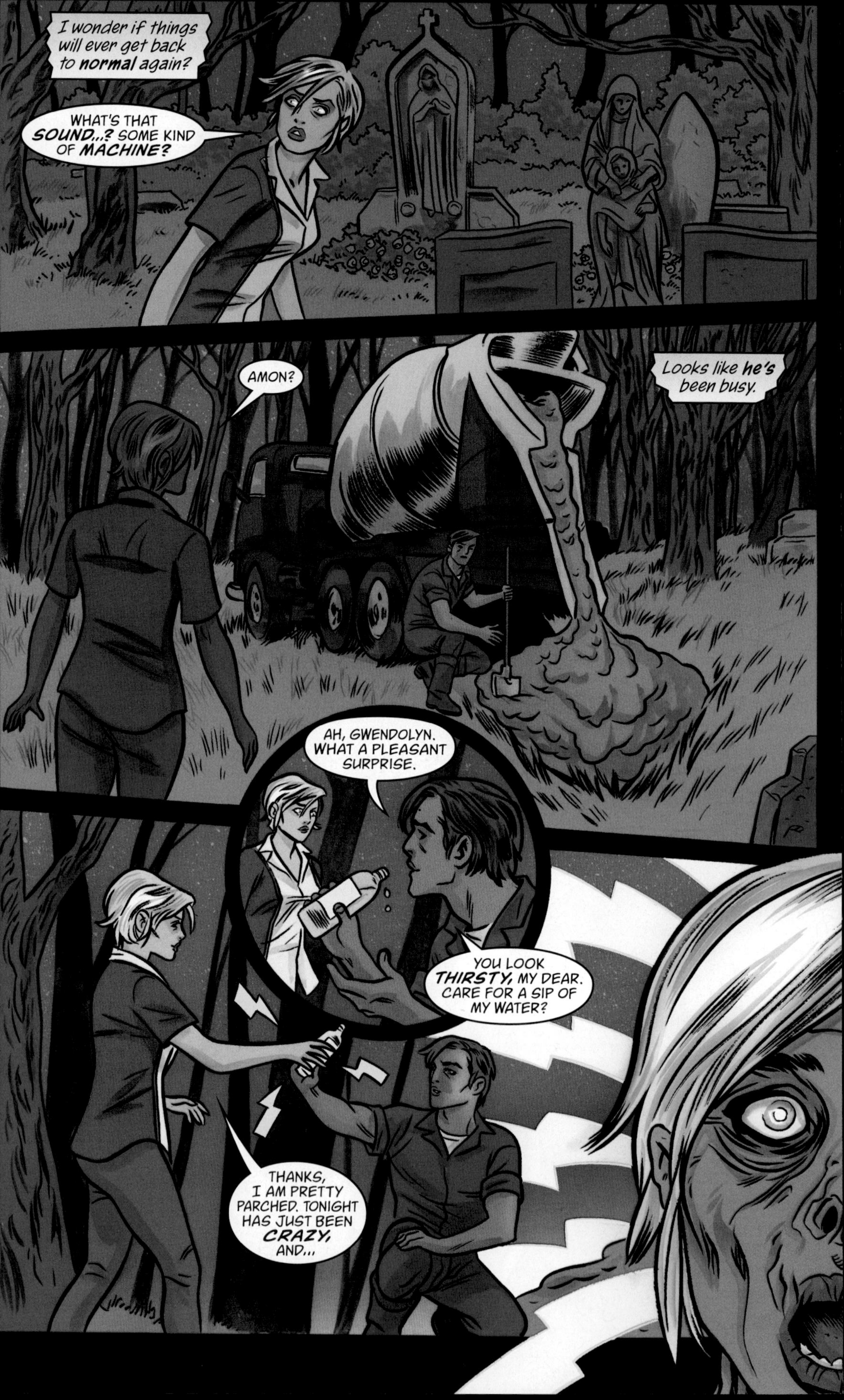
I wonder if things will ever get back to **normal** again?
WHAT'S THAT **SOUND...?** SOME KIND OF **MACHINE?**
AMON?
Looks like **he's** been busy.
AH, GWENDOLYN. WHAT A PLEASANT SURPRISE.
YOU LOOK **THIRSTY,** MY DEAR. CARE FOR A SIP OF MY WATER?
THANKS, I AM PRETTY PARCHED. TONIGHT HAS JUST BEEN **CRAZY,** AND...

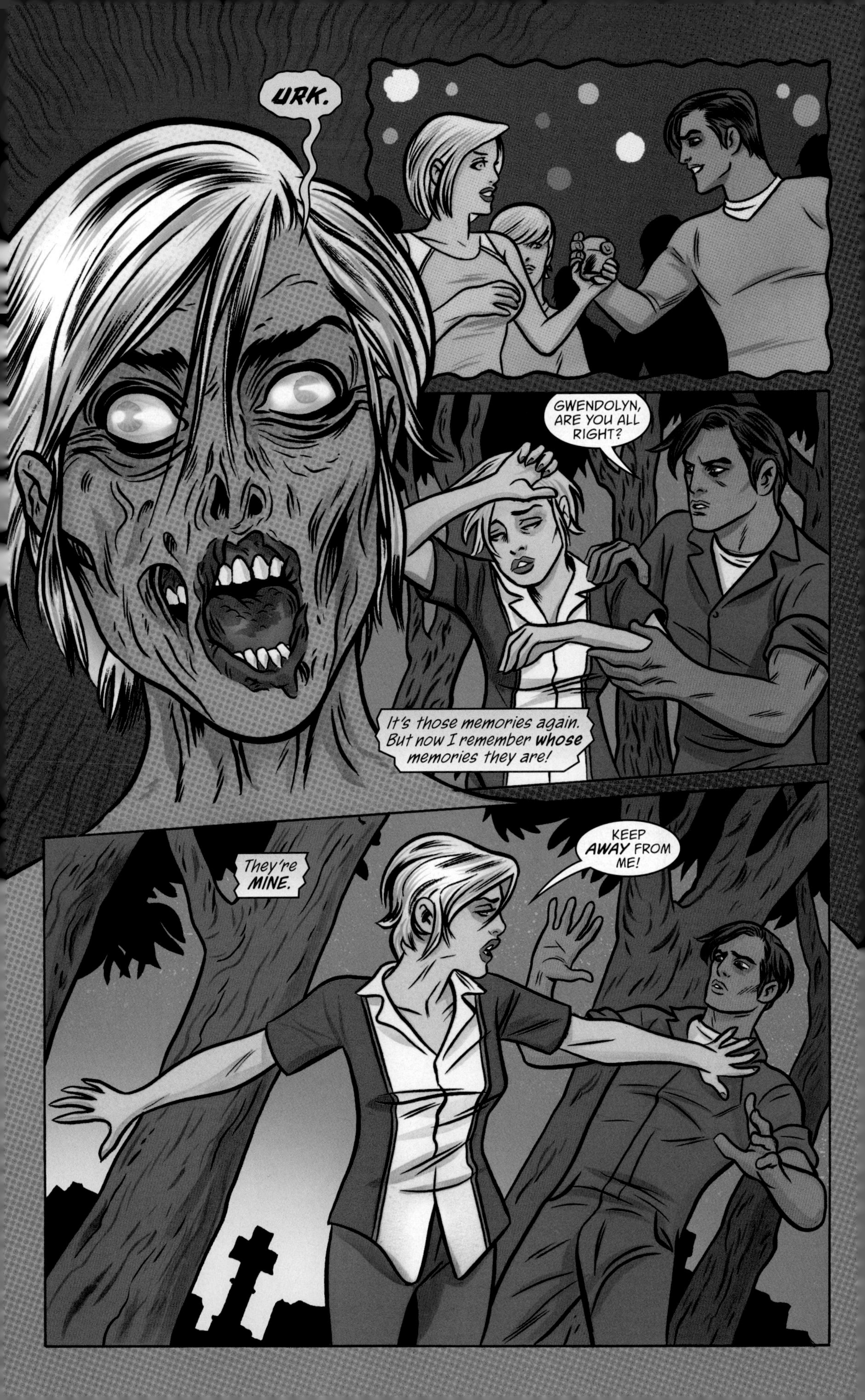
URK.
GWENDOLYN, ARE YOU ALL RIGHT?
It's those memories again. But now I remember **whose** memories they are!
They're **MINE.**
KEEP **AWAY** FROM ME!

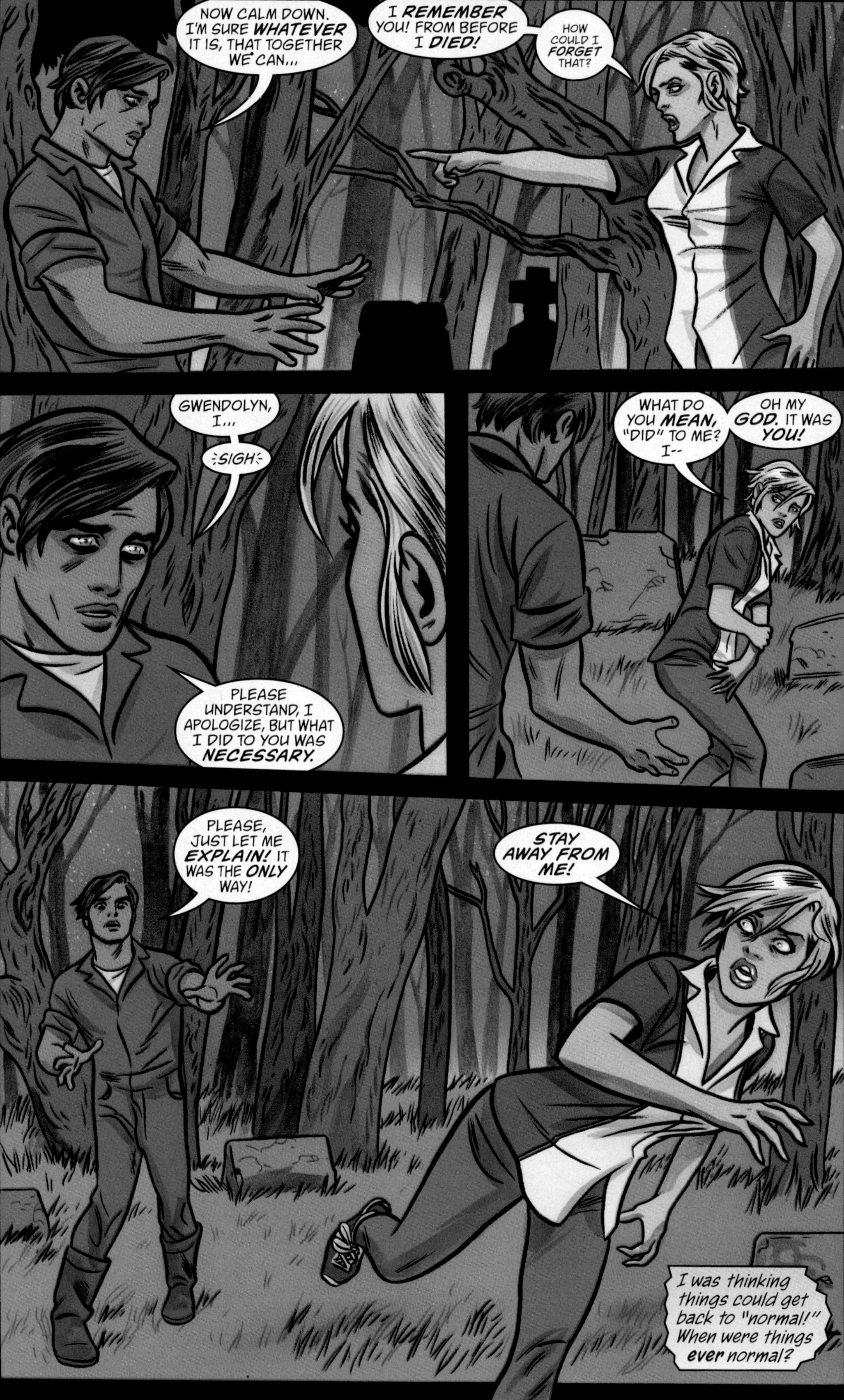
NOW CALM DOWN. I'M SURE WHATEVER IT IS, THAT TOGETHER WE CAN...
I REMEMBER YOU! FROM BEFORE I DIED!
HOW COULD I FORGET THAT?
GWENDOLYN, I...
SIGH
PLEASE UNDERSTAND, I APOLOGIZE, BUT WHAT I DID TO YOU WAS NECESSARY.
WHAT DO YOU MEAN, "DID" TO ME? I--
OH MY GOD. IT WAS YOU!
PLEASE, JUST LET ME EXPLAIN! IT WAS THE ONLY WAY!
STAY AWAY FROM ME!
I was thinking things could get back to "normal!" When were things ever normal?

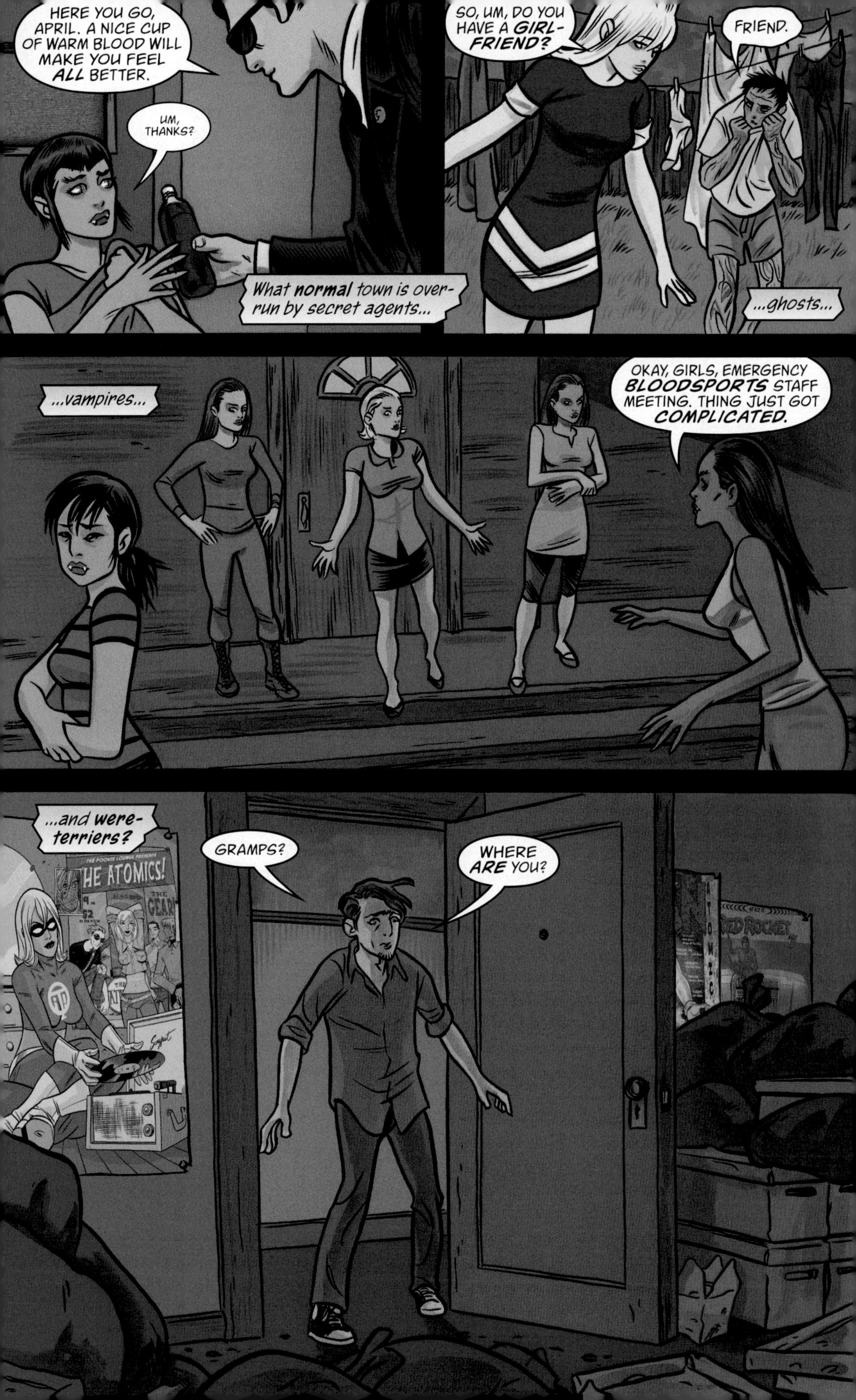

HERE YOU GO, APRIL. A NICE CUP OF WARM BLOOD WILL MAKE YOU FEEL ALL BETTER.
UM, THANKS?
What normal town is over-run by secret agents...
SO, UM, DO YOU HAVE A GIRL-FRIEND?
FRIEND.
...ghosts...
...vampires...
OKAY, GIRLS, EMERGENCY BLOODSPORTS STAFF MEETING. THING JUST GOT COMPLICATED.
...and were-terriers?
THE ATOMICS!
GRAMPS?
WHERE ARE YOU?
RED ROCKET

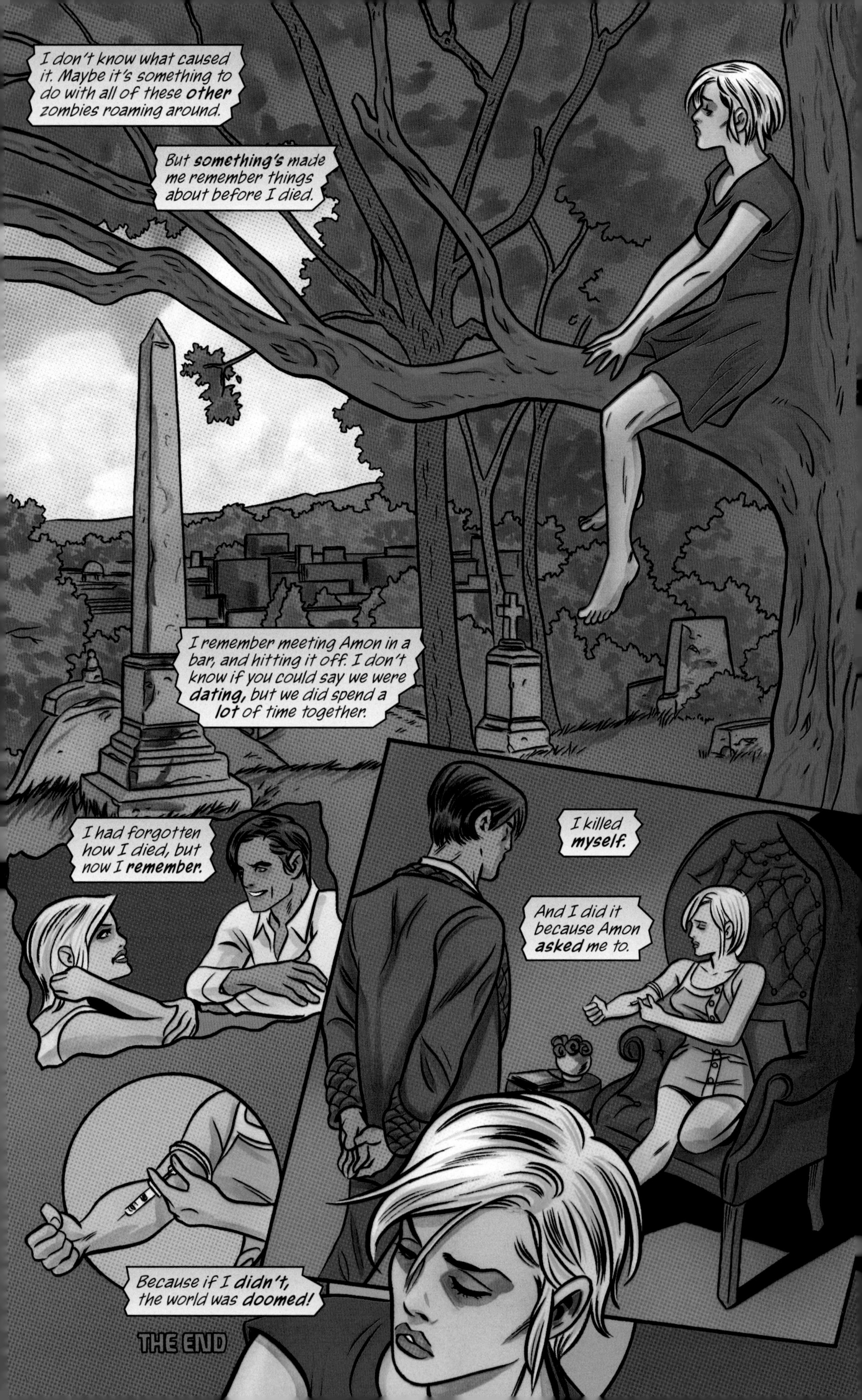
I don't know what caused it. Maybe it's something to do with all of these **other** zombies roaming around.
But **something's** made me remember things about before I died.
I remember meeting Amon in a bar, and hitting it off. I don't know if you could say we were **dating,** but we did spend a **lot** of time together.
I had forgotten how I died, but now I **remember.**
I killed **myself.**
And I did it because Amon **asked** me to.
Because if I **didn't,** the world was **doomed!**
THE END

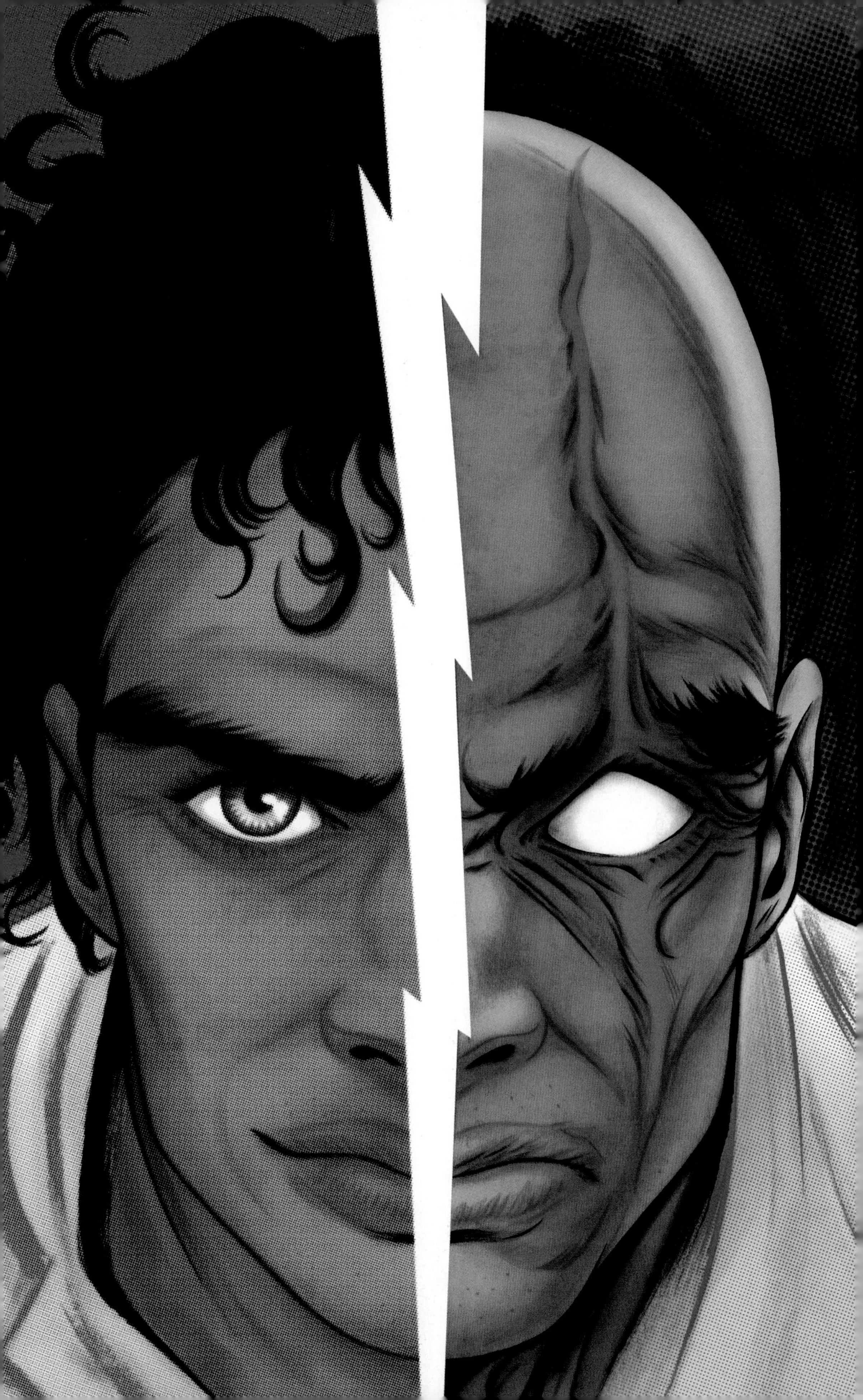

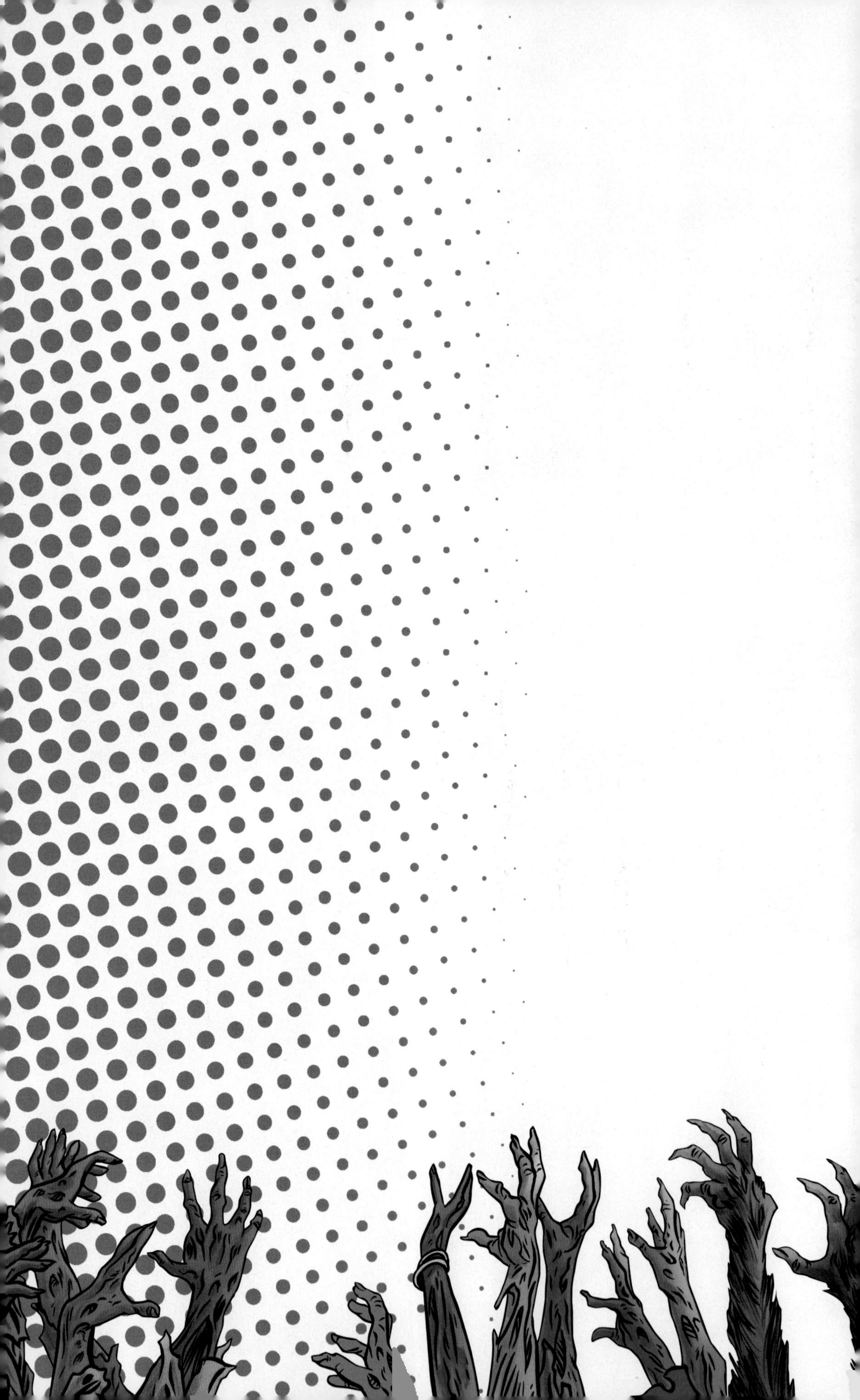

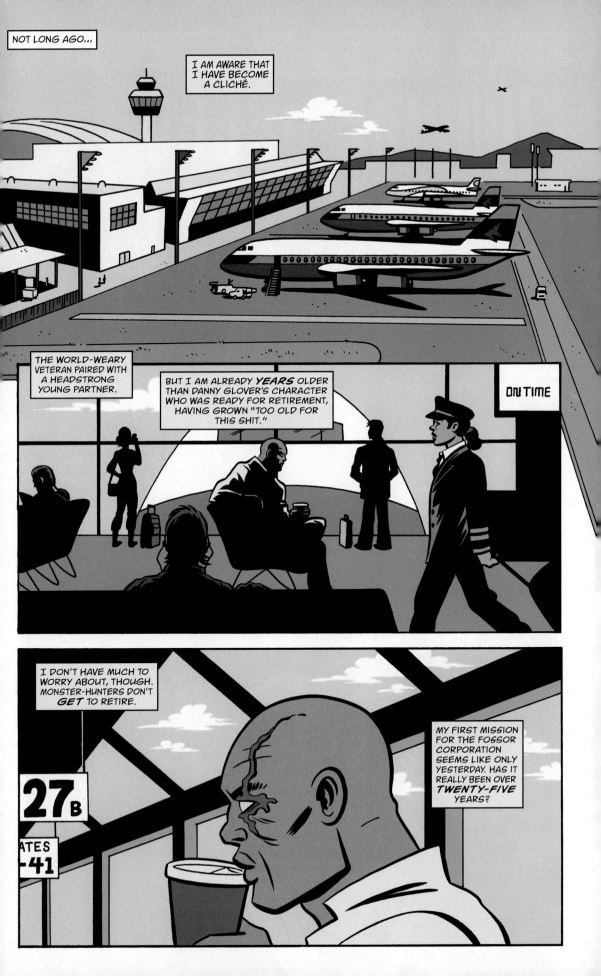

NOT LONG AGO...

I AM AWARE THAT I HAVE BECOME A CLICHÉ.

THE WORLD-WEARY VETERAN PAIRED WITH A HEADSTRONG YOUNG PARTNER.

BUT I AM ALREADY *YEARS* OLDER THAN DANNY GLOVER'S CHARACTER WHO WAS READY FOR RETIREMENT, HAVING GROWN "TOO OLD FOR THIS SHIT."

ON TIME

I DON'T HAVE MUCH TO WORRY ABOUT, THOUGH. MONSTER-HUNTERS DON'T *GET* TO RETIRE.

MY FIRST MISSION FOR THE FOSSOR CORPORATION SEEMS LIKE ONLY YESTERDAY. HAS IT REALLY BEEN OVER *TWENTY-FIVE* YEARS?

27B

ATES
-41

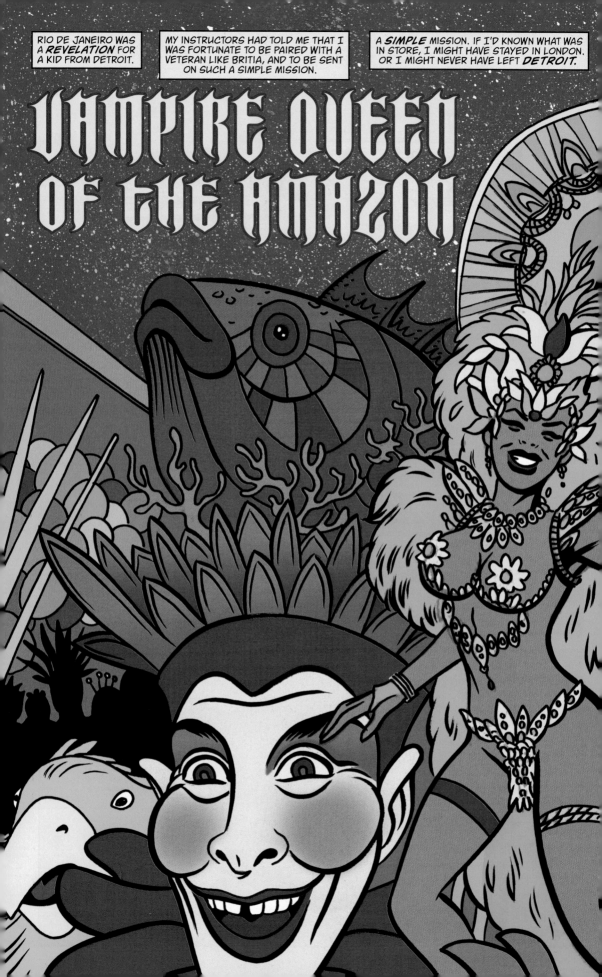

RIO DE JANEIRO WAS A *REVELATION* FOR A KID FROM DETROIT.

MY INSTRUCTORS HAD TOLD ME THAT I WAS FORTUNATE TO BE PAIRED WITH A VETERAN LIKE BRITIA, AND TO BE SENT ON SUCH A SIMPLE MISSION.

A *SIMPLE* MISSION. IF I'D KNOWN WHAT WAS IN STORE, I MIGHT HAVE STAYED IN LONDON. OR I MIGHT NEVER HAVE LEFT *DETROIT.*

VAMPIRE QUEEN OF THE AMAZON

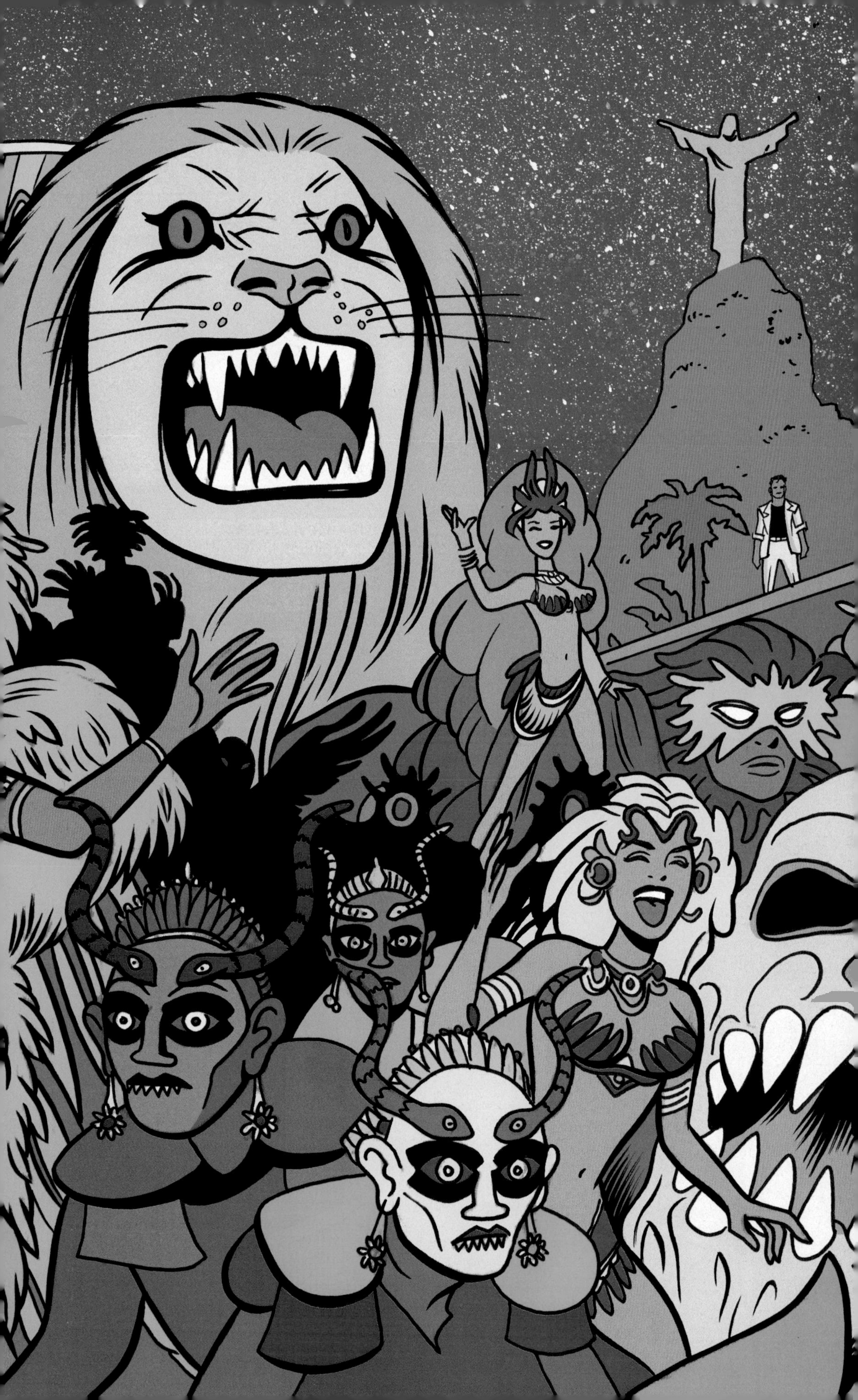

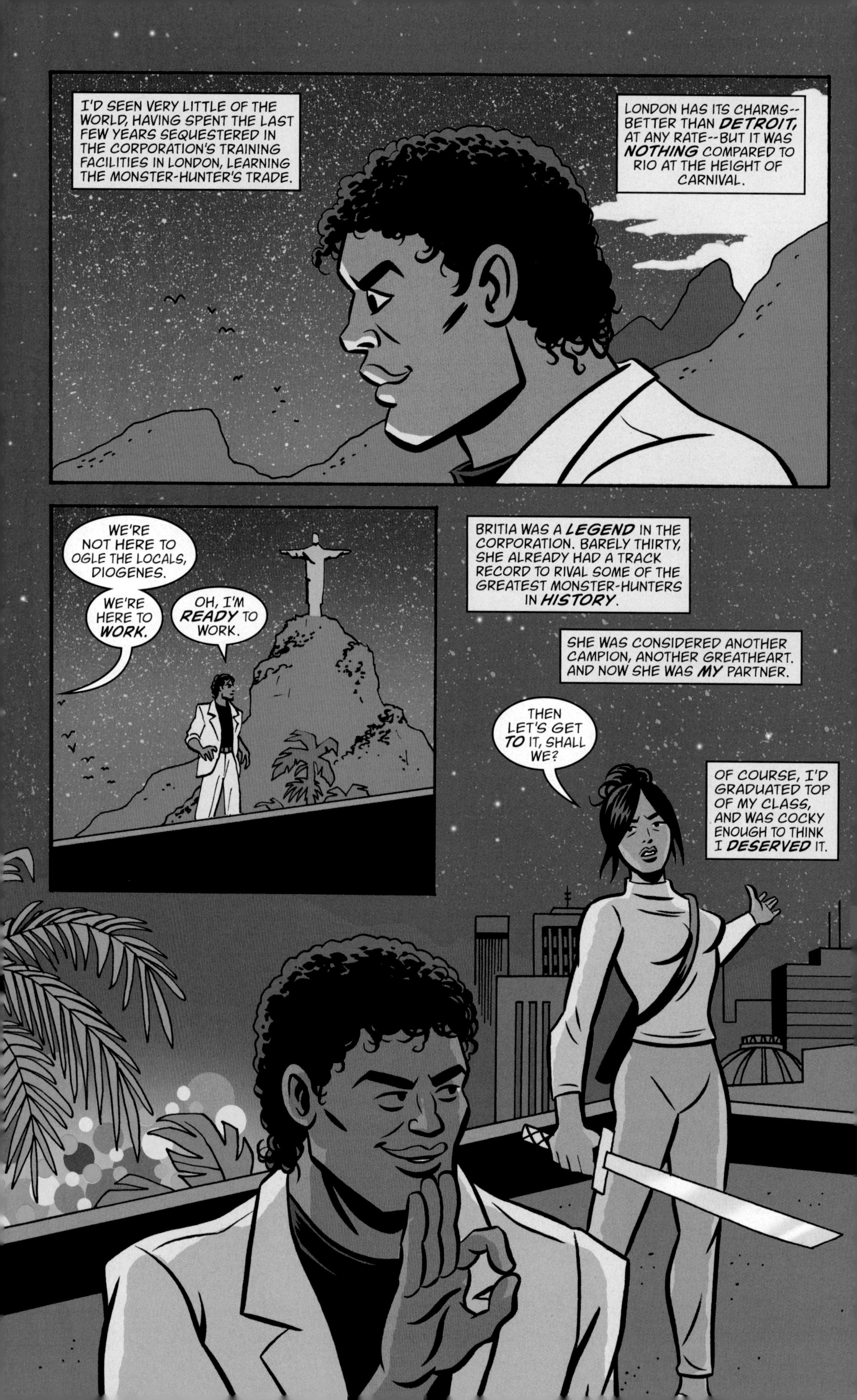
I'D SEEN VERY LITTLE OF THE WORLD, HAVING SPENT THE LAST FEW YEARS SEQUESTERED IN THE CORPORATION'S TRAINING FACILITIES IN LONDON, LEARNING THE MONSTER-HUNTER'S TRADE.
LONDON HAS ITS CHARMS-- BETTER THAN DETROIT, AT ANY RATE--BUT IT WAS NOTHING COMPARED TO RIO AT THE HEIGHT OF CARNIVAL.
WE'RE NOT HERE TO OGLE THE LOCALS, DIOGENES.
WE'RE HERE TO WORK.
OH, I'M READY TO WORK.
BRITIA WAS A LEGEND IN THE CORPORATION. BARELY THIRTY, SHE ALREADY HAD A TRACK RECORD TO RIVAL SOME OF THE GREATEST MONSTER-HUNTERS IN HISTORY.
SHE WAS CONSIDERED ANOTHER CAMPION, ANOTHER GREATHEART. AND NOW SHE WAS MY PARTNER.
THEN LET'S GET TO IT, SHALL WE?
OF COURSE, I'D GRADUATED TOP OF MY CLASS, AND WAS COCKY ENOUGH TO THINK I DESERVED IT.

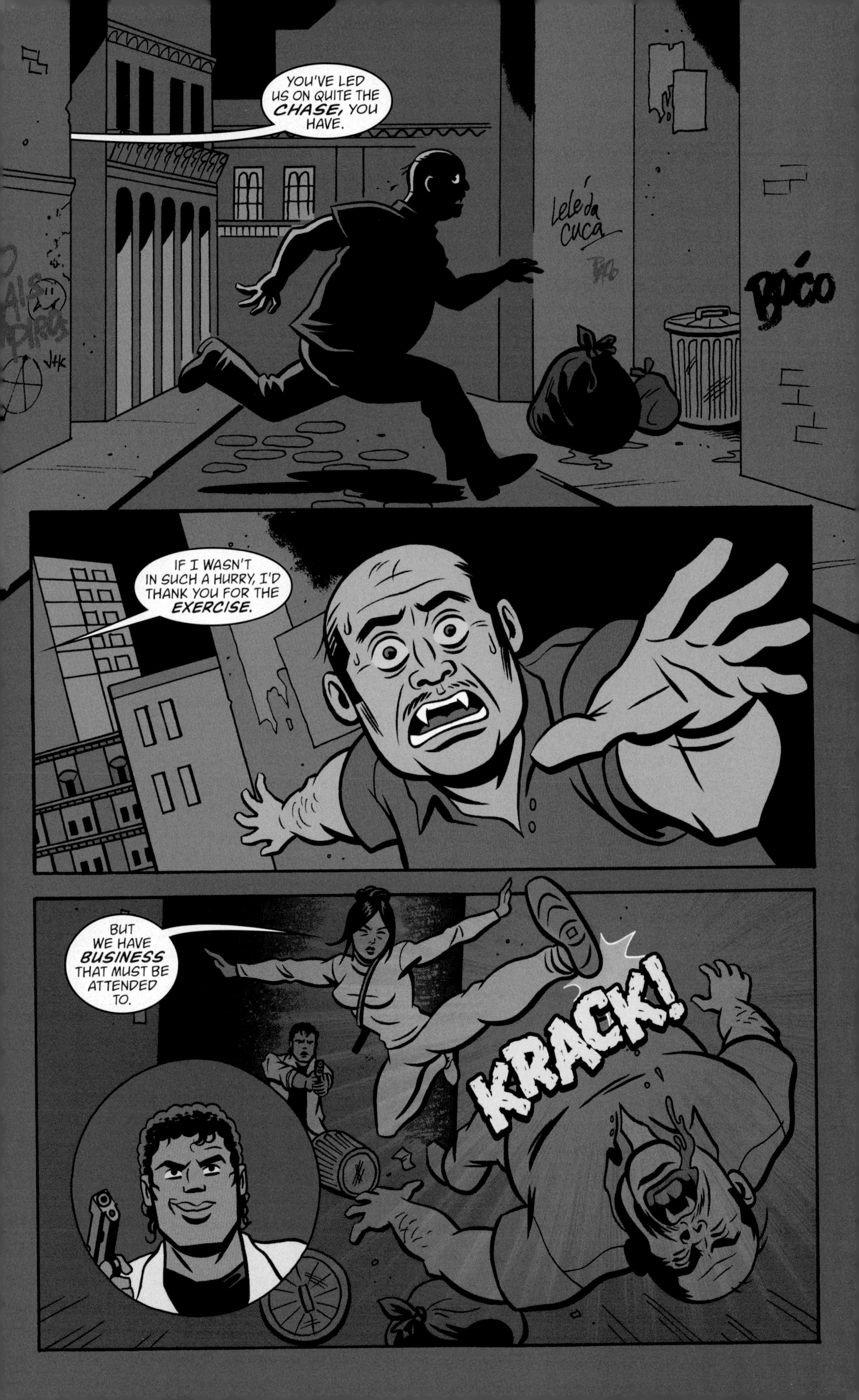
YOU'VE LED US ON QUITE THE CHASE, YOU HAVE.
IF I WASN'T IN SUCH A HURRY, I'D THANK YOU FOR THE EXERCISE.
BUT WE HAVE BUSINESS THAT MUST BE ATTENDED TO.
KRACK!

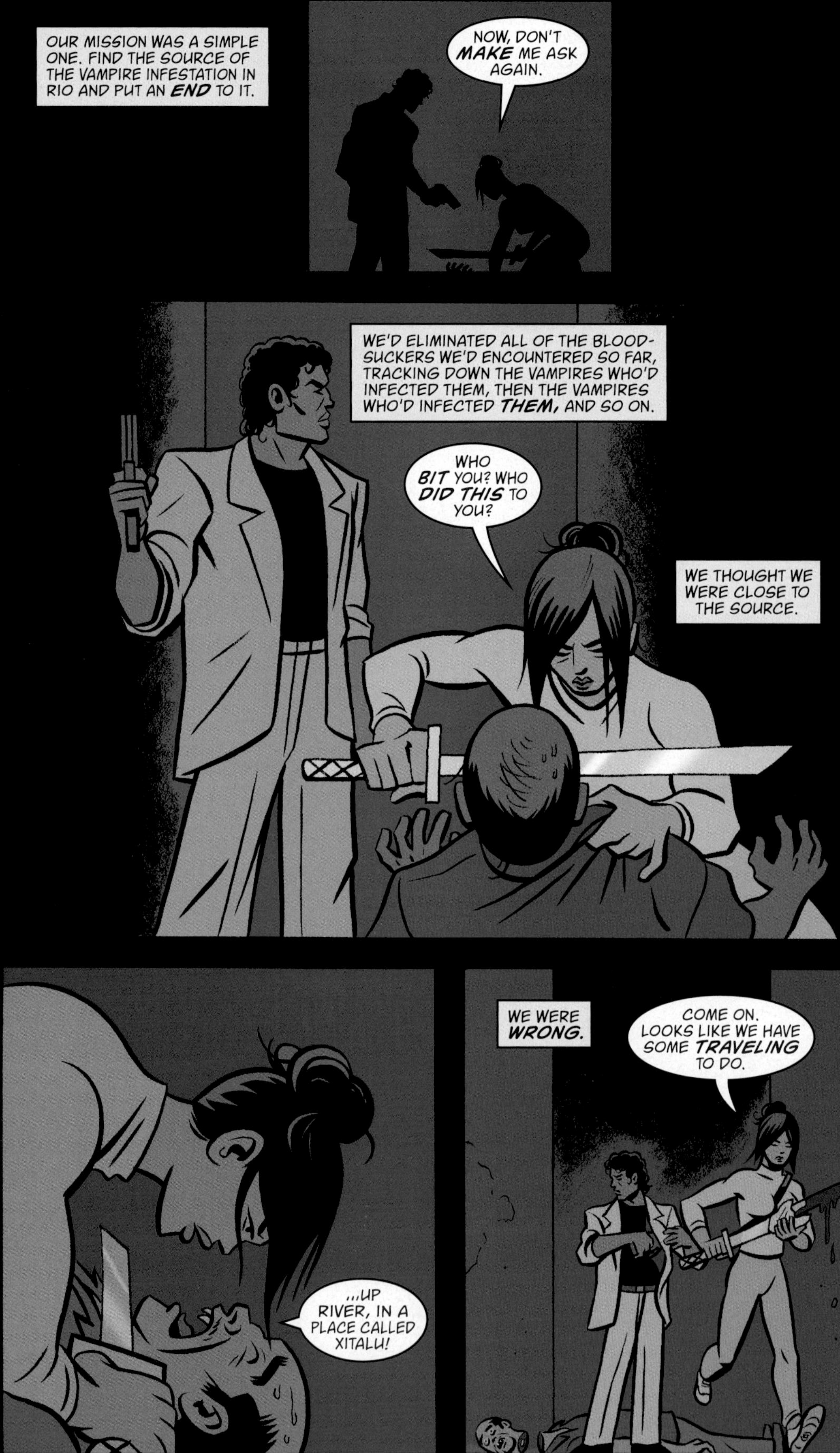
OUR MISSION WAS A SIMPLE ONE. FIND THE SOURCE OF THE VAMPIRE INFESTATION IN RIO AND PUT AN END TO IT.
NOW, DON'T MAKE ME ASK AGAIN.
WE'D ELIMINATED ALL OF THE BLOOD-SUCKERS WE'D ENCOUNTERED SO FAR, TRACKING DOWN THE VAMPIRES WHO'D INFECTED THEM, THEN THE VAMPIRES WHO'D INFECTED THEM, AND SO ON.
WHO BIT YOU? WHO DID THIS TO YOU?
WE THOUGHT WE WERE CLOSE TO THE SOURCE.
...UP RIVER, IN A PLACE CALLED XITALU!
WE WERE WRONG.
COME ON. LOOKS LIKE WE HAVE SOME TRAVELING TO DO.

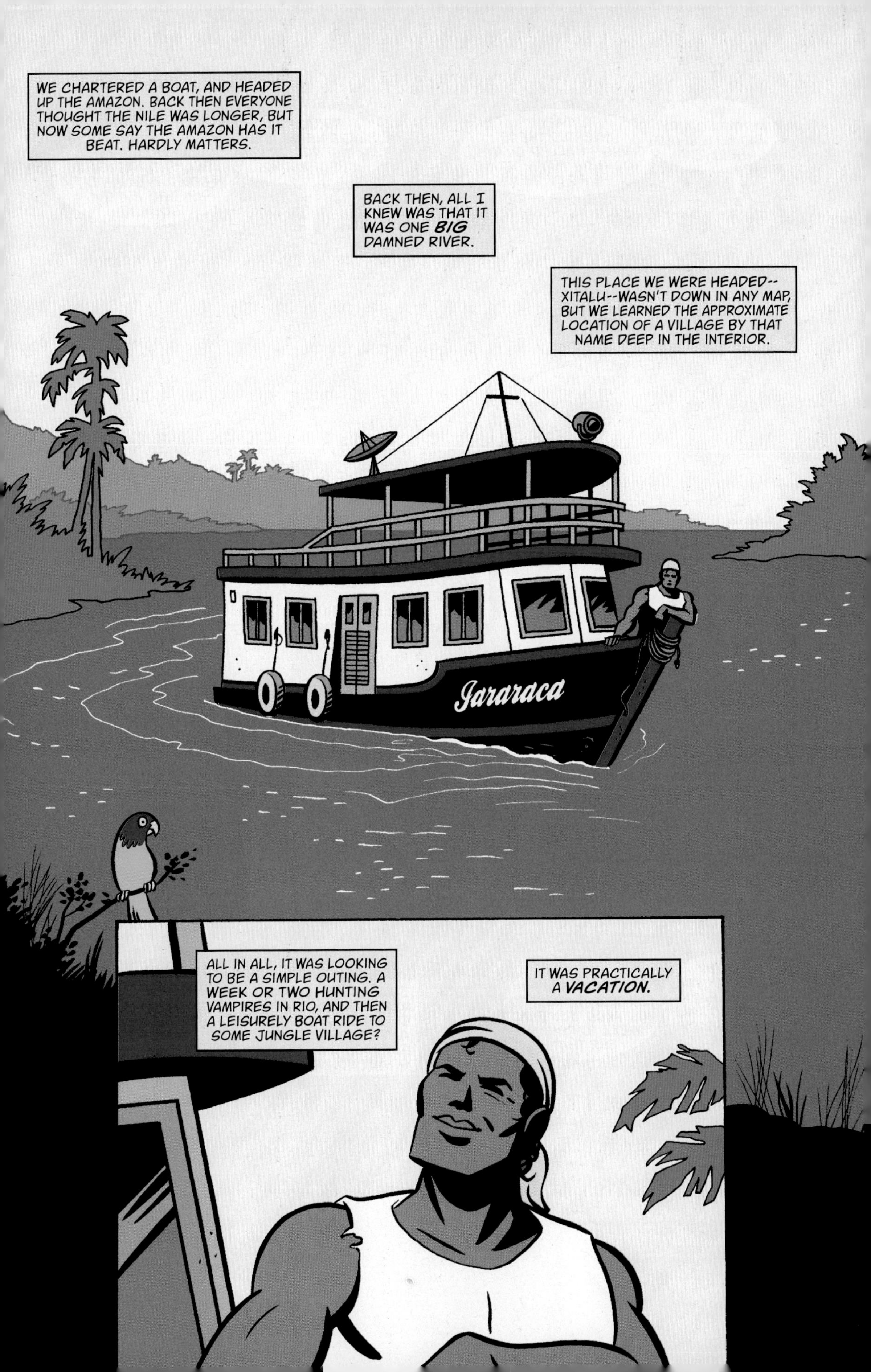
WE CHARTERED A BOAT, AND HEADED UP THE AMAZON. BACK THEN EVERYONE THOUGHT THE NILE WAS LONGER, BUT NOW SOME SAY THE AMAZON HAS IT BEAT. HARDLY MATTERS.
BACK THEN, ALL I KNEW WAS THAT IT WAS ONE *BIG* DAMNED RIVER.
THIS PLACE WE WERE HEADED--XITALU--WASN'T DOWN IN ANY MAP, BUT WE LEARNED THE APPROXIMATE LOCATION OF A VILLAGE BY THAT NAME DEEP IN THE INTERIOR.
Jararaca
ALL IN ALL, IT WAS LOOKING TO BE A SIMPLE OUTING. A WEEK OR TWO HUNTING VAMPIRES IN RIO, AND THEN A LEISURELY BOAT RIDE TO SOME JUNGLE VILLAGE?
IT WAS PRACTICALLY A *VACATION.*

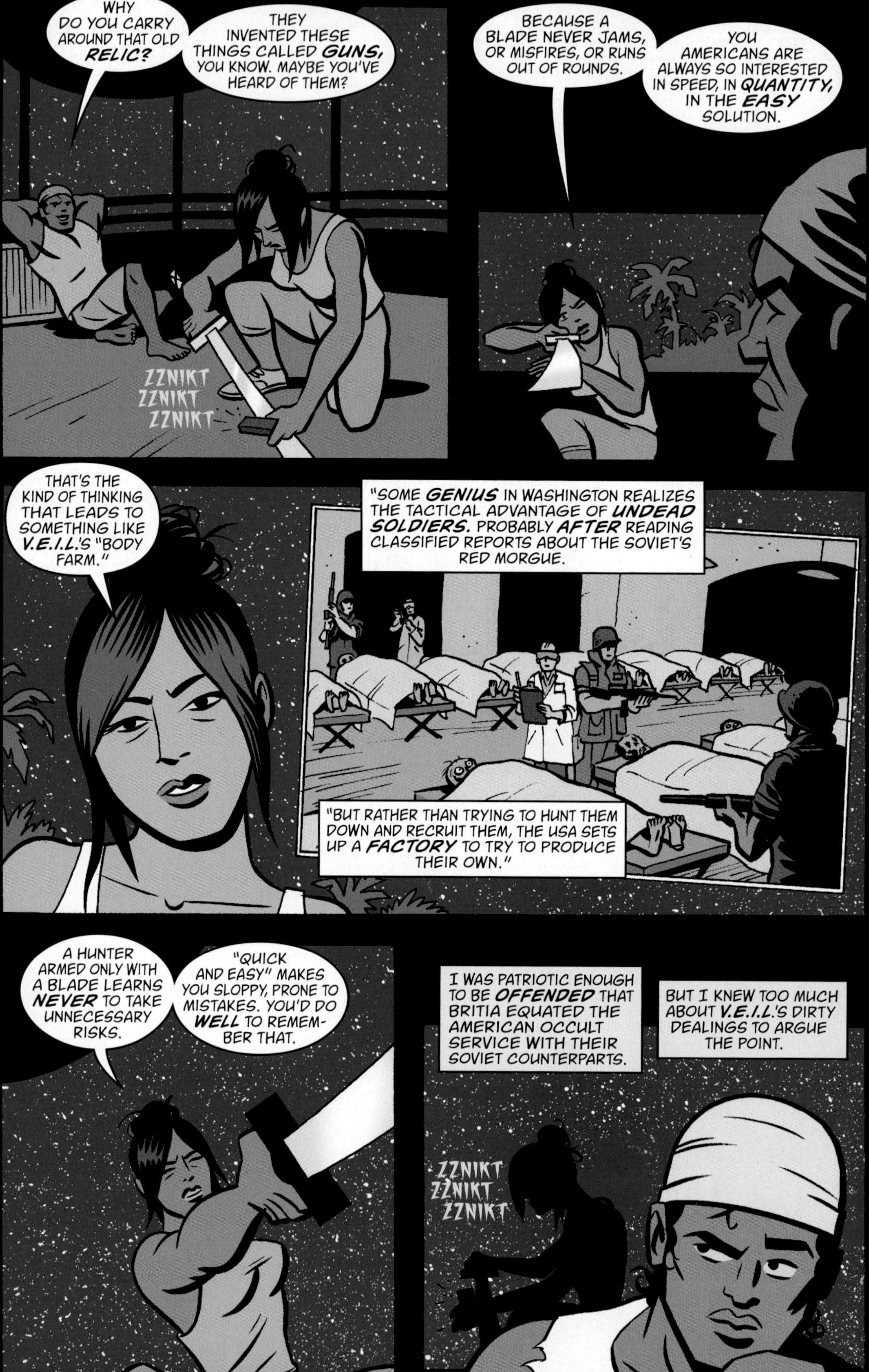
WHY DO YOU CARRY AROUND THAT OLD RELIC?
THEY INVENTED THESE THINGS CALLED GUNS, YOU KNOW. MAYBE YOU'VE HEARD OF THEM?
ZZNIKT ZZNIKT ZZNIKT
BECAUSE A BLADE NEVER JAMS, OR MISFIRES, OR RUNS OUT OF ROUNDS.
YOU AMERICANS ARE ALWAYS SO INTERESTED IN SPEED, IN QUANTITY, IN THE EASY SOLUTION.
THAT'S THE KIND OF THINKING THAT LEADS TO SOMETHING LIKE V.E.I.L.'S "BODY FARM."
"SOME GENIUS IN WASHINGTON REALIZES THE TACTICAL ADVANTAGE OF UNDEAD SOLDIERS. PROBABLY AFTER READING CLASSIFIED REPORTS ABOUT THE SOVIET'S RED MORGUE.
"BUT RATHER THAN TRYING TO HUNT THEM DOWN AND RECRUIT THEM, THE USA SETS UP A FACTORY TO TRY TO PRODUCE THEIR OWN."
A HUNTER ARMED ONLY WITH A BLADE LEARNS NEVER TO TAKE UNNECESSARY RISKS.
"QUICK AND EASY" MAKES YOU SLOPPY, PRONE TO MISTAKES. YOU'D DO WELL TO REMEMBER THAT.
I WAS PATRIOTIC ENOUGH TO BE OFFENDED THAT BRITIA EQUATED THE AMERICAN OCCULT SERVICE WITH THEIR SOVIET COUNTERPARTS.
BUT I KNEW TOO MUCH ABOUT V.E.I.L.'S DIRTY DEALINGS TO ARGUE THE POINT.
ZZNIKT ZZNIKT ZZNIKT

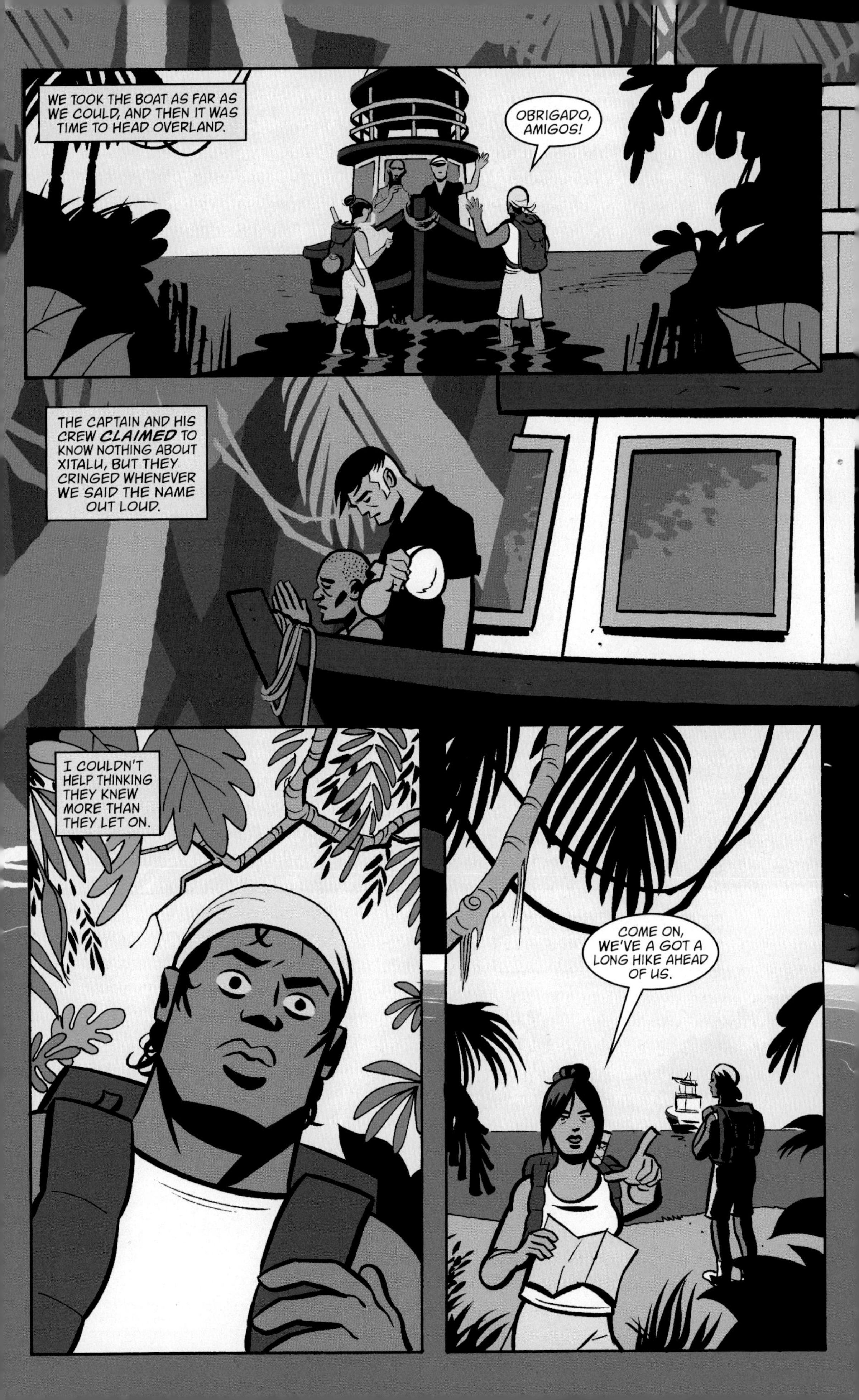
WE TOOK THE BOAT AS FAR AS WE COULD, AND THEN IT WAS TIME TO HEAD OVERLAND.
OBRIGADO, AMIGOS!
THE CAPTAIN AND HIS CREW CLAIMED TO KNOW NOTHING ABOUT XITALU, BUT THEY CRINGED WHENEVER WE SAID THE NAME OUT LOUD.
I COULDN'T HELP THINKING THEY KNEW MORE THAN THEY LET ON.
COME ON, WE'VE A GOT A LONG HIKE AHEAD OF US.

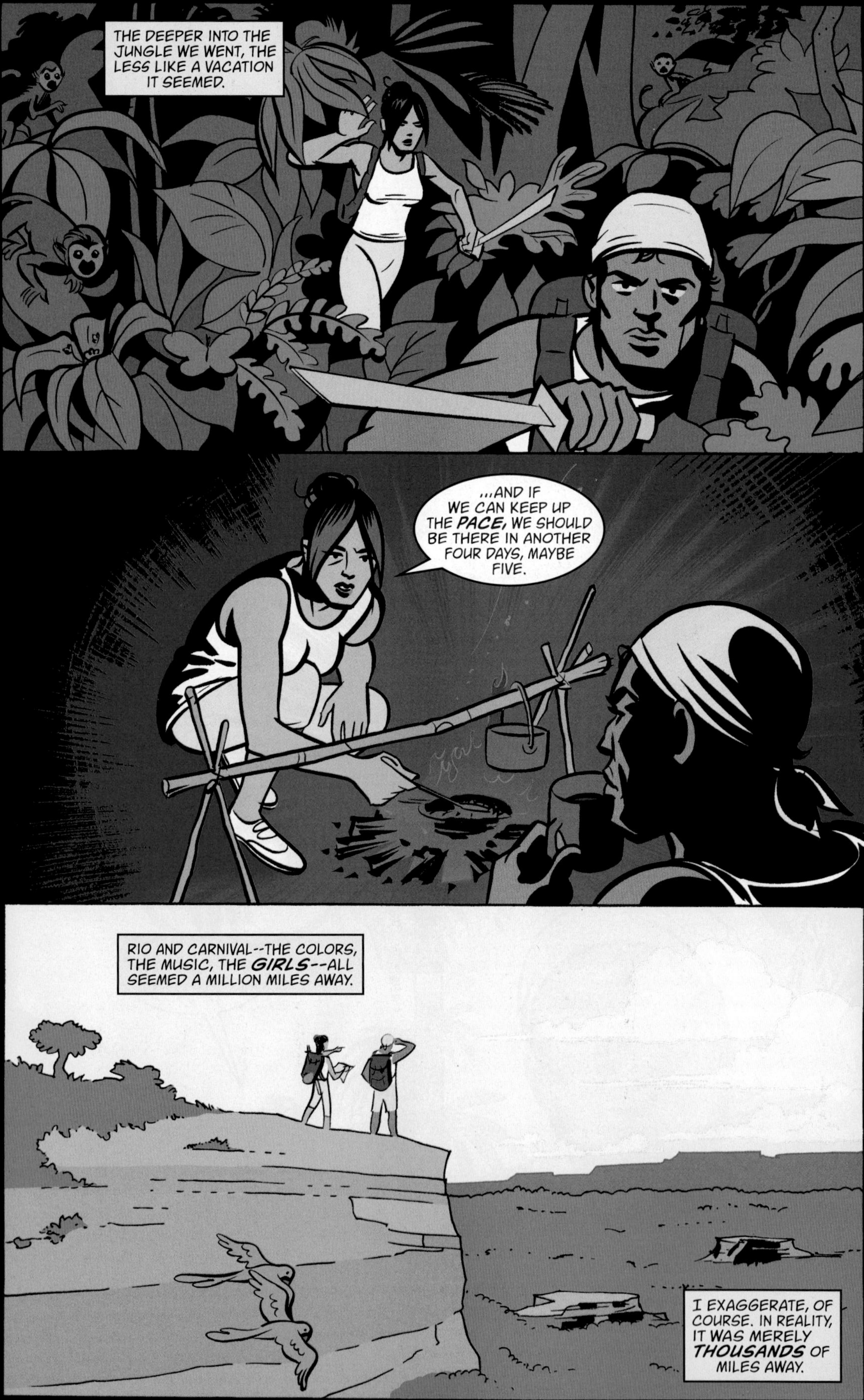
THE DEEPER INTO THE JUNGLE WE WENT, THE LESS LIKE A VACATION IT SEEMED.
...AND IF WE CAN KEEP UP THE *PACE,* WE SHOULD BE THERE IN ANOTHER FOUR DAYS, MAYBE FIVE.
RIO AND CARNIVAL--THE COLORS, THE MUSIC, THE *GIRLS*--ALL SEEMED A MILLION MILES AWAY.
I EXAGGERATE, OF COURSE. IN REALITY, IT WAS MERELY *THOUSANDS* OF MILES AWAY.

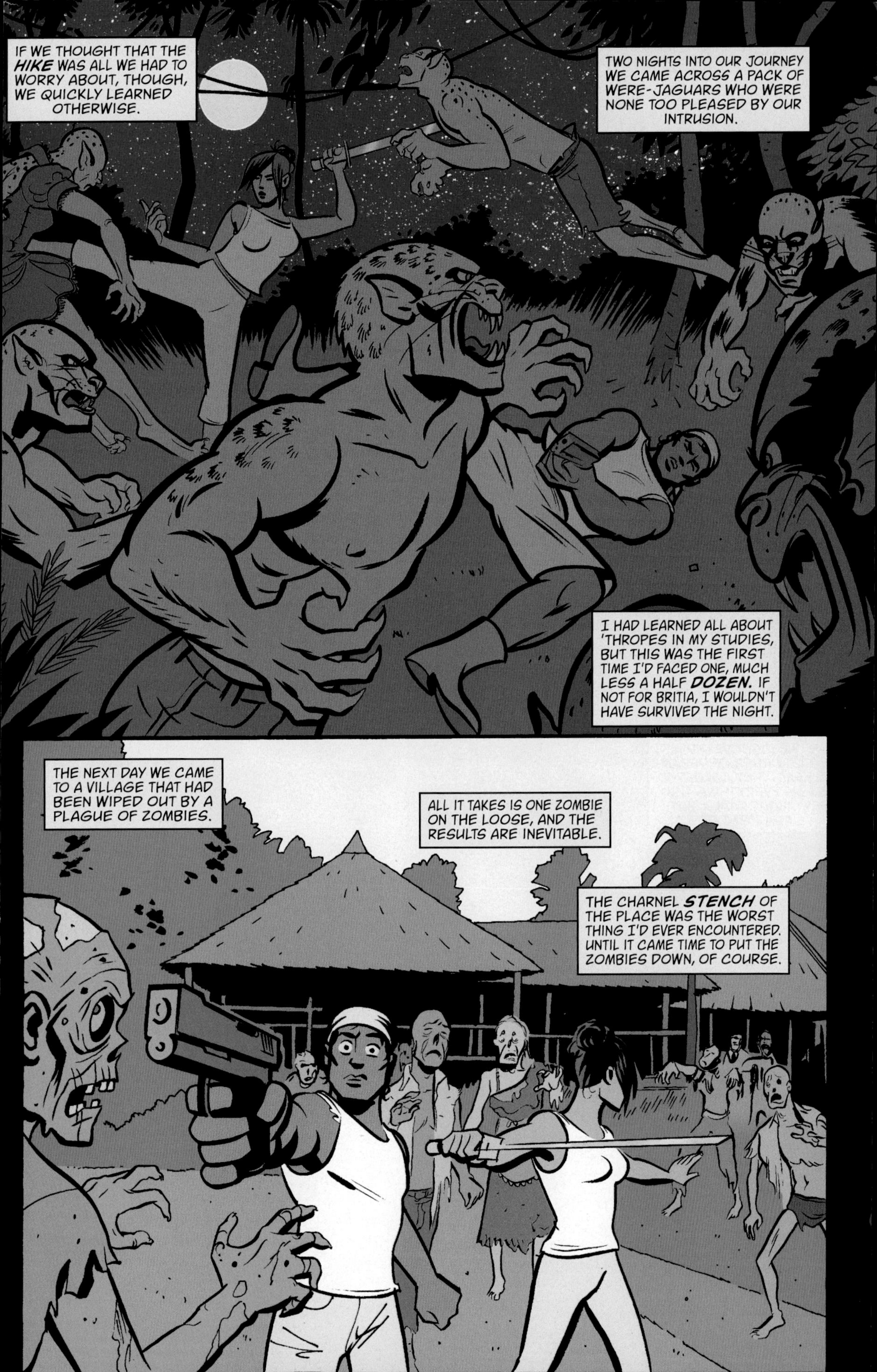
IF WE THOUGHT THAT THE HIKE WAS ALL WE HAD TO WORRY ABOUT, THOUGH, WE QUICKLY LEARNED OTHERWISE.
TWO NIGHTS INTO OUR JOURNEY WE CAME ACROSS A PACK OF WERE-JAGUARS WHO WERE NONE TOO PLEASED BY OUR INTRUSION.
I HAD LEARNED ALL ABOUT 'THROPES IN MY STUDIES, BUT THIS WAS THE FIRST TIME I'D FACED ONE, MUCH LESS A HALF DOZEN. IF NOT FOR BRITIA, I WOULDN'T HAVE SURVIVED THE NIGHT.
THE NEXT DAY WE CAME TO A VILLAGE THAT HAD BEEN WIPED OUT BY A PLAGUE OF ZOMBIES.
ALL IT TAKES IS ONE ZOMBIE ON THE LOOSE, AND THE RESULTS ARE INEVITABLE.
THE CHARNEL STENCH OF THE PLACE WAS THE WORST THING I'D EVER ENCOUNTERED. UNTIL IT CAME TIME TO PUT THE ZOMBIES DOWN, OF COURSE.

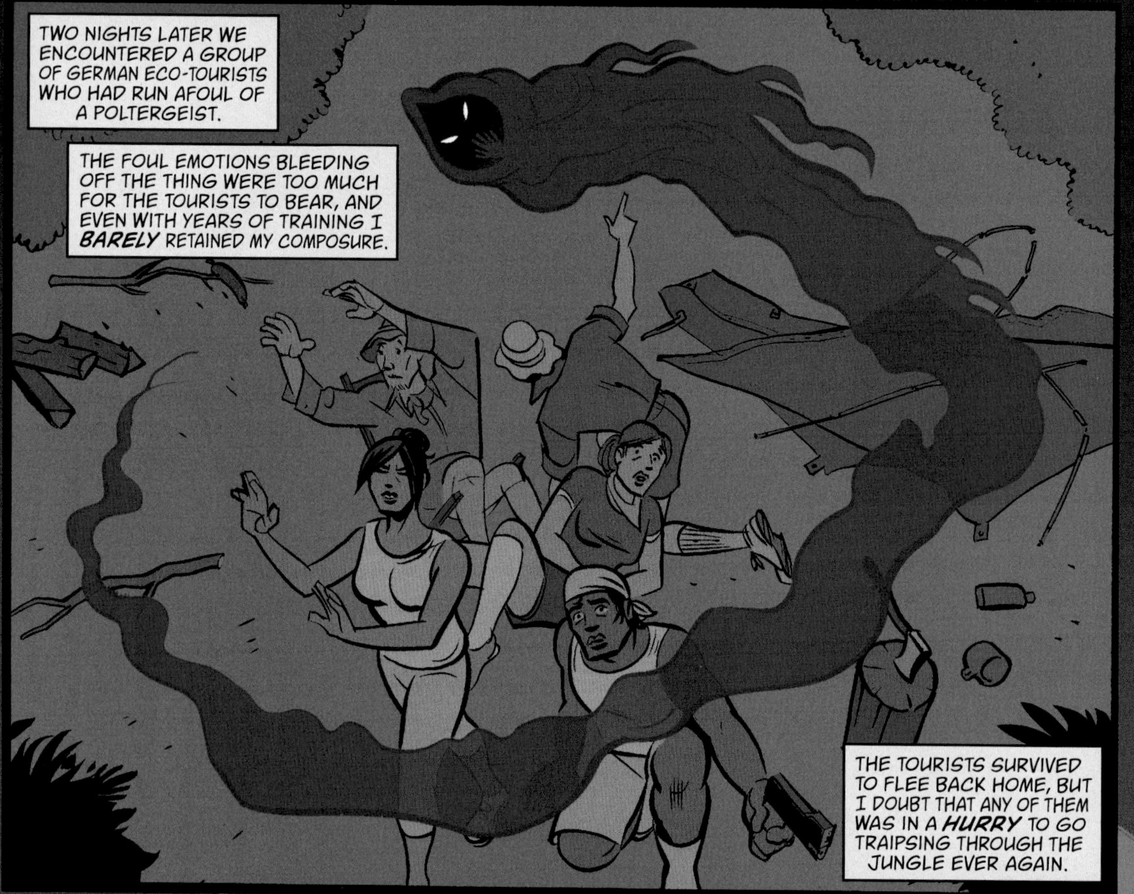
TWO NIGHTS LATER WE ENCOUNTERED A GROUP OF GERMAN ECO-TOURISTS WHO HAD RUN AFOUL OF A POLTERGEIST.
THE FOUL EMOTIONS BLEEDING OFF THE THING WERE TOO MUCH FOR THE TOURISTS TO BEAR, AND EVEN WITH YEARS OF TRAINING I BARELY RETAINED MY COMPOSURE.
THE TOURISTS SURVIVED TO FLEE BACK HOME, BUT I DOUBT THAT ANY OF THEM WAS IN A HURRY TO GO TRAIPSING THROUGH THE JUNGLE EVER AGAIN.

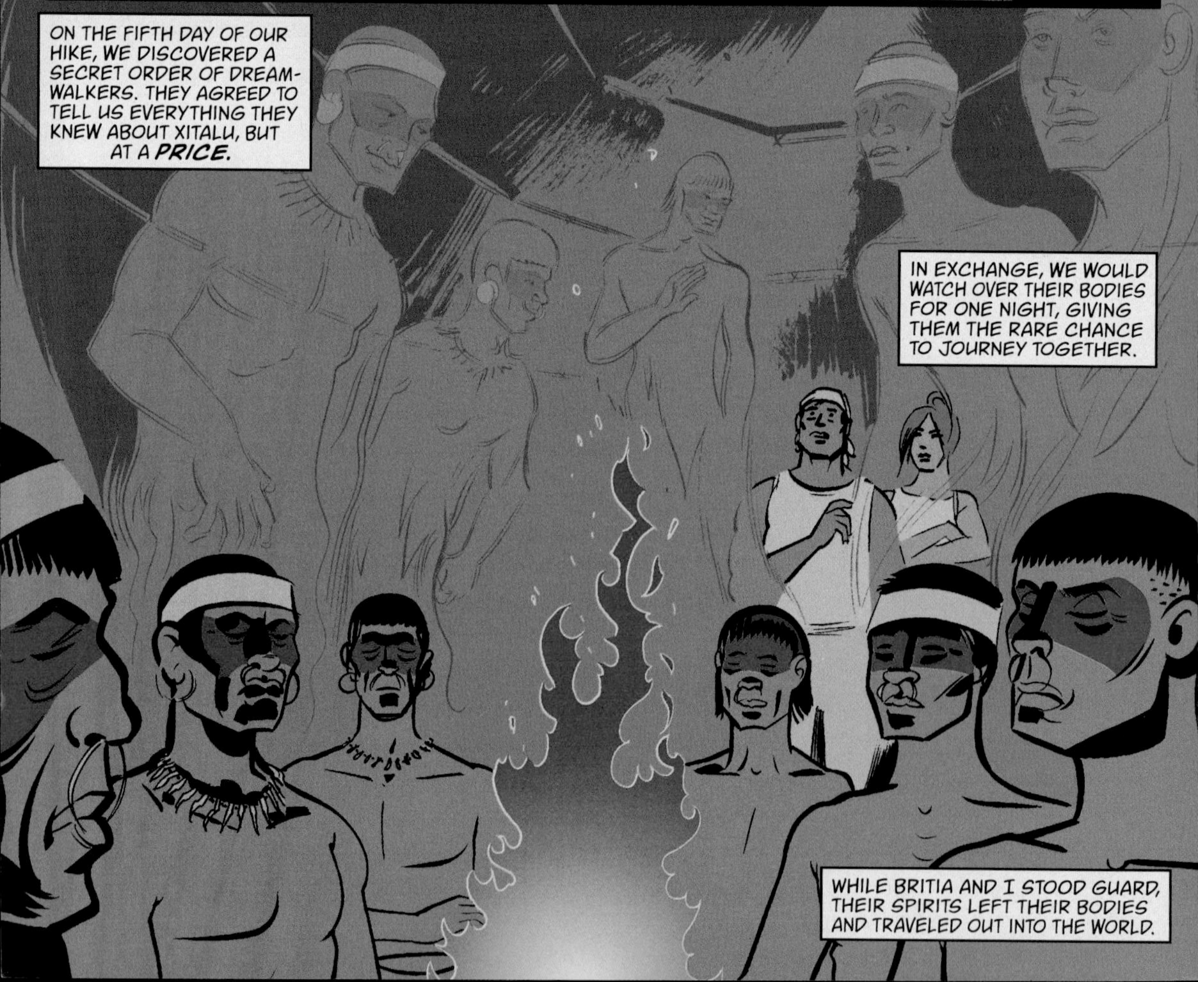
ON THE FIFTH DAY OF OUR HIKE, WE DISCOVERED A SECRET ORDER OF DREAM-WALKERS. THEY AGREED TO TELL US EVERYTHING THEY KNEW ABOUT XITALU, BUT AT A PRICE.
IN EXCHANGE, WE WOULD WATCH OVER THEIR BODIES FOR ONE NIGHT, GIVING THEM THE RARE CHANCE TO JOURNEY TOGETHER.
WHILE BRITIA AND I STOOD GUARD, THEIR SPIRITS LEFT THEIR BODIES AND TRAVELED OUT INTO THE WORLD.

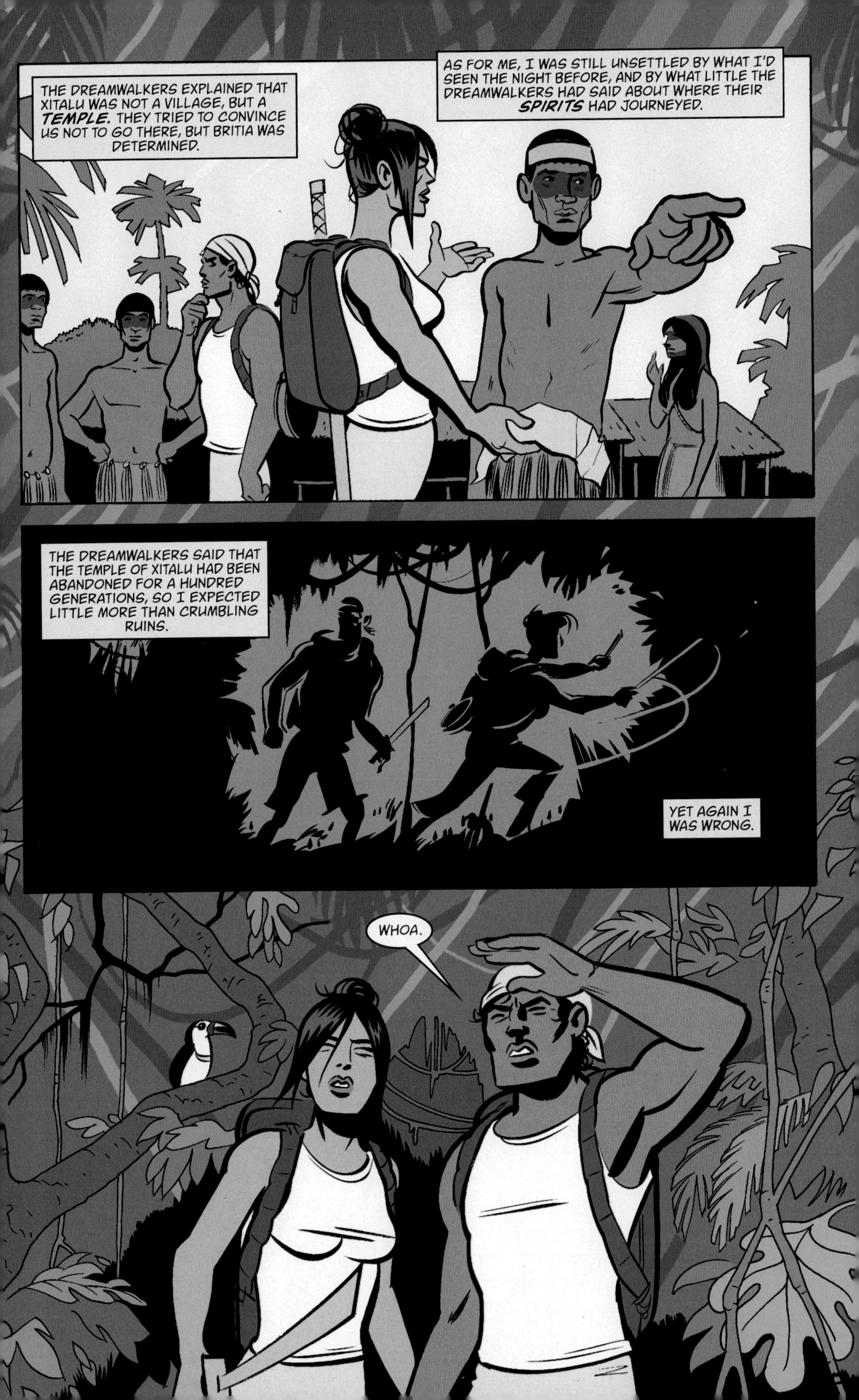
THE DREAMWALKERS EXPLAINED THAT XITALU WAS NOT A VILLAGE, BUT A TEMPLE. THEY TRIED TO CONVINCE US NOT TO GO THERE, BUT BRITIA WAS DETERMINED.
AS FOR ME, I WAS STILL UNSETTLED BY WHAT I'D SEEN THE NIGHT BEFORE, AND BY WHAT LITTLE THE DREAMWALKERS HAD SAID ABOUT WHERE THEIR SPIRITS HAD JOURNEYED.
THE DREAMWALKERS SAID THAT THE TEMPLE OF XITALU HAD BEEN ABANDONED FOR A HUNDRED GENERATIONS, SO I EXPECTED LITTLE MORE THAN CRUMBLING RUINS.
YET AGAIN I WAS WRONG.
WHOA.

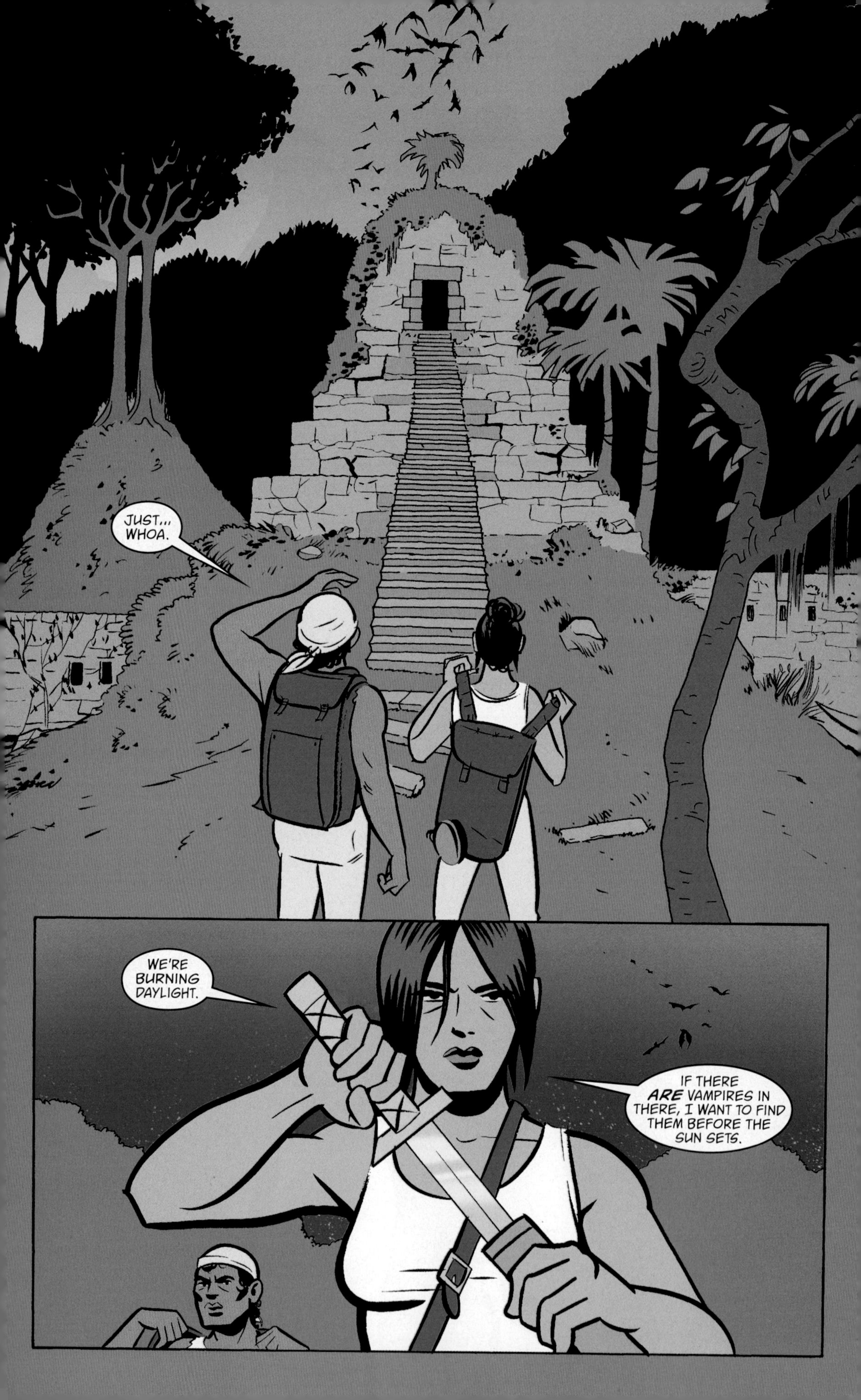
JUST... WHOA.
WE'RE BURNING DAYLIGHT.
IF THERE ARE VAMPIRES IN THERE, I WANT TO FIND THEM BEFORE THE SUN SETS.

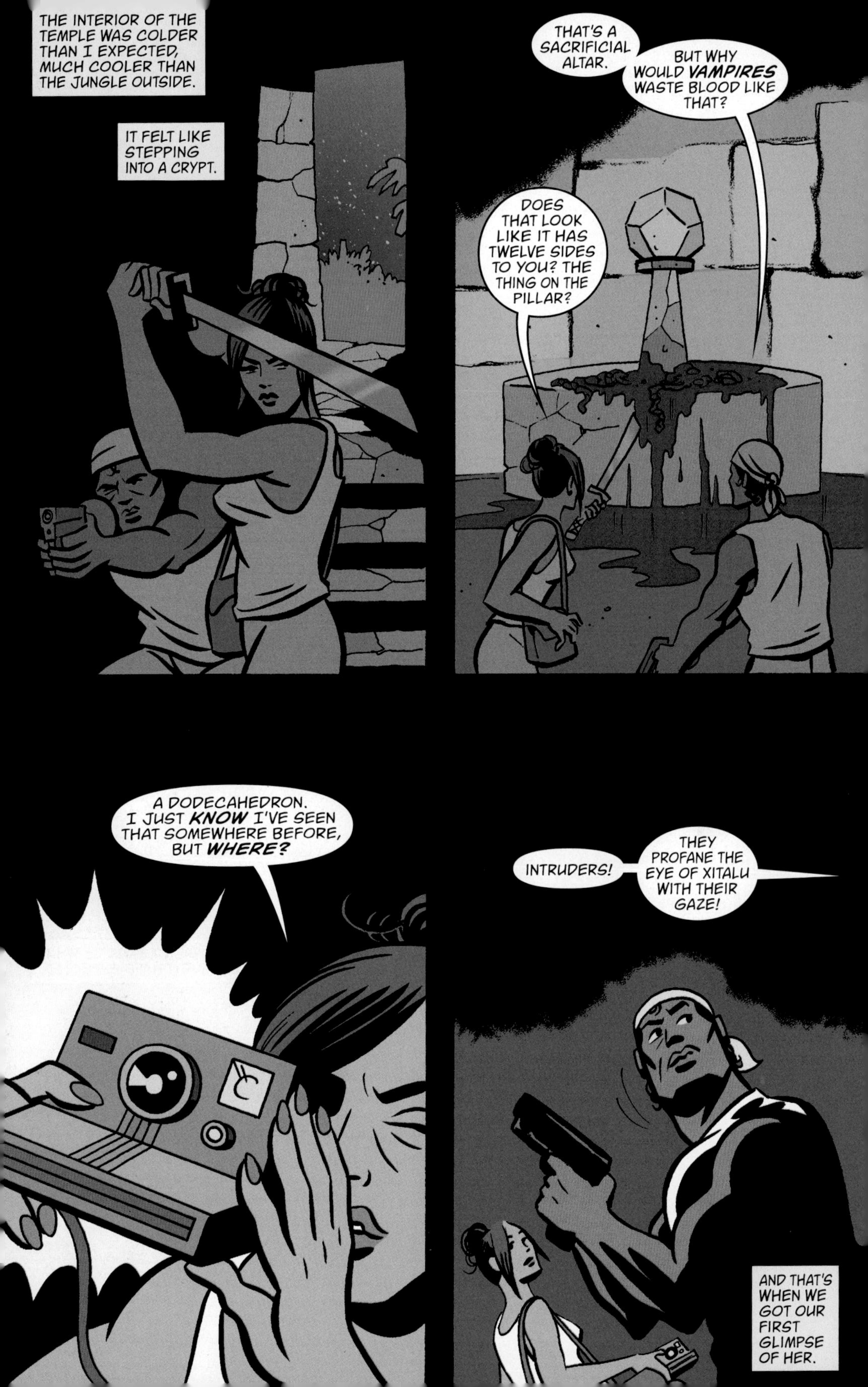
THE INTERIOR OF THE TEMPLE WAS COLDER THAN I EXPECTED, MUCH COOLER THAN THE JUNGLE OUTSIDE.
IT FELT LIKE STEPPING INTO A CRYPT.
THAT'S A SACRIFICIAL ALTAR.
BUT WHY WOULD VAMPIRES WASTE BLOOD LIKE THAT?
DOES THAT LOOK LIKE IT HAS TWELVE SIDES TO YOU? THE THING ON THE PILLAR?
A DODECAHEDRON. I JUST KNOW I'VE SEEN THAT SOMEWHERE BEFORE, BUT WHERE?
INTRUDERS!
THEY PROFANE THE EYE OF XITALU WITH THEIR GAZE!
AND THAT'S WHEN WE GOT OUR FIRST GLIMPSE OF HER.

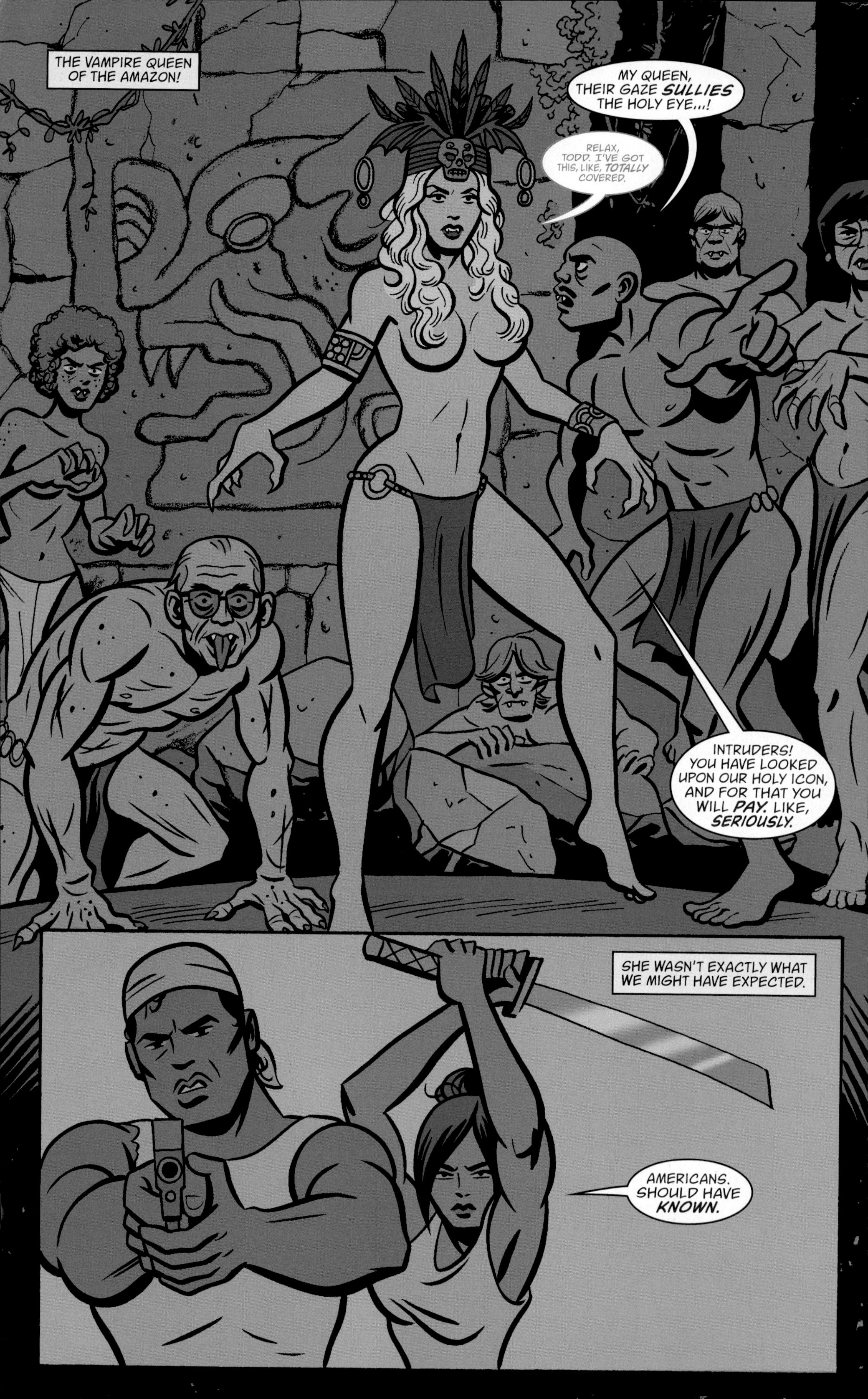
THE VAMPIRE QUEEN OF THE AMAZON!
MY QUEEN, THEIR GAZE SULLIES THE HOLY EYE...!
RELAX, TODD. I'VE GOT THIS, LIKE, TOTALLY COVERED.
INTRUDERS! YOU HAVE LOOKED UPON OUR HOLY ICON, AND FOR THAT YOU WILL PAY. LIKE, SERIOUSLY.
SHE WASN'T EXACTLY WHAT WE MIGHT HAVE EXPECTED.
AMERICANS. SHOULD HAVE KNOWN.

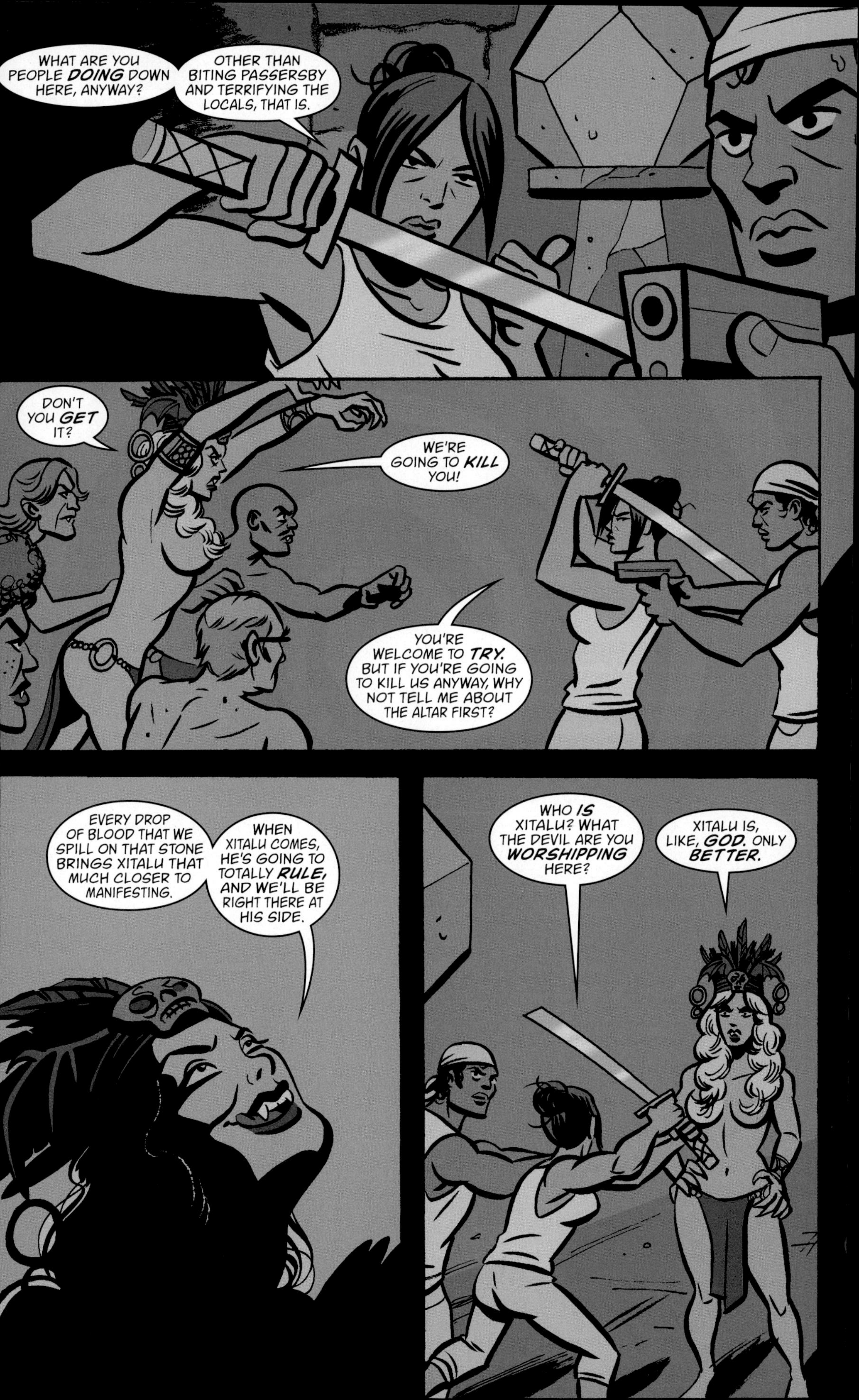
WHAT ARE YOU PEOPLE **DOING** DOWN HERE, ANYWAY?
OTHER THAN BITING PASSERSBY AND TERRIFYING THE LOCALS, THAT IS.
DON'T YOU **GET** IT?
WE'RE GOING TO **KILL** YOU!
YOU'RE WELCOME TO **TRY.** BUT IF YOU'RE GOING TO KILL US ANYWAY, WHY NOT TELL ME ABOUT THE ALTAR FIRST?
EVERY DROP OF BLOOD THAT WE SPILL ON THAT STONE BRINGS XITALU THAT MUCH CLOSER TO MANIFESTING.
WHEN XITALU COMES, HE'S GOING TO TOTALLY **RULE,** AND **WE'LL** BE RIGHT THERE AT HIS SIDE.
WHO **IS** XITALU? WHAT THE DEVIL ARE YOU **WORSHIPPING** HERE?
XITALU IS, LIKE, **GOD.** ONLY **BETTER.**

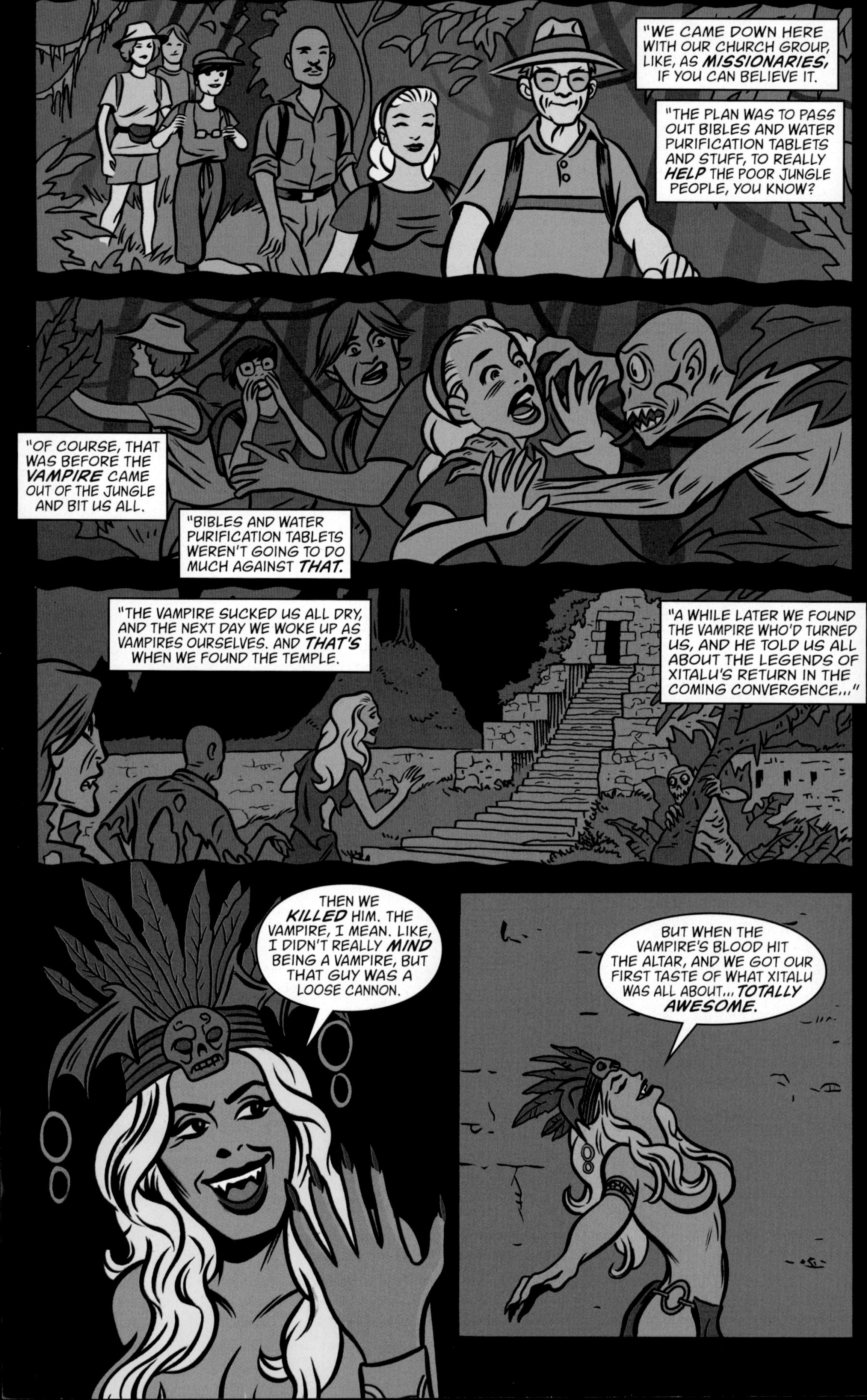
"WE CAME DOWN HERE WITH OUR CHURCH GROUP, LIKE, AS *MISSIONARIES,* IF YOU CAN BELIEVE IT.
"THE PLAN WAS TO PASS OUT BIBLES AND WATER PURIFICATION TABLETS AND STUFF, TO REALLY *HELP* THE POOR JUNGLE PEOPLE, YOU KNOW?
"OF COURSE, THAT WAS BEFORE THE *VAMPIRE* CAME OUT OF THE JUNGLE AND BIT US ALL.
"BIBLES AND WATER PURIFICATION TABLETS WEREN'T GOING TO DO MUCH AGAINST *THAT.*
"THE VAMPIRE SUCKED US ALL DRY, AND THE NEXT DAY WE WOKE UP AS VAMPIRES OURSELVES. AND *THAT'S* WHEN WE FOUND THE TEMPLE.
"A WHILE LATER WE FOUND THE VAMPIRE WHO'D TURNED US, AND HE TOLD US ALL ABOUT THE LEGENDS OF XITALU'S RETURN IN THE COMING CONVERGENCE..."
THEN WE *KILLED* HIM. THE VAMPIRE, I MEAN. LIKE, I DIDN'T REALLY *MIND* BEING A VAMPIRE, BUT THAT GUY WAS A LOOSE CANNON.
BUT WHEN THE VAMPIRE'S BLOOD HIT THE ALTAR, AND WE GOT OUR FIRST TASTE OF WHAT XITALU WAS ALL ABOUT... *TOTALLY AWESOME.*

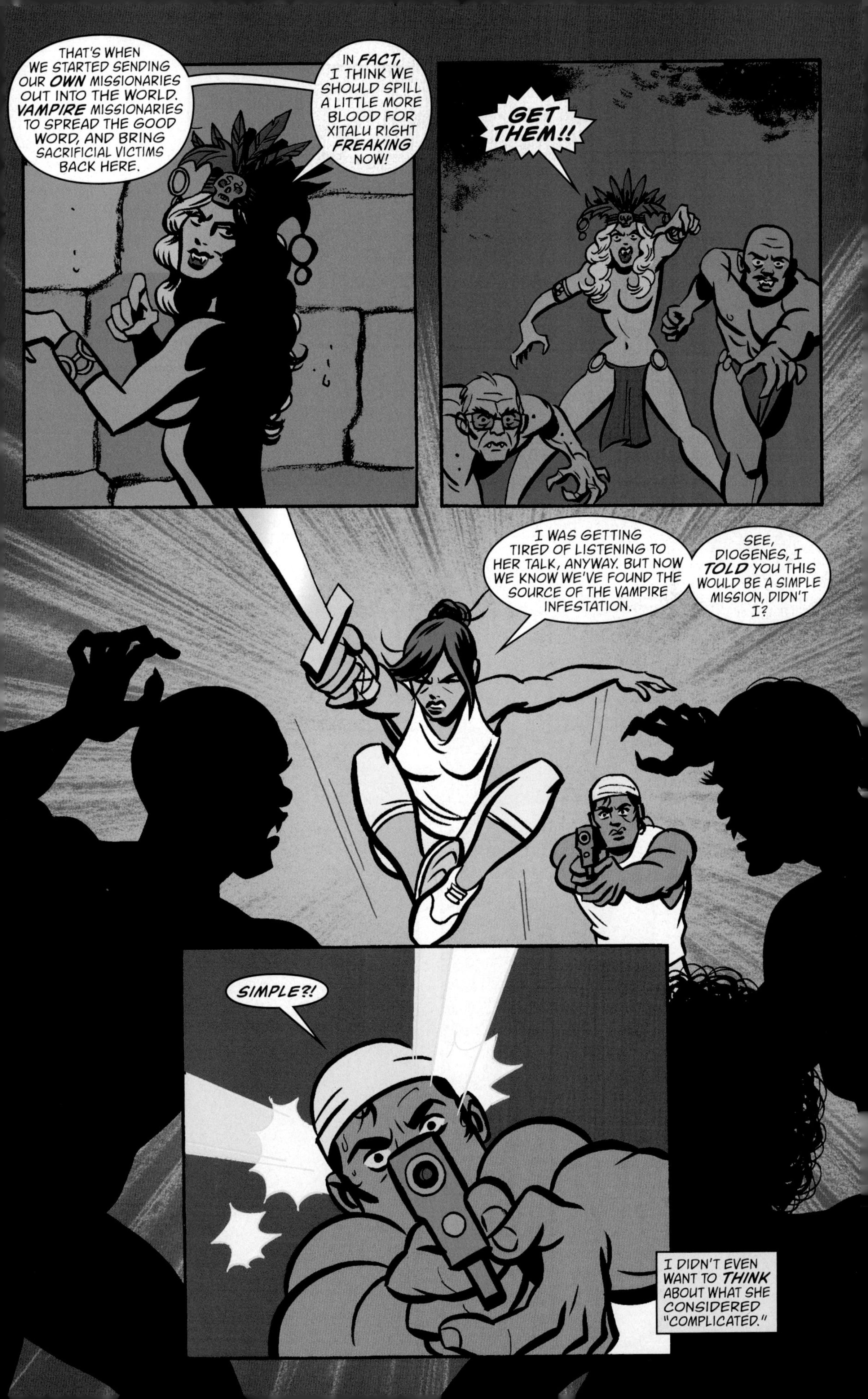
THAT'S WHEN WE STARTED SENDING OUR OWN MISSIONARIES OUT INTO THE WORLD. VAMPIRE MISSIONARIES TO SPREAD THE GOOD WORD, AND BRING SACRIFICIAL VICTIMS BACK HERE.
IN FACT, I THINK WE SHOULD SPILL A LITTLE MORE BLOOD FOR XITALU RIGHT FREAKING NOW!
GET THEM!!
I WAS GETTING TIRED OF LISTENING TO HER TALK, ANYWAY. BUT NOW WE KNOW WE'VE FOUND THE SOURCE OF THE VAMPIRE INFESTATION.
SEE, DIOGENES, I TOLD YOU THIS WOULD BE A SIMPLE MISSION, DIDN'T I?
SIMPLE?!
I DIDN'T EVEN WANT TO THINK ABOUT WHAT SHE CONSIDERED "COMPLICATED."

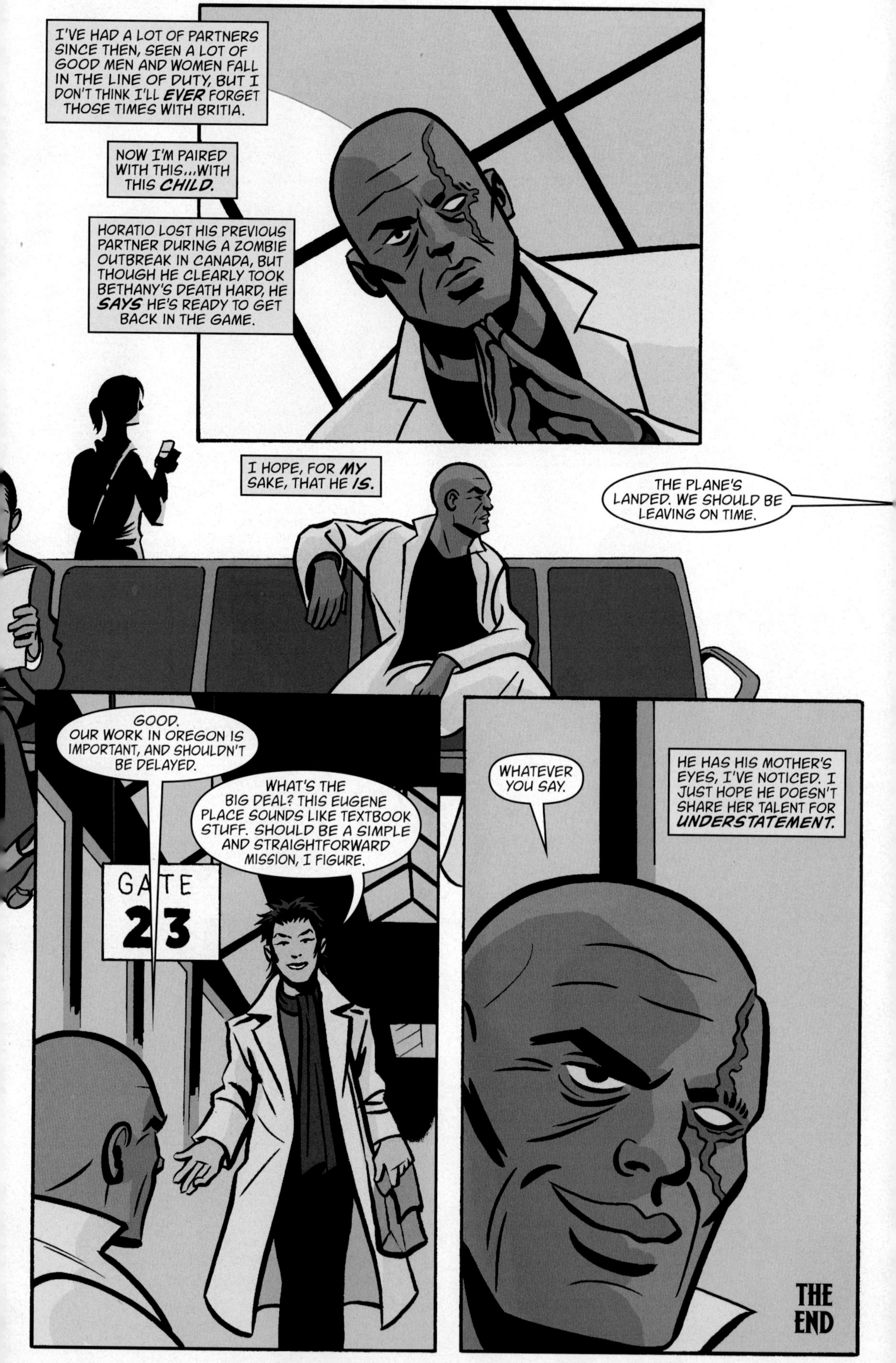
I'VE HAD A LOT OF PARTNERS SINCE THEN, SEEN A LOT OF GOOD MEN AND WOMEN FALL IN THE LINE OF DUTY, BUT I DON'T THINK I'LL EVER FORGET THOSE TIMES WITH BRITIA.
NOW I'M PAIRED WITH THIS...WITH THIS CHILD.
HORATIO LOST HIS PREVIOUS PARTNER DURING A ZOMBIE OUTBREAK IN CANADA, BUT THOUGH HE CLEARLY TOOK BETHANY'S DEATH HARD, HE SAYS HE'S READY TO GET BACK IN THE GAME.
I HOPE, FOR MY SAKE, THAT HE IS.
THE PLANE'S LANDED. WE SHOULD BE LEAVING ON TIME.
GOOD. OUR WORK IN OREGON IS IMPORTANT, AND SHOULDN'T BE DELAYED.
WHAT'S THE BIG DEAL? THIS EUGENE PLACE SOUNDS LIKE TEXTBOOK STUFF. SHOULD BE A SIMPLE AND STRAIGHTFORWARD MISSION, I FIGURE.
GATE
23
WHATEVER YOU SAY.
HE HAS HIS MOTHER'S EYES, I'VE NOTICED. I JUST HOPE HE DOESN'T SHARE HER TALENT FOR UNDERSTATEMENT.
THE END

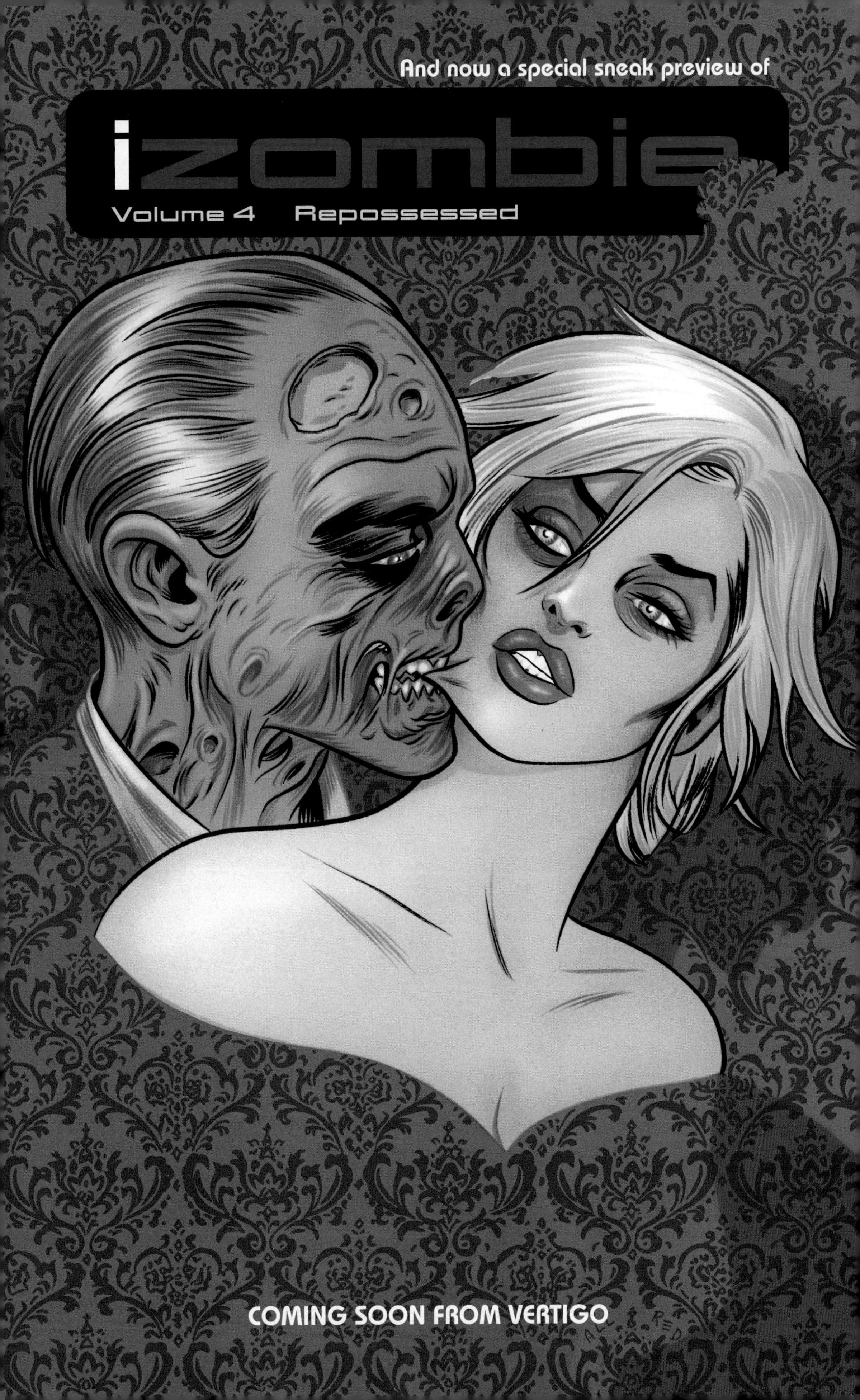
And now a special sneak preview of
izombie
Volume 4 Repossessed
COMING SOON FROM VERTIGO

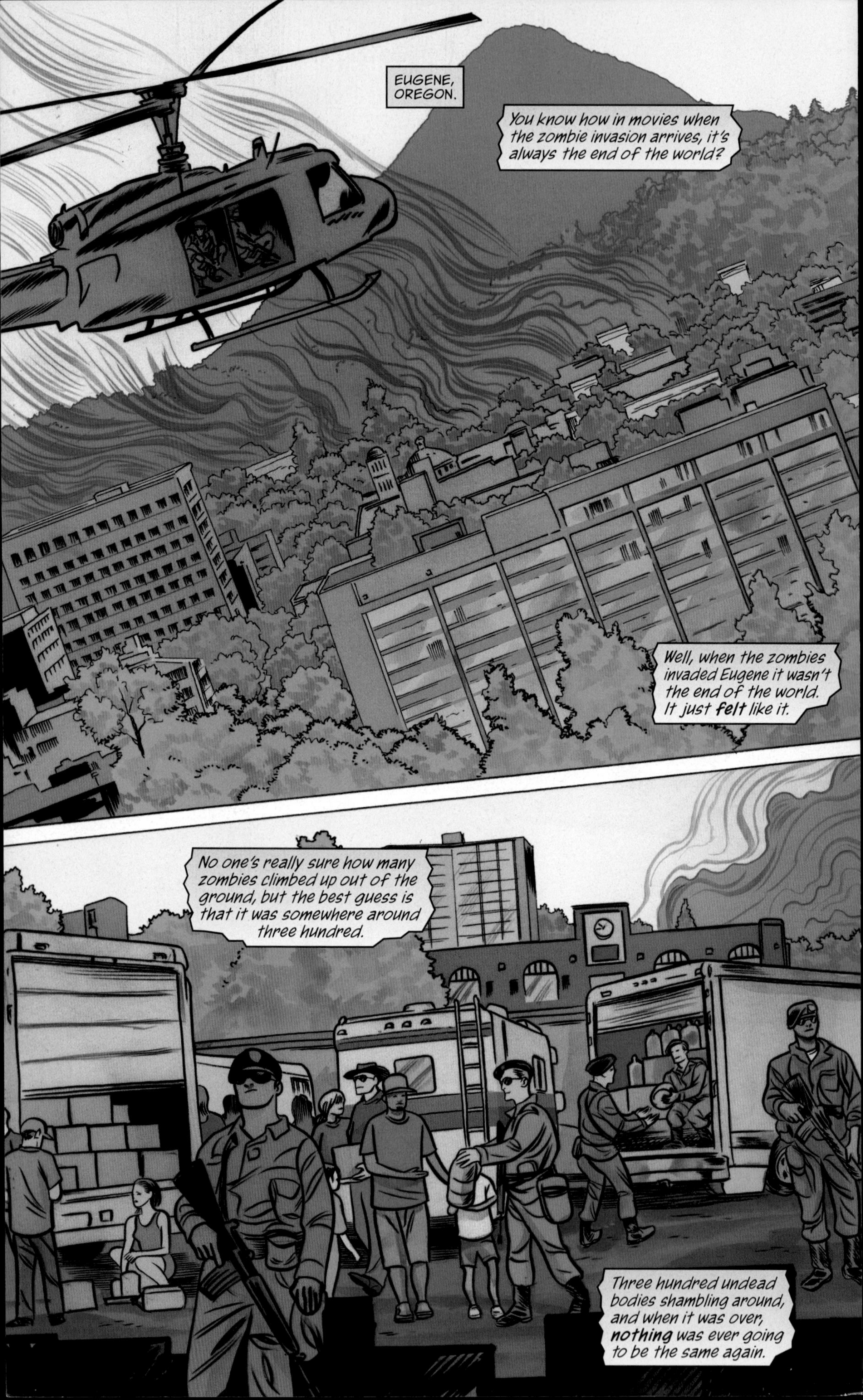
EUGENE, OREGON.
You know how in movies when the zombie invasion arrives, it's always the end of the world?
Well, when the zombies invaded Eugene it wasn't the end of the world. It just **felt** like it.
No one's really sure how many zombies climbed up out of the ground, but the best guess is that it was somewhere around three hundred.
Three hundred undead bodies shambling around, and when it was over, **nothing** was ever going to be the same again.

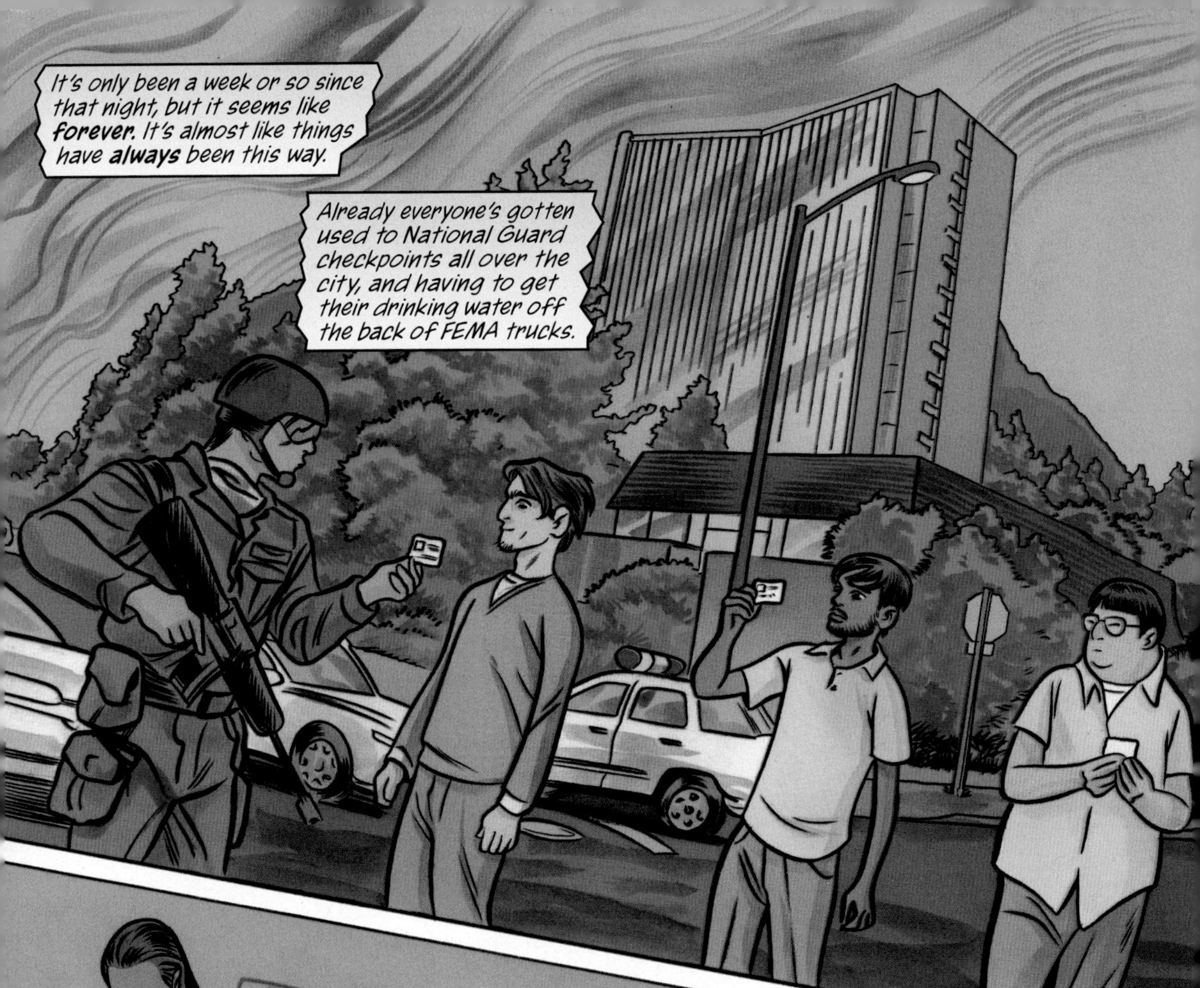
It's only been a week or so since that night, but it seems like **forever**. It's almost like things have **always** been this way.
Already everyone's gotten used to National Guard checkpoints all over the city, and having to get their drinking water off the back of FEMA trucks.

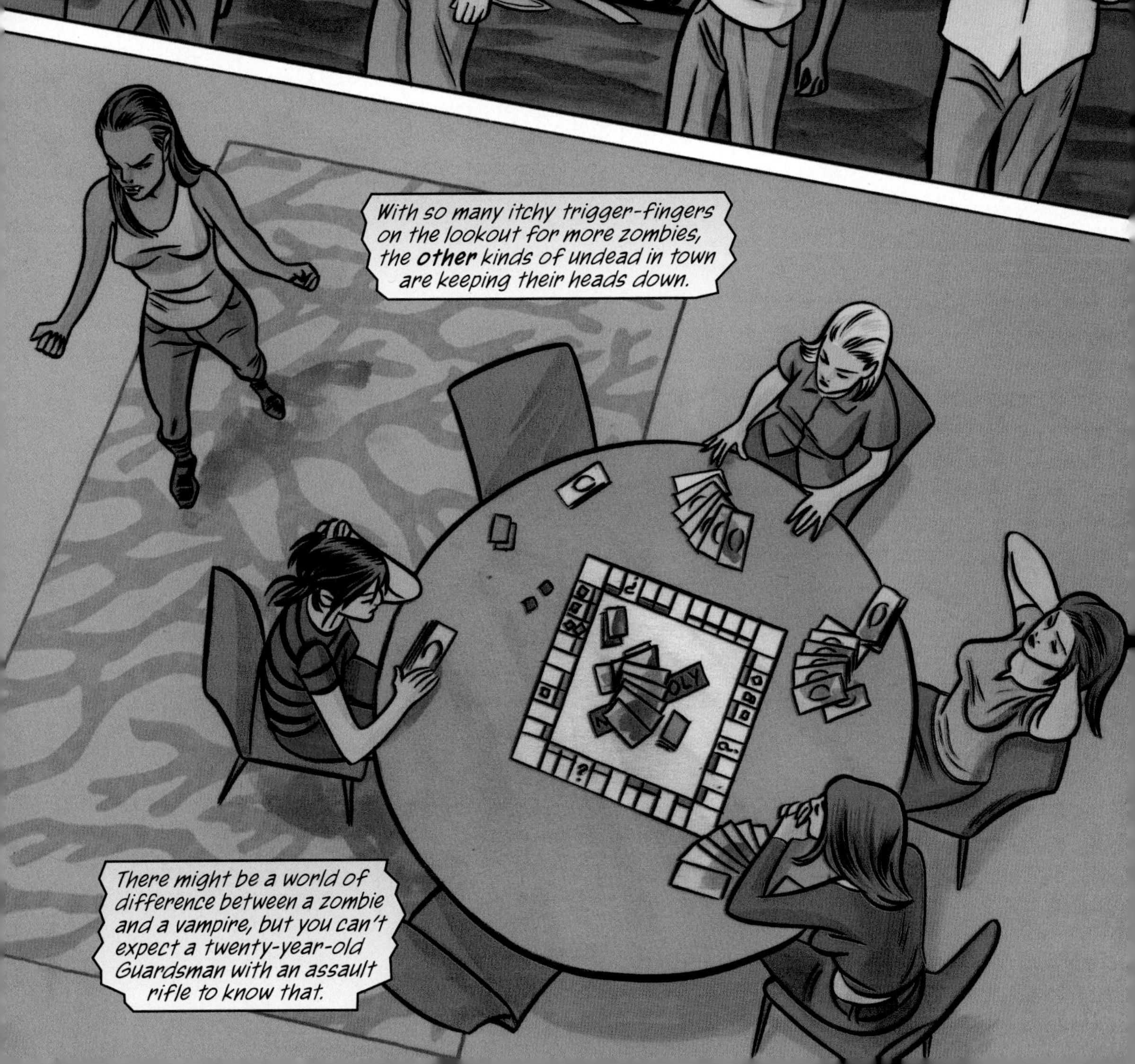
With so many itchy trigger-fingers on the lookout for more zombies, the **other** kinds of undead in town are keeping their heads down.
There might be a world of difference between a zombie and a vampire, but you can't expect a twenty-year-old Guardsman with an assault rifle to know that.

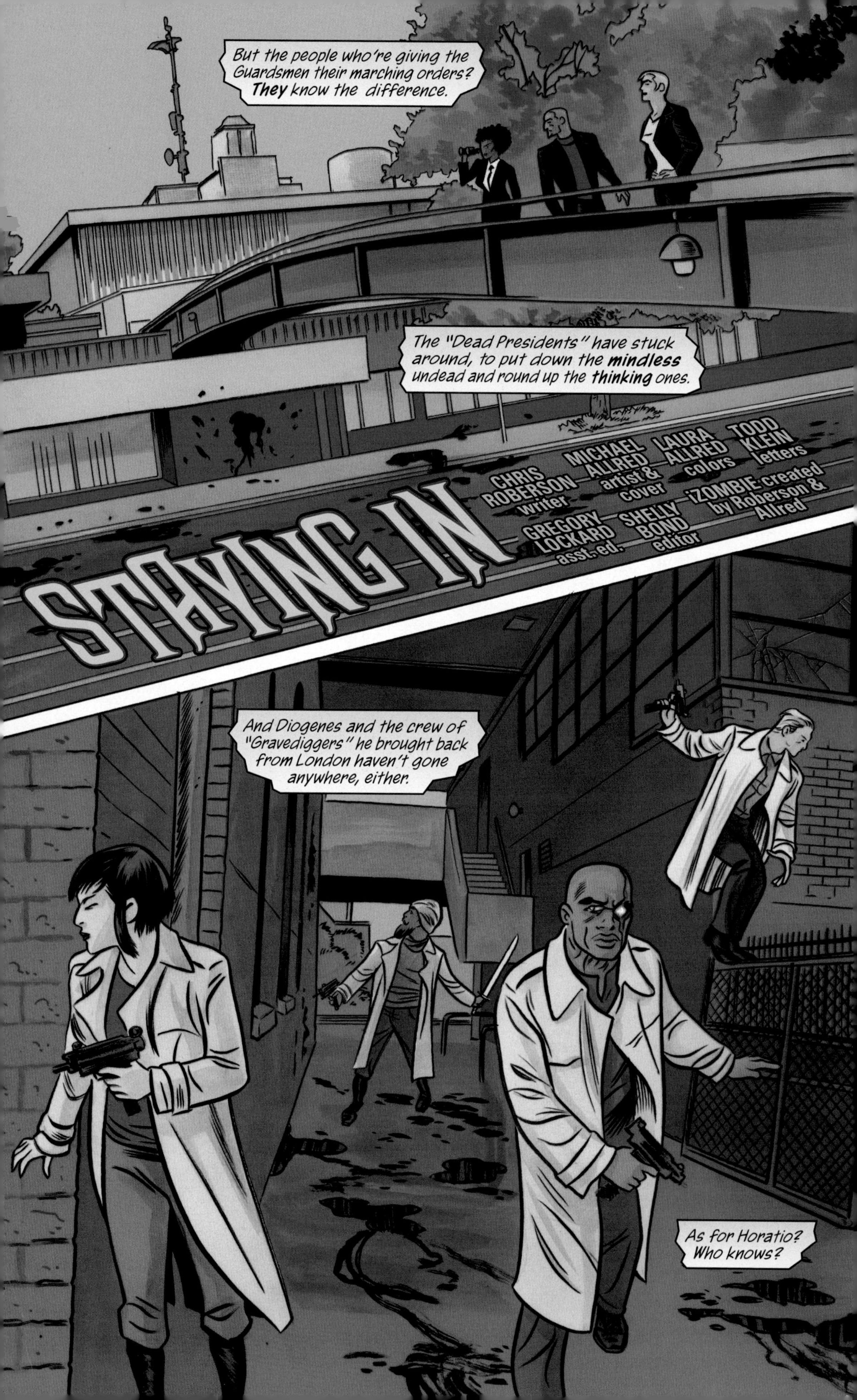
But the people who're giving the Guardsmen their marching orders? They know the difference.
The "Dead Presidents" have stuck around, to put down the mindless undead and round up the thinking ones.
STAYING IN
CHRIS ROBERSON writer
MICHAEL ALLRED artist & cover
LAURA ALLRED colors
TODD KLEIN letters
GREGORY LOCKARD asst. ed.
SHELLY BOND editor
iZOMBIE created by Roberson & Allred
And Diogenes and the crew of "Gravediggers" he brought back from London haven't gone anywhere, either.
As for Horatio? Who knows?

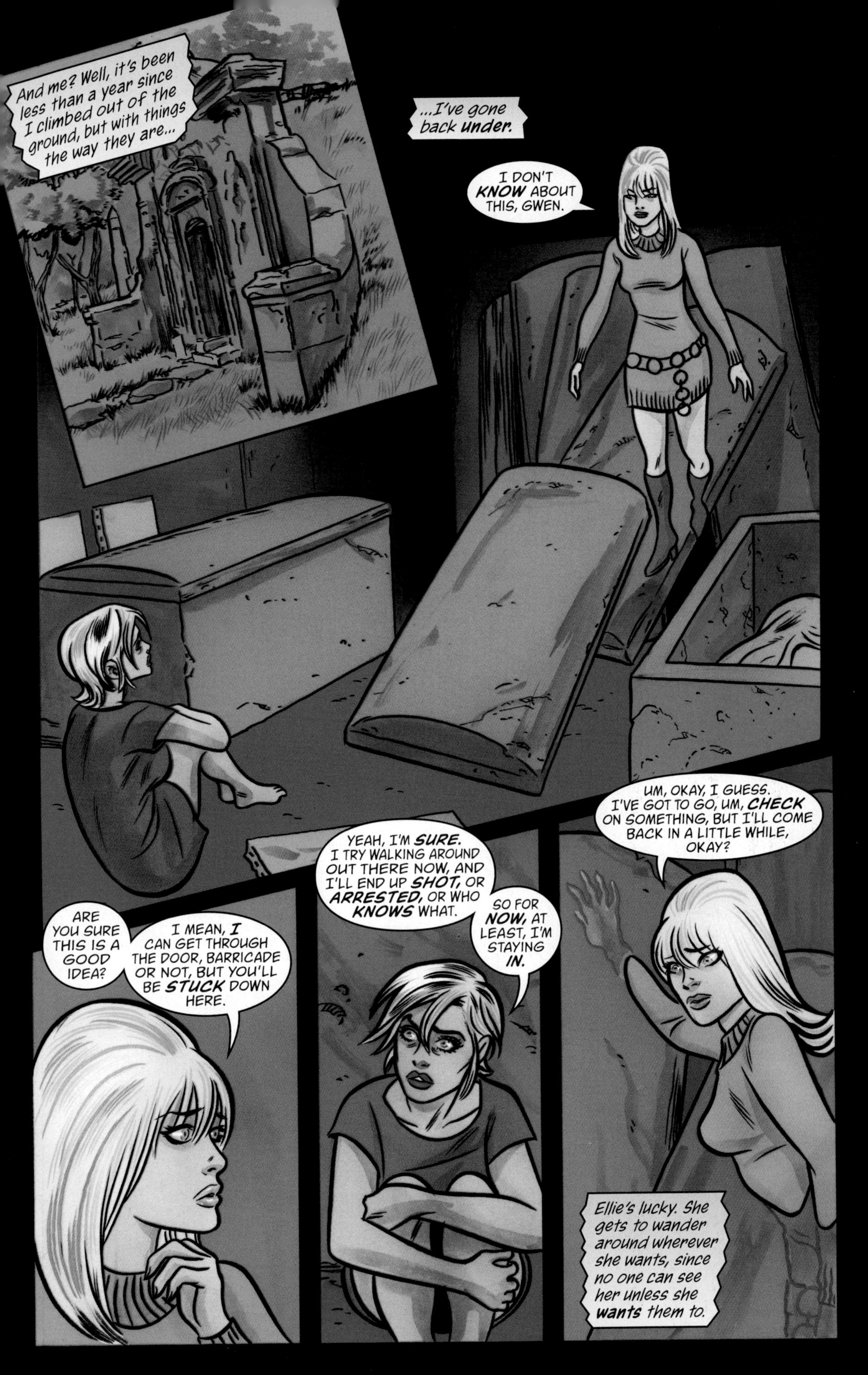
And me? Well, it's been less than a year since I climbed out of the ground, but with things the way they are...
...I've gone back under.
I DON'T KNOW ABOUT THIS, GWEN.
ARE YOU SURE THIS IS A GOOD IDEA?
I MEAN, I CAN GET THROUGH THE DOOR, BARRICADE OR NOT, BUT YOU'LL BE STUCK DOWN HERE.
YEAH, I'M SURE. I TRY WALKING AROUND OUT THERE NOW, AND I'LL END UP SHOT, OR ARRESTED, OR WHO KNOWS WHAT.
SO FOR NOW, AT LEAST, I'M STAYING IN.
UM, OKAY, I GUESS. I'VE GOT TO GO, UM, CHECK ON SOMETHING, BUT I'LL COME BACK IN A LITTLE WHILE, OKAY?
Ellie's lucky. She gets to wander around wherever she wants, since no one can see her unless she wants them to.

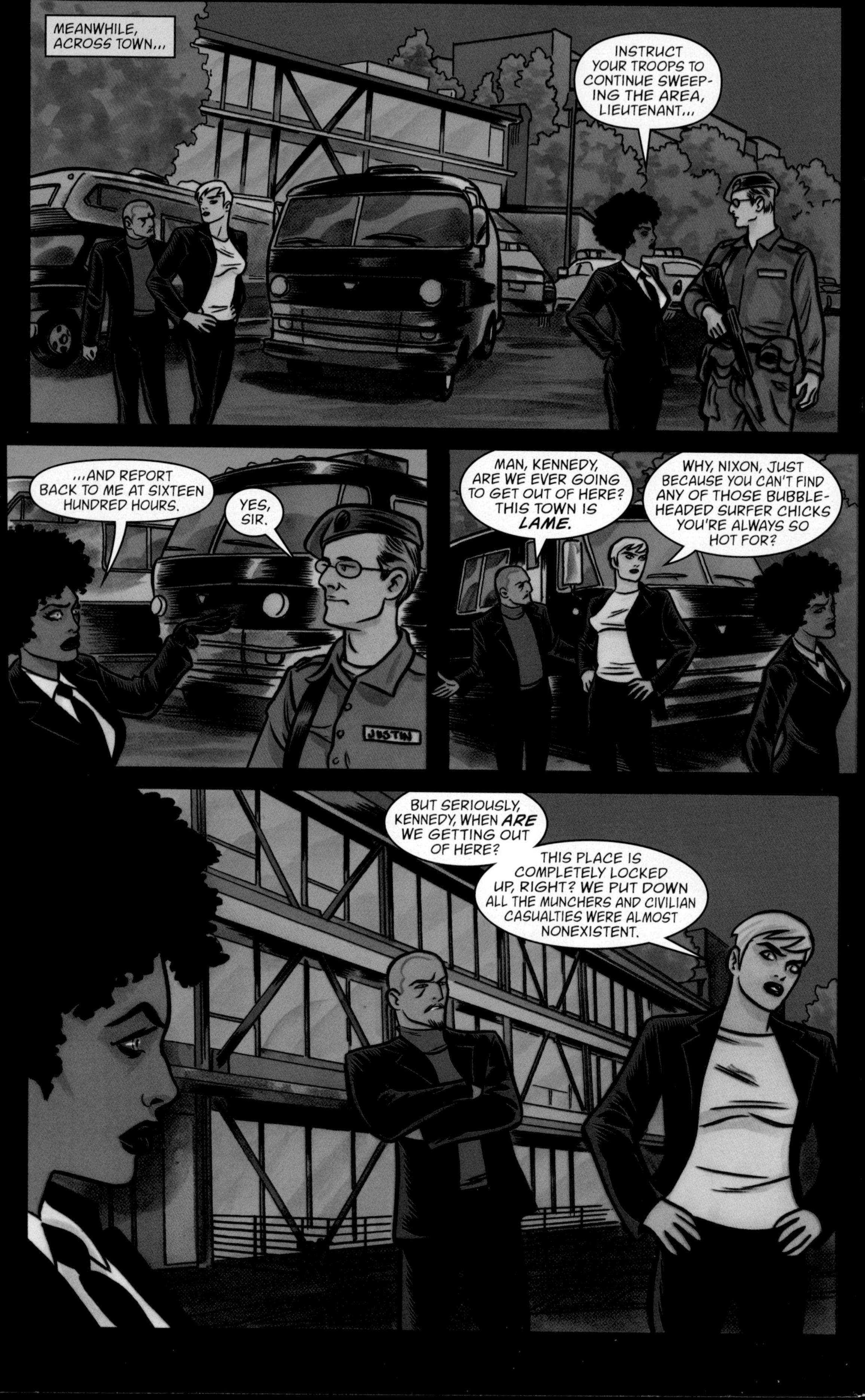
MEANWHILE, ACROSS TOWN...
INSTRUCT YOUR TROOPS TO CONTINUE SWEEP-ING THE AREA, LIEUTENANT...
...AND REPORT BACK TO ME AT SIXTEEN HUNDRED HOURS.
YES, SIR.
JUSTIN
MAN, KENNEDY, ARE WE EVER GOING TO GET OUT OF HERE? THIS TOWN IS *LAME.*
WHY, NIXON, JUST BECAUSE YOU CAN'T FIND ANY OF THOSE BUBBLE-HEADED SURFER CHICKS YOU'RE ALWAYS SO HOT FOR?
BUT SERIOUSLY, KENNEDY, WHEN *ARE* WE GETTING OUT OF HERE?
THIS PLACE IS COMPLETELY LOCKED UP, RIGHT? WE PUT DOWN ALL THE MUNCHERS AND CIVILIAN CASUALTIES WERE ALMOST NONEXISTENT.

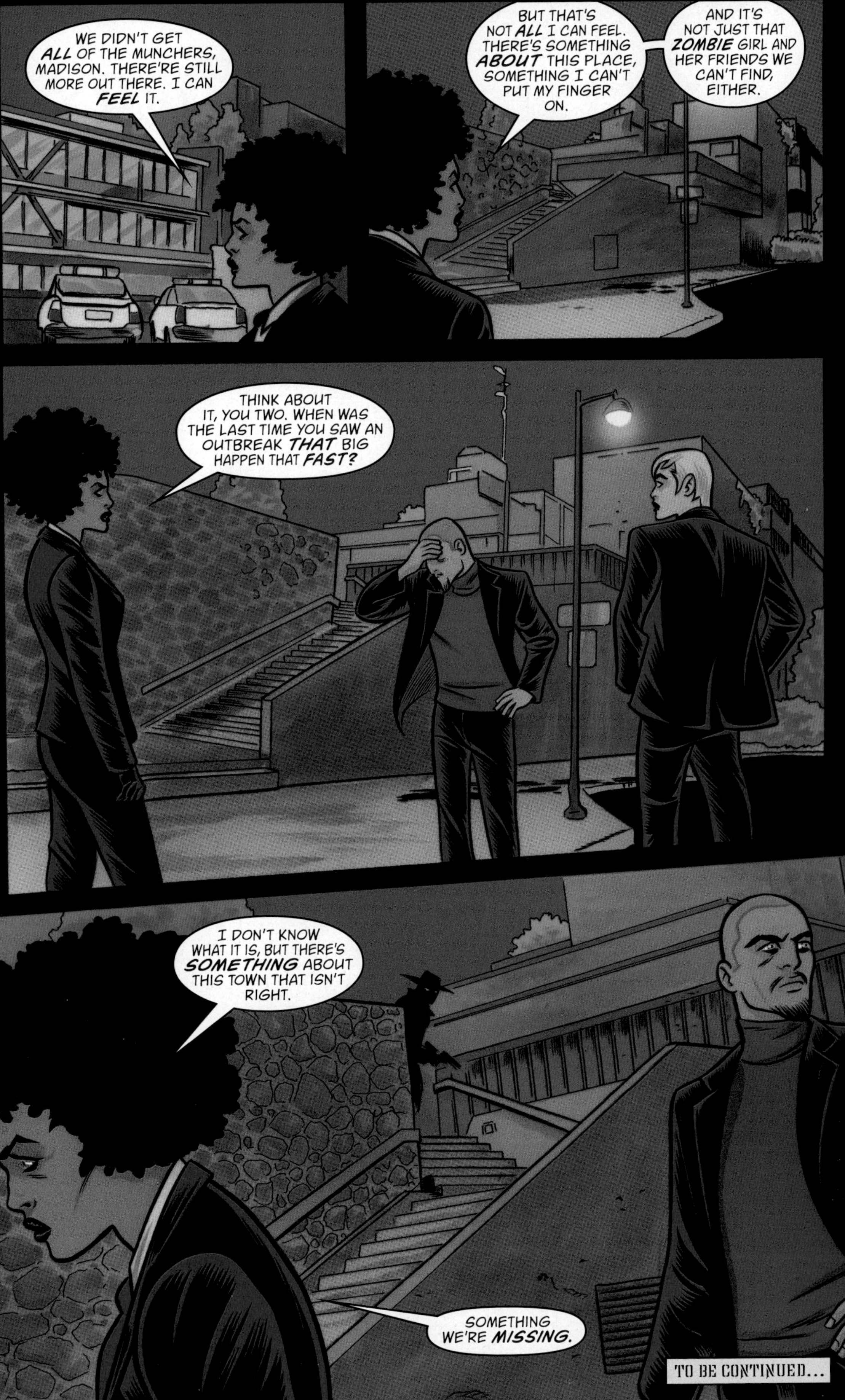
WE DIDN'T GET ALL OF THE MUNCHERS, MADISON. THERE'RE STILL MORE OUT THERE. I CAN FEEL IT.
BUT THAT'S NOT ALL I CAN FEEL. THERE'S SOMETHING ABOUT THIS PLACE, SOMETHING I CAN'T PUT MY FINGER ON.
AND IT'S NOT JUST THAT ZOMBIE GIRL AND HER FRIENDS WE CAN'T FIND, EITHER.
THINK ABOUT IT, YOU TWO. WHEN WAS THE LAST TIME YOU SAW AN OUTBREAK THAT BIG HAPPEN THAT FAST?
I DON'T KNOW WHAT IT IS, BUT THERE'S SOMETHING ABOUT THIS TOWN THAT ISN'T RIGHT.
SOMETHING WE'RE MISSING.
TO BE CONTINUED...

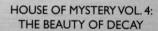

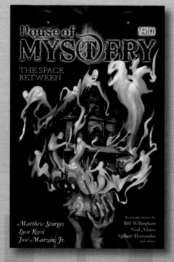